Oklahoma Tough

Also by Ron Padgett

Oklahoma Tough

MY FATHER,
KING OF THE TULSA BOOTLEGGERS

Ron Padgett

UNIVERSITY OF OKLAHOMA PRESS • NORMAN

LIBRARY OF CONGRESS CATALOGING-IN-PUBLICATION DATA

Padgett, Ron, 1942–
    Oklahoma tough : my father, king of the Tulsa
bootleggers / Ron Padgett.
        p.   cm.
    Includes bibliographical references.
    ISBN 978-0-8061-3509-0 (cloth)
    ISBN 978-0-8061-3732-2 (paper)
        1. Padgett, Wayne Merriott, 1922–1991. 2. Criminals—
Oklahoma—Tulsa—Biography. 3. Organized crime—
Oklahoma—Tulsa. I. Title.

HV6248.P234 A3 2003
364.1'092—dc21
[B]

                                                    2002026715

The paper in this book meets the guidelines for permanence
and durability of the Committee on Production Guidelines
for Book Longevity of the Council on Library Resources. ∞

This book is dedicated to the memory of my mother
Lucille Huey
and to the memory of my grandmother
Verna Padgett.

Contents

Illustrations

ILLUSTRATIONS

Preface

I think that this book began to germinate in the sudden feeling that came over me years ago one night in New York City. I had left my hometown of Tulsa some twenty-five years before that, at the age of eighteen, to attend college in New York, where I stayed thereafter, though I had returned to Tulsa to visit my family almost every year. On the night in question, in the middle of preparing a midnight snack, I had a Proustian flashback that I wrote about in a short piece called "Coors":

> When I laid out the slices of olive loaf next to the can of Coors, I was hit with an intense sensation of being around three or four years old, in Howard Donahue's welding shop in the afternoon, with my father and some guys standing around shooting the breeze. It was a very empty feeling, imbued with ignorance. The heavy shadows cast by cylinders of compressed gas echoed with pointlessness. Still, among the grease spots and dusty tools, there was a sense that life was going strong, no questions asked. These guys didn't have any idea why they were on the face of the earth, nor had it occurred to them to wonder why. Hell, they had things to do. Slick back their hair. Punch some son of a bitch in the nose. Laugh. Say "much obliged." Pop the clutch and roar off down the street on a wave of energy.
>
> The warm summer breeze pours around my head and whips my hair around into my face when I turn it just a little. I am flying through the air, me and the air. The '49 Ford has disappeared. My daddy is happy behind the wheel. In the back seat are forty-two boxes of Tide. "Lifetime supply," he laughs.
>
> Since then he has spent his life trying to obtain a lifetime supply of everything. All that time, he never put lettuce on his sandwiches. Just lunchmeat between two pieces of white bread.

Which is how I had mine tonight, with this Coors, a beer I didn't think they sold this far east, until I discovered it in a new supermarket today. And when I laid out the slices of olive loaf next to the can of Coors, I was hit with an intense sensation, the pang of loving someone I don't really know.

When I started writing the piece (around 1984), I didn't know that it was going to lead to the realization in its final sentence. I had lived in the same house with my father for the first eighteen years of my life, and we had visited and talked many times after that, but there was still so much about him I didn't know. Many people have a similar realization when a parent dies, along with the regret of not having expressed one's love abundantly or clearly enough. Although my father was still alive, writing the piece suddenly reoriented me toward him by making me ask myself: who was he, and why was I feeling this mysterious pang?

A few years later, I had the idea that he and I—a career criminal and his poet son—should write a book about his life, which had been adventurous and colorful. As Tulsa's "King of the Bootleggers," he had inside knowledge of the secret workings of people from every stratum of Tulsa life, from mayor to murderer. Now, with most of his criminal life behind him and with his cancer in remission, I thought that he could tell his life story and I could write it down. It would make a good book, and I could learn more about him in the process.

"I have a great idea. Let's you and me write the story of your life. You talk and I write."

"No, son, I can't do that."

"Why not?"

"Too many people would get hurt. I mean *hurt*."

By this he meant physically. He had many friends, criminal and otherwise, who had confided in him over the years. Betraying their confidence—a serious violation of his moral code—could result in deadly reprisals against them. In retrospect, I've wondered if he weren't saying more than he knew: that certain people would be hurt emotionally as well. There were things that he didn't want his mother to know, and, although I didn't suspect it until after his death, there were things he didn't want me to know, either. Ultimately, although he once told me that he had no regrets, I know there were some parts of his life that he preferred to leave unexamined, even by himself.

A couple of years went by, during which I made the acquaintance of Elmore ("Dutch") Leonard, the author of crime novels. Over dinner, the subject of my father came up, and I rattled on about Daddy's exploits. "Sounds like a good subject," Dutch said. "You should write a book about him."

My father already knew about Elmore Leonard. I had sent him a copy of *Glitz*, in which a character named LaDonna Holly Padgett, a former Miss Tulsa Raceway and Miss Oklahoma, talks about her life, the details of which Leonard had based on a piece I had written about Tulsa stock car racing. Daddy had gotten a kick out of LaDonna Padgett and *Glitz* in general. Dutch's encouragement caused me to start thinking of other ways to convince Daddy to collaborate with me.

"I've figured out a way that we can write the book," I told him. "I'll interview you on tape. You can leave out the names of the people involved in anything that might be dangerous to publish. Then, I'll store the tapes in a safe deposit box in New York for as long as you want. Only if you give me the go-ahead will I put the book together. And the best part is that I now have a Hollywood connection"—I fudged things here—"and I think we could make some money on a film deal." I was trying to appeal to Daddy's lifelong interest in deals and profits. "How does that sound?"

"I still can't do it," he said. "But I'll tell you what: after I die, you can write anything you want about me."

When he did die, in 1991, I started to face the prospect of writing the book on my own. But his death had changed my purpose. I now had the mental image of a book that would rise like a granite monument so massive that no one would ever forget him, a monument built from the details of his fascinating life. But there were problems. Without my prime source, how would I ever be able to untangle the Gordian knot of a life based on secrecy? Aside from key figures, which people, among the vast numbers who knew him, would I choose to interview? Who would be willing to talk? How would I distinguish fact from rumor? How would I handle finding out things that are perhaps better left unknown? What kind of emotional wear and tear might be involved in interviewing those who loved him? Added to these worries was the awareness that I was a poet, not a biographer. The immensity of the job was daunting, but by then I was afraid of *not* tackling it. I had already been telling people I was working on a biography of my father. I had said it so many times to so many people that now I *had* to write it, or at least try. Finally, I talked myself into getting on a plane and going back to Tulsa to start interviewing people who had known him.

Fortunately, many of them—relatives, acquaintances, colleagues, friends, and adversaries—proved generous in providing information, photographs, and other documents. Some spoke with abandon, offering information and insights I hadn't expected. Others were cautious. In only a few instances did I sense evasiveness or disingenuousness. In all cases, it was intriguing to see how each interviewee gave his or her information a particular slant. Many of them wanted not only to create a portrait of the subject, but also, being human, to create a favorable impression of themselves. But, in writing this book, what of the impression *I* would give?

In midcourse, I realized that my image of the book as a monument had faded, and that I had started to think of it as a rebuttal to my classmates in elementary school who had snickered about Daddy's bootlegging. It was as if I were now replying to them, "But look, he was also an extraordinary, generous, exciting, charismatic man—a good man. He was better than your boring fathers, so don't make fun of him!" In other words, I had begun this project as a biographer and ended it as a child, which may account for the book's somewhat dual point of view. Most of the accounts written by children of criminal fathers are memoirs; that is, they include biographical information mostly as background for the parent-child relationship. I wanted the main focus to be on my father, not on our relationship. I think I took this position because it was one that would enable me to distance my emotions. Once I started writing, though, the emotions found their own way in, at least some of them.

So after all this, do I now understand Wayne Merriott Padgett, the man who was my father? Yes and no. Yes in the sense that I know a lot more about him and I think I see why he did some of the things he did—both good and bad. No in the sense that no one can ever get inside the dazzling complexity of someone else's spirit. Wiser or not, I've tried to be honest and forthcoming, to avoid romanticizing or glorifying my father's life, but the truth is that, despite all his faults, he was a hero to me, and he still is.

Acknowledgments

I am grateful to the many people and organizations that helped make this book possible: Lorine Allen; Joan Brix Banks; Al Benningfield; Keith Binning, *Tulsa Daily World*; Bobby Bluejacket; Cecile Bowers; the late Joe Brainard; Mary Jane Brown; Chief Ralph Brown, Tulsa Fire Department; the office staff of Dr. Richmond Brownson; Tracy Cabanis; the late Raymond Clark; Louise Clark; B. T. Cook; Gene Curtis, *Tulsa Daily World*; Loretta Day, Tulsa Public Schools; Bob Dumont; Howard Donahue; Lee Eller; Kenward Elmslie; S. M. "Buddy" Fallis; the Federal Bureau of Investigation, Oklahoma City and Washington, D.C.; Homer Gafford; Dick Gallup; Edna Gallup; the late John Gallup; Barry Gifford; the Greenwood Cultural Center; the late Al Haddock; Geof Hewitt; Jess "Logchain" Hunter; Pete James; Merilark Johnson-Padgett; Jeff Kaufmann, Tulsa Historical Society; the Kellogg-Hubbard Library, Montpelier, Vermont; Hugh Hamilton; Nancy Hamilton; Bill Martin; Robbie Matthis; Dr. Michael Maxwell; Bobbie Mitchell; Alma Montgomery; the Research Division of the New York Public Library; Pete Nicklau; Dean and Shelley Padgett; Mary Margaret Padgett; Penny Padgett; Robert Padgett, Jr.; the late Gladys Pilkington; John Pilkington; James Pilkington; Robert Polito; Robert Powers, Tulsa Historical Society; Elda Powers; George Schneeman; Steven Shapiro, New York Civil Liberties Union; Dr. Richard Shildt; the office of Gene Stipe; Robert Tucker; and the Tulsa County Public Library reference librarians. Phillip Lopate was encouraging and helpful far beyond the call of duty. I am particularly grateful for the help of Kam Wygant.

At the University of Oklahoma Press, I thank the entire staff, in particular Daniel Simon, who welcomed this project, and the design staff of Gail Carter and Tony Roberts. Many thanks go to copyeditor Jay Fultz for his clarity and critical good sense. All authors should be so lucky to have a copyeditor like him.

I also thank my friend and agent Robert Cornfield and my wife, Patricia. Inexpressible is my debt to my late mother, Lucille Huey, and to my late grandmother Verna Padgett.

Quotations from print materials are referenced in the text or in notes at the end of the book. Quotations from individuals are from interviews I conducted with them.

The names of key people in this book are listed in Appendix B.

Oklahoma Tough

Composite map of TULSA (1921–1991)

Streets roughly to scale of 1" = 1 mile

Streets (horizontal): Pine St., Admiral Pl., 3rd St., 11th St., 21st St., 31st St.

Streets (vertical): Memorial, Sheridan, Yale, Harvard, Lewis, Peoria, Main

To Collinsville ⇦

To Claremore, Grand Lake, Baxter Springs (KS), & Joplin (MO) ⇨

To Hot Springs (AR) ⇧

His last house

To The Sheridan Club ⇨

Sears warehouse

race track

The Fairgrounds

Stokes farm

The Buckhorn ■ The Music Box

Rose Hill Cemetery

Will Rogers High School

King St. house

Cleveland Jr. High

Grover & Verna's

Archer Park

Whittier Sq. area

2733 E. 4th St.

Noah & Daisy's

Donahue's garage

Whittier Elementary

car lot

"Mom's"

Virgil Edgar's Conoco

St. John's Hospital

The East Side

The South Side

The North Side

Independence

"Little Africa"

1st St.

Police station

Central Park

Central High School

Downtown

Ritz Theater

To Sand Springs ⇦

⇦ To West Tulsa, Sapulpa, & Oklahoma City

Arkansas River

N
W — E
S

Composite map of Tulsa, 1921–1991.

1
Sunday Morning

VERNA WENT OUT TO FEED THE CHICKS. Eight A.M. was a little later than usual, but she had stayed up last night ironing, first Grover's uniforms and khakis, then the boys' clothes, with a little starch for the shirts. And as she ironed she had worried. Why hadn't Grover met her after the movie? Why hadn't he come home? Was he with another woman? In their more than thirteen years of marriage, he had stayed out all night like this only once. It had hurt her feelings terribly, but she had said nothing. Where *was* he?

It was a quiet Sunday morning. This whole May had been a bad month for tornadoes. The air was getting sultry as Verna stepped off the back porch and onto the gravel path that led to the garage door a few feet away. Ten years ago, when construction on the house had begun, this had been just a big field, with a farmhouse in the distance and one other house, newly built. Now, in 1933, Grover and Verna's house was surrounded by others, part of a neighborhood. It even had a paved street and city water.

Verna noticed that the padlock on the garage door was unlocked and that the door was ajar, but she couldn't remember whether or not she had closed it the day before. It didn't matter. There wasn't anything inside worth stealing. As she swung the door open, she could hear the baby chicks cheeping.

It took a moment for her eyes to adjust to the dark. Then she saw Grover lying on a makeshift pallet on the floor, his blue coat folded neatly under his head.

"Why . . . honey, did you sleep all night out here?" she asked.

Grover didn't budge.

When she knelt down and gently shook his shoulder, his head lolled to one side and saliva spilled from the corner of his mouth.

In shock, Verna ran next door and told the neighbors. Then she rushed back to the house, woke the boys, and told them straight out that their father was dead.

It must have been the neighbors who called the fire station where Grover worked, Engine Company Number 11, and at 8:10 the station called the police. In no time Verna's backyard was filled with people.

Assistant Fire Chief L. J. Bullock, County Investigator Jack Bonham, and an unidentified third official arrived at the scene and conducted an investigation. Then the body was removed to a funeral home.

The next morning, the front page of the *Tulsa World* announced: "Mystery Shrouds Fireman's Death." The article stated that Grover F. Padgett, for eleven years a member of the Tulsa fire department, had been found dead under mysterious circumstances in his garage. Grover's car "was locked and the motor not running, which eliminated monoxide gas as a cause of the death. There was not a mark upon the body to indicate violence . . . [and because] the man might have taken poison, a thorough search was made of the premises for some container in which it might have been carried. None was found. Also the physician who examined Padgett pointed out that there were no traces about the man's mouth to indicate that he had poisoned himself." The position of Grover's body pretty much ruled out death by natural causes.

Later that same day, the unnamed third official wrote a report to the fire and police commissioner, saying, perhaps in response to the wording of the *World* headline, that he and County Inspector Bonham were "satisfied that the death was not shrouded in mystery." However, his report made no attempt to explain the death.

The death certificate did, though, at least partially. Dated May 31, 1933, and signed by F. E. Rushing, the autopsy physician, the certificate listed the cause of death as "carbolic acid poisoning (suicide)." Grover's brother Roy had been present at the autopsy. "Grover's insides were cooked," he told a relative.

Carbolic acid is a powerful antiseptic that was discovered in coal tar in 1834. By the early 1900s, ingesting it was a common method of suicide. In 1933 carbolic acid solution was available over the counter at any pharmacy, and twenty cents' worth was enough to kill a grown man.

But where was the bottle that had held the poison? If Grover had killed himself, he couldn't have done it in the garage. If he had killed himself, where had he done it? If he had killed himself, how did he get home? He couldn't have done all of it by himself. It just didn't add up.

Maybe he hadn't killed himself at all. Maybe someone had "helped" him swallow the poison by forcing a funnel down his throat.

Verna's three sons quickly came to believe that their father had been murdered. One of them, barely eleven years old, had heard things to that effect at the funeral. Week after week he lay in bed at night listening to his mother's sobbing, and vowed revenge on the murderers. No matter how long it took, he would find them. Wayne would track them down and kill every last one of those sons of bitches.

2 *Background*

GROVER FLOYD PADGETT WAS BORN on October 14, 1888, near Versailles, Missouri, to George Padgett, a farmer, and Laura Merriott. George had migrated from North Carolina. Laura was a native of Missouri. Their marriage produced five children, but Laura died when Grover was three, and George remarried and had three more children. Grover and his seven siblings were raised by his father and stepmother.

When Grover was six, the family moved to the then small town of Tulsa (population ca. 500), in Indian Territory, where his father opened a livery stable. But because the town was rather wild and Grover's sister Maggie, then age twelve, started running the streets and acting up, George soon moved the family about twenty-five miles east of town, to live on the Rucker Ranch, until the kids were grown. It was on the ranch that young Grover learned to ride. "He broke all the horses for people," Verna said. One time he got thrown, and "it tore the muscles off his shoulder, and it never did get completely normal." But that didn't stop him from riding or, at the age of twenty-one, from enlisting in the United States Army for the first of three tours of duty. For two years he served in the Philippines, in the aftermath of a series of uprisings there. As sergeant first class in 1917, he was stationed at Camp Shelby, near Hattiesburg, Mississippi, where he drilled black cavalrymen for combat in World War I. Furloughed to the Army Reserves in 1919, he returned to his family, which had moved to a farm six miles north of Claremore, Oklahoma (ca. 2,500).

Shortly after Grover's return, two of his sisters talked him into accompanying them to visit their friends, the Tucker girls. One of those girls, barely nineteen, was Verna. She recalled that first meeting: "I knew right then that Grover was trying to notice me and it didn't faze me a bit."

Grover was thirty. He wasn't particularly tall (5 feet 9¾ inches), but he was muscular and he had a strong jaw. His light brown hair was cut short, and his blue eyes seemed even bluer against his deeply tanned face. He held his head and neck as if he were standing at attention.

Verna had long blond hair and blue-gray eyes. She was eleven years younger than Grover, but only a quarter of an inch shorter. Height ran in her family.

Her father, Jesse Tucker, stood a lanky six foot three. He had grown up in northwestern Arkansas. Like most men of his time and place, he had many skills—at various times he was a farmer, a drugstore owner, a justice of the peace, and a traveling salesman for a nursery—but he was unusual in that he also liked to read, think, and discuss social, religious, and philosophical issues. He subscribed to the *Congressional Record* and the *National Rip-Saw*, a socialist publication. At some point, Jesse declared himself a socialist. He was a great admirer of what used to be called freethinkers: Voltaire, socialist Eugene V. Debs, and Robert Ingersoll, the nineteenth-century American agnostic and critic of Christianity. As a child, Jesse had gone to school only three months each year, as was typical in farm communities where every worker was necessary, but he had educated himself. He also enjoyed chewing tobacco, spitting arcs of juice from across the living room to the spitoon next to the wood stove. He claimed he never missed, but his wife, Eva, occasionally asked him to shorten the distance.

Also a native of northwestern Arkansas, Eva was typical of many women of her time and place: unassuming, quiet, and, with six children to take care of—not to mention her huge vegetable patches—incredibly hardworking. Though married to a freethinker, Eva, the daughter of a

Baptist minister and farmer, quietly went to church, when possible. Free-thinkers or not, the Tuckers' word was their bond, a character trait that Verna prized.

All of Verna's life had been spent either on a farm, where she and her siblings had worked alongside their parents, or in small towns in north-western Arkansas. Her older sisters, Dahna and Grace, had taken teacher training at the normal institute in Claremore, and Dahna had started teaching grade school in Oolagah. But Verna was never encouraged to follow their lead. She had completed the eighth grade, which was as far as you could go in her neck of the woods, so she repeated eighth grade—twice—reviewing last year's courses and then studying more advanced material on her own. It was a sheltered existence. "I can't make people believe how isolated we were," she said.

Grover, on the other hand, had been all over, not only the western United States and the South, but as far as the Philippines, maybe even Japan! At thirty, he exuded a quiet confidence. The jut of his jaw reinforced his aura of determination. Grover, staying with his father and step-mother on his mustering-out pay, had all day and night to pursue the attractive Verna, who already had several other young Claremore suitors. His parents' farm was only two miles north of the Tuckers' ten acres. He called on Verna often, and gradually she became interested in him.

Grover was mad about her, but he couldn't marry her while penniless. So he went down to Texas briefly to wildcat the new oil rigs there, taking a room above a bar in some rural outpost. In his room he wrote to Verna, describing the hard work on the rig and the nightly sounds from the bar below, the sounds of drinking, gambling, and occasional fighting. The letters also described his loneliness and his absolute conviction that Verna was the only girl for him.

During that summer, she went to stay with an aunt and uncle in Fayet-teville for about ten days. Now back from Texas, Grover wrote more love letters to her, one of them a nine-page epistle sent special delivery. Verna took the train back to Claremore, where Grover was expecting her.

As the train approached the station, it got sidetracked to wait for another train to pass. Night was setting in. Verna recalled: "Grover walked down the railroad track and got on the train and came in and sat down beside me. He said, 'Are we going to go home tonight as two or one?' Very slowly, I said, 'One.' When we pulled into the station and got off the train, his sister Opal, the postman, the lady that writes the marriage licenses, and a Masonic judge were waiting: he had it all planned. That's how he took things in hand. We went right to the courthouse and got married."

The marriage license was issued, the marriage performed, and the license recorded, all on September 30, 1919, though Verna later recalled it as September 1. She also distinctly remembered that Grover's date of birth was November 19, not the October 14 date his father would later supply for the death certificate. On the marriage license, Grover is listed as being twenty-eight years old, whereas according to his army records he would have been thirty-one. With no official record of his birth extant, we can only wonder whether or not Grover wanted the army to think he was older or the justice of the peace to think he was younger. Verna always suspected Grover was a little older than he had let on, but she never mentioned it to him. The tight-lipped Grover never told. It was only one of the mysteries he would take to the grave.

3   *Grover and Verna: Married Life*

WHEN GROVER AND VERNA arrived at the Tuckers' farm that night and told her parents that they had just gotten married, Verna's mother said nothing; tears came to her father's eyes. But the newlyweds were welcome—as was everyone—to stay at the Tucker house.

Grover was getting seventeen dollars a month from the Army Reserves, not nearly enough to support a family. Soon he found work doing carpentry, and he and Verna moved into Claremore, renting a room from Verna's sister Dahna. In the spring of 1920, Grover was honorably discharged from the service, and he and Verna rented a small frame house, where their first child, Robert Floyd Padgett, was born, on June 2, only eight months after their rather precipitous marriage. Although it is tempting to speculate, Verna's upbringing and character make a premarital conception unlikely.

A month after Robert's birth Grover took a job as a migrant worker, part of a crew of twelve men who began the season harvesting wheat in Kansas and worked their way north, perhaps as far as Montana, into September, when Grover returned to Claremore.

But he could see no future there, and so he moved the family the twenty-nine miles down to Tulsa, a town that had been growing quickly since his brief stay there as a child. In 1900, the year of its first U.S. census, Tulsa had 1,390 people. Successive census figures were 7,298 (1907), 18,182 (1910), 28,240 (1915), 58,782 (1919), and 72,075 (1920), but unofficial figures placed the numbers higher. Between 1910 and 1920, the national urban population increased by 29 percent. Tulsa's jumped 400 percent. People were pouring into the city, where jobs were plentiful.

Grover found employment in a furniture store, but soon switched to laying oil and gas pipe. He and Verna and baby Robert were renting two rooms, until Grover's half-sister Opal and Verna's little sister Tenna came down from Claremore and suggested that together they could afford a large place. Grover found such an apartment not far from downtown Tulsa. Most of the neighborhood was of well-built one- and two-story homes with small yards. It's possible that the owner was a Mason, or that Grover found the apartment through one of his fellow Masons. He had joined the society about three years before.

Grover had joined the Masons, the Saba Grotto (also known as The Mystic Order of Veiled Prophets of the Enchanted Realm), and the Shriners for "advancement." He even got Verna to join the Eastern Star, the equivalent Shriners group for women. At that time, the mayor of Tulsa was a Mason, as were a large number of public officials and businessmen. Early in 1921, Grover's membership paid off: he went down to City Hall a manual laborer and came back a policeman.

Not that the job was a plum. The officers not only had to work twelve-hour shifts seven days a week, they had to pay for their own uniforms and revolvers. But to Grover it was preferable to harvesting wheat or laying pipe, and he must have enjoyed being in uniform again.

His first assignment was the First Street beat, where, twenty-seven years before, his father had opened the livery stable. Now the area's prostitution, liquor trade, and gambling were more flagrant, and there were cocaine and paregoric addicts to contend with. Because public officials were on the take, all Grover had to do was to keep things from getting completely out of hand. But in May of 1921, things in Tulsa ran amok, even beyond the control of the city's entire police force.

Tulsa, first as part of Indian Territory and then, with statehood in 1907, as part of Oklahoma, had had a checkered history of law enforcement (see Appendix A). With the discovery of oil near Tulsa on June 25, 1901, Tulsa's boom period began, attracting not only bankers, businesspeople, shop-keepers, and people looking for an honest job, but also various "drifters, grifters, grafters, gamblers, loafers, idlers, and flim-flams."[1] By 1914, the city was wide open.

The time was ripe for vigilante action. The Ku Klux Klan, founded during the Reconstruction Era after the Civil War, had pretty much subsided by the end of the nineteenth century. But by 1915 it had reawakened, this time in response to what it considered to be lawlessness and political radicalism. In addition to Jews, blacks, and Catholics, the rise of Communism, socialism, and unionism posed a new threat to those Americans who believed in "pure" Americanism, which of course included white supremacy.

In August of 1916, the Tulsa City Commission passed an ordinance that required blacks to live in a separate part of town. The Klan became active in Tulsa the following year. In 1917, a group of Wobblies—members of the radical Industrial Workers of the World—were arrested, mainly for political reasons, and quickly convicted of bombing the home of an oil executive. While the police were transferring the prisoners to the county jail, a black-robed group called the Knights of Liberty seized the Wobblies and took them to the edge of town, beat them, tarred and feathered them, and ran them off. The Klan itself was responsible for dragging any number of people, black and white, from their homes and beating them. A police strike in 1919 and mass resignations in 1920 weakened local law enforcement. In August of 1920, a mob of two thousand people dragged a confessed murderer from his cell, took him to the scene of the crime, and hanged him while police watched. There were reports that the police had even directed traffic. Chief of Police John Gustafson—who had campaigned with the pledge "I'll clean up the city or quit!"—piously described the matter as "regrettable, but probably inevitable." But all this paled in comparison to what lay ahead.

On the afternoon of May 30, 1921, a few months after Grover had joined the force, a young black man was accused of attempting to molest a white girl in the elevator she operated. The next day, police took him to jail, where he was questioned and held. The *Tulsa Tribune* hit the stands at 3:15

OKLAHOMA TOUGH

P.M. with a biased and distorted account of the incident, stating that there were rumors of a lynching.* If there hadn't been rumors, there certainly were some now! The rumors reached what whites called Little Africa, the black neighborhood, near downtown. Throughout the afternoon, the rumors and groups of blacks and whites had increased until, outside the jail, one white man got into a struggle with a black man who refused to surrender his gun and the weapon went off, serving as a sort of nightmarish starter's pistol. The Tulsa Race Riot—the most violent and disgraceful chapter in the city's history—had begun.

It was a one-sided contest. After some gun battles in the center of town, the heavily outnumbered blacks retreated to their neighborhood, whose entire population numbered around eleven thousand. At dawn, approximately fifteen thousand enraged white men attacked, looting and burning virtually every building in the entire thirty-five-square-block area. The official account stated that they burned 1,115 houses to the ground, as well as all the black churches and businesses. After the National Guard restored order, the official death toll listed nine white men and boys, and sixty-eight black men, women, and children. Many people still maintain that the death toll among blacks was considerably higher, and that there were atrocities that went unmentioned in the press.[2]

At this point Grover may have questioned his career move. During the first night of rioting, he had come to the window of his apartment and told Verna, "We're having a race riot," and instructed her to stay indoors until it was over. "Little Africa" wasn't very far away. Verna could hear the gunshots. It was impossible for the police to stop the rioting, once it had begun: there were only about thirty officers on the entire force. According to eyewitness accounts, some policemen took part in the rioting. Some guarded important buildings and facilities. Others rounded up blacks, making sure they were unarmed, and transported them to enclosed areas, partly for their own protection. Apparently, Grover had escorted blacks to Convention Hall, located between his own apartment and "Little Africa." The role must have felt familiar to this former army sergeant who had drilled black recruits. But witnessing armed combat for the first time—and on one's native soil—and being powerless before it, must have come as a shock.

---

* In its November 9, 1917, editorial about the Tulsa Wobblies, the *Tulsa World* had actually called for a lynching, urging citizens to buy some rope and "kill 'em dead."

Grover shared some of the racism of his time and place, although there is no evidence that he was virulent about it. Ostensibly, he had joined fraternal groups to get a better job, but the fact is that, after the riot, many members of those groups joined the Klan. "It was the thing to do," Verna said. Grover, ever tight-lipped, never told her whether he joined the Klan. Tulsa quickly became a strong Klan city, and the neighborhood he and Verna lived in has been described as Klan territory.[3] But Verna never saw any sign of his being a Klansman. It's possible that he joined and then simply remained inactive. What is certain is that Grover's family looked down on—and sometimes feared—blacks, as did a great many other white Tulsans.

In any case, Grover soon joined the fire department. Why? "I don't know," Verna said. "Never did know. It's funny, I never pinned him down for nothing and asked him." He then moved the family to the home of fellow fireman Andy Woods, at 2008 East Archer, in a respectable working-class neighborhood about a mile and a half east of downtown. A widower, Mr. Woods rented out the house, reserving one room for himself. It was in this house that Verna gave birth to her second child, on March 4, 1922.

Verna and Grover named him Wayne Merriott Padgett, after the son of one of Verna's friends. Grover, who bore a tattoo of a cross with a banner across it that read "Mother," picked Merriott, the maiden name of his mother, who had died when he was three. Grover himself would not live to see his new son grow up and become one of the shrewdest and most elusive criminals in Oklahoma history.

Within two and a half years Grover had gone from being single to married with two children, and in that period he had gone from town to town, job to job, lodging to lodging. Maybe it was time to settle down and stay put.

Grover bought a building lot from a farmer who was parceling out his fields on the east side of town. The farmer's own two-story farmhouse was visible from the lot, as was one other house, newly built. Verna's father and a carpenter set to work putting up the house, along with an outhouse in the back; Grover helped when he was off work. Five other houses were going up at the same time, mostly on weekends. In May of 1923, when Wayne was fourteen months old, the family moved into their new home, the first home that belonged to them, all two rooms of it. They furnished it with a used bed from an auction and some donated chairs. For a total of four dollars Grover bought a used stove and an icebox, the kind cooled by ice. At first the house had no electricity, only gas. The street out front was still a dirt road, soft from years of plowing, muddy in the rain. Even Admiral Place, the thoroughfare two blocks south, wasn't paved, and the jitney service from downtown came out only as far as Lewis, three-quarters of a mile away. Eventually, Grover fenced in the backyard, built a rabbit hutch and chicken pen, and, in an open patch behind the yard, he grew potatoes, okra, and onions.

A year later Grover made the final payment on the lot and the lumber, then took out another loan and hired a contractor, who added two bedrooms, a dining room, a kitchen, a back porch, and a room for a future indoor bathroom. The Padgetts didn't yet have a radio or a car, but things were going along pretty well at 153 North Florence Avenue.

The two boys were healthy but had different personalities. Robert was quieter, the thoughtful, studious type. Wayne walked at nine months, and from the time he started growing he was very active. Verna recalled, "When he got his first tricycle, he tore it down and put it back together. I seen him out in the backyard and he was taking the wheels off. I said, 'What are you doing?' and he said, 'I'm trying to see how this thing works.' He was about four. He was up and around and at 'em, played a lot, liked to throw rocks and do all the things little boys do."

On October 14, 1926, Verna gave birth to her third and last child, Tommie Gene.

The year before, Robert had started kindergarten at Whittier Elementary School, a long, one-story red brick building. Wayne entered kindergarten there in September of 1927. Verna said that "he didn't learn as fast as Robert did, but he made his grades every year. Robert was more studious, and didn't get out and do the things that Wayne did. Wayne would climb trees and do things like that, just like any regular boy."

And like any "regular" boy of that time and place, he never avoided a fight. Verna said, "One time he had a fight with a little boy. I was mowing the lawn, and a couple come down with their little boy and said, 'I'd like you to look at what Wayne did to our boy.' So I said, 'Well, a boy pushed my son Robert off the gate up at Whittier and put him in the hospital unconscious, and I never went to *his* parents.'" (Robert had been hospitalized with a fractured skull.) Verna acknowledged that Wayne did get in fights with boys his own age. Even Wayne and Robert duked it out at home from time to time, prompting their Aunt Tenna to buy them boxing gloves. A photograph taken around 1930 shows the tow-headed boys in bathing suits out in the backyard, striking a boxing pose. Robert is facing his opponent, but Wayne has turned to flash a charming smile to the photographer. He is roughly the same size as his older brother.

From time to time Verna took the boys to a Baptist church a mile away, and because there was no church in her neighborhood, she started a Sunday school in her home, in 1925 or 1926. "I ordered some cards that had pictures of angels or Jesus on them, with a little scripture at the bottom. The first thing I knew, I had a bunch of little kids every Sunday." Eventually, a church opened in the neighborhood. "Wayne got a plaque for never missing a Sunday. He couldn't wait to go there every Sunday morning."

For his part, Grover wasn't a bad father. According to Verna, "He was a pretty good provider, but he didn't seem to have patience. He had been a sergeant in World War I and he spoke to the boys like they were soldiers, in a strong voice. He was all right, about like the average dad, I guess. He seemed to think a lot of the boys, took them to get their shoes, and helped buy their clothes."

There was one bad habit, though, that Grover had picked up in the army. Verna explained, "Of course we lived very close [economically] then, trying to pay for the house. He was gone a lot." Gone where? "I didn't know. I never did ask him. He was gambling. I suspicioned it, because he would borrow money—and not for us." She knew because it was she who answered the phone when various loan companies called to dun him. "I never asked him where he'd been. I knew better than to. See, when you're tied down with three little children, you're at everybody's mercy. Especially your husband's. You *can't* be independent. You *can't* give orders or ask questions. That's the way I was raised, I guess. I never remember my mother asking Dad for anything. Grover was about twelve years older than me and had been a bachelor, so he knew how to take the lead."

Around the house, he didn't say much, unless Verna's dad or Grover's brother Roy—who now lived just a few blocks away—or another man dropped by. But Verna herself wasn't very talkative. Grover wasn't openly affectionate, either. "Before I married him, he acted like the world would come to an end if I didn't marry him. He said, 'Whoever gets you will get a premium' and all that kind of stuff. And then after we got married, I can't remember him ever telling me he loved me. I'll say one thing about him, he was like Wayne: he wouldn't *say* I love you, but he'd *do* something for you. He was always bringing something home, like a box of candy, something like that. He never did mistreat me, ever. He never even threatened to hit me."

But he could be extremely jealous, although Verna never gave him any cause to be. One time a door-to-door salesman knocked on the door and asked Verna for the lady of the house. She replied that *she* was the lady. "You can't be the lady of the house—you don't look any older than a schoolgirl." In a flash Grover bounded out the front door and socked the guy in the jaw, knocking him off the porch. The salesman beat a hasty retreat as Grover glowered at him, with clenched fists.

Grover's switch to the fire department seemed an improvement. No longer was he stuck with the night shift; the fire department work shifts rotated. No longer did he have to deal with the riffraff along First Street, not to mention mass rioting. Instead, he had the companionship of the other men in the firehouse—not unlike army life. But it was a dangerous job.

In late 1926 or in 1927, Grover was injured by a car that plowed into the rear of his fire truck. The collision left a nasty gash in the heel of his right foot. When the wound refused to heal, he was sent to the Mayo Clinic in Rochester, Minnesota. In early December of 1927, Wayne, now in his third month of kindergarten, sent him a letter: "DEAR DADDY I AM A ƆOOD BOY, I LOVE YOU. WAYNE." But Grover's suppurating heel continued to give him problems. He didn't complain about pain, but he did limp.

With an insurance settlement from the accident, Grover put a large down payment on a new $695 Ford—a 1930 Model A, the standard one. That is, it had a simple Briggs body, without cowl lights, mohair upholstery, interior light, and armrests, all of which came with the fancier version of the same car. But the new car was fine, and in it the family started to take weekend trips, Grover driving, Verna at his side, and the three boys in the back seat, where, if they wanted, they could pull down the windowshades. There is a photograph of them parked at what appears to be a picnic area; they are sitting on the car's running board. The picture was probably taken in 1930, because the fenders show no signs of the dents that quickly accumulated from the loose stones on the roads in those days.

In addition to a telephone, they bought a Philco radio in Whittier Square, which, only a few blocks from Whittier school, was Tulsa's first shopping area outside of downtown.

Gradually they settled into a family routine. Grover worked his shift, came home, slept, and ate. Sometimes he spent time with his brother Roy. The two got along well, though they were different types: Roy was modest, gentle, and hardworking, very much a family man. Grover "smoked, drank, and ran around," as Roy's daughter Alma put it. Verna stayed at home, tended the garden and chickens, cleaned the house, washed the clothes by hand and ironed them, cooked, and looked after the three boys: "My boys were always neat. I bathed them and put Johnson's baby powder on them." She also kept them well fed, with three meals a day, and she made sure they had oranges.

But Grover had other routines. To help pay off his gambling debts, at one point he even pawned his revolver. Finally, Verna worked up her nerve and told him that if he would turn over his paycheck to her every week, she would have them out of debt within six months. To Grover such an abdication of control was unthinkable. So, in the early 1930s, Verna took a part-time job in a downtown clothing store. The children were either in school or with a babysitter, never alone.

When Robert and Wayne were about ten and eight, they attended a tent meeting, and, caught up in the fervor of the revival, were baptized on the spot. At another meeting there they heard Billy Sunday preach, and, as Verna put it, "Boy, he really laid it on." But their religious enthusiasm was to subside and then be dashed by what was to come.

Grover's heel continued to bother him. In September of 1932, he saw several new doctors. It's possible that he had a double motive for doing so: relief from his injury and a disability pension. In those days there was no worker's compensation or Social Security disability payments. In any event, these new medical visits, in light of what happened soon after, take on an ominous shading.

On a weekend morning a few months later, Grover told Verna to get the boys ready. They were all going out to Mohawk Park. He wanted to hunt squirrel. Verna thought it odd that he wanted to take the entire family along, but as usual she didn't question him.

Mohawk Park is described in a 1938 Federal Writers' Project book called *Tulsa: A Guide to the Oil Capital*, the authorship of which has been ascribed to Jim Thompson, who later wrote such hard-boiled chillers as *The Killer Inside Me* and *The Grifters*: "Mohawk Park is a municipally owned recreation area of 2,400 acres, with protected woodland, landscaped gardens, lakes, lagoons, bridle paths, and zoological gardens. Other recreational features are picnic grounds with stone shelters and fireplaces, a polo field, tennis courts, golf course, and an archery range. . . . The zoo is probably the most popular feature in the park."[4] Work on Mohawk Park had begun in 1924, and by the early 1930s it was a popular local attraction for families.

But Grover did not take the boys to see the animals. Instead, he parked on the edge of a heavily wooded, remote area, telling Verna and the boys to wait in the car. Then he disappeared into the woods with his squirrel rifle. When he returned ten or fifteen minutes later, his hand was wrapped in a bloody handkerchief. He had had an accident. His little finger and part of his ring finger were gone. Verna would have to drive him to the hospital.

No one recalls Wayne's ever having mentioned this incident. It's possible he took it in stride, since safety standards were much lower in those days, and accidental maiming was not uncommon. But it's also possible that the incident left its emotional mark on him, later motivating him unconsciously to become a crack shot who would thereby "rectify" this violent visitation on his family.

Now with both a defective foot *and* a defective hand, Grover applied for a pension. But fire department officials denied it, deciding that his medical problems would in no way affect him in the performance of his duties.

In retrospect, the "accident" seemed suspicious to Verna. With a rifle you might accidentally shoot yourself in the foot, or shoot someone else, but how do you shoot yourself in the *hand*? Besides, like most country boys, Grover had learned to hunt at an early age, and had abundant training and experience with firearms in the military. Accidental or not, the incident had left Grover "nervous," according to Verna, a condition that later seemed pronounced to his fellow firemen. However, he didn't seem depressed or gloomy.

Oklahoma spring weather tends to be volatile, but May of 1933 had seen an unusual number of windstorms and tornados, with hail and sudden drops in barometric pressure. Before a tornado hits, the air sometimes turns a dusky yellow, and there is a sudden silence and eerie stillness to everything.

However, the only tornado on May 27 was to be an emotional one. Grover decided to take that Saturday off. Verna needed some new shoes, so that afternoon he drove her and the boys downtown, where he parked the car and suggested that, after shopping, she take the boys to see the new movie at the Ritz. The other movies in town weren't suitable for the boys. He'd meet them at the car after the show.

The Ritz was the nicest movie theater in town. Ornately decorated in an Art Deco combination of Spanish-Moorish and crypto-American Indian styles, it had beautiful mosaic floors and walls, dual stairways to the balcony, and a booming organ. And when the lights went down, you could gaze straight up and see stars glittering in the night sky. Of course, they were just little lights twinkling in the ceiling, but the effect was uncanny.

It was opening day for *Hell Below,* a submarine warfare drama starring Robert Montgomery, Walter Huston, Madge Evans, Jimmy Durante, and Eugene Pallette. The staggering combination of Durante (who played the part of "Ptomaine") and Pallette provided "the comic relief against such thrills as torpedoing enemy destroyers, fighting off enemy aircraft, and the hair-raising episode in which Montgomery rams a fort with an explosive-laden submarine," according to the *Tulsa Daily World* review. The feature film came with a Mickey Mouse cartoon and Paramount News.

Verna and the boys took in the 3:25 show, which let out a little less than two hours later. When they got back to the car, Grover wasn't there, but he knew what time the show ended, so he would be along soon. They waited. And waited. For over an hour. Finally, Verna took the boys home on the bus. After dinner, she put them to bed and ironed until 10 or 10:30. She was usually in bed by 8:30.

Where Grover had gone immediately after he left Verna and the boys is unknown, but by that evening he was on the tenth floor of the Bliss Hotel, playing cards in a game run by a thirty-four-year-old gambler, sportsman, and former fireman named J. N. (Ned) VanDeventer. Apparently, Grover lost, and lost heavily, not only his paycheck but the paychecks of some of his fellow firemen, which he was supposed to cash for them. Losing more than you can afford causes a kind of emotional pressure drop, and my guess is that whatever drove Grover to shoot off part of his hand also caused him to go downstairs to the lobby pharmacy, buy a bottle of carbolic acid, go back to the room and into the bathroom, close the door, and drink the fatal liquid.

When the other players discovered him, they realized they had to get him out of the hotel. VanDeventer had a nice thing going there, and he didn't need this kind of trouble. So they must have bundled him up, put him in his car, and driven him home, discarding the carbolic acid bottle along the way. It's likely that one of the other gamblers was a fireman, who could recognize Grover's car and knew where he lived. Neighbors later said that about 3 A.M. Sunday morning they had heard and then seen a car slowly coming down the dark street with the headlights off. The men had turned off the engine and pushed the car the final few hundred feet to the garage, where they took out Grover's body and arranged it as nicely as they could on the floor. About eight o'clock that morning, Verna went out to feed the chicks.

4 *Growing Up*

THE ELEVEN-YEAR-OLD BOY WHO lay in bed vowing revenge was enraged not only by his father's death, but also by his mother's grief. Verna had not told the boys anything about the cause of death. She had simply handed Grover's suicide note to the police.

Written on laundry cardboard, the note said that he had lost money to a Mr. VanDeventer and others, listing the amount of his paycheck and the checks of some of his fellow firemen and telling Verna to collect his death pension, around one hundred and fifty dollars. He also stated that he couldn't raise three boys on a wooden leg, adding, "You tried and I wouldn't listen," a reference to her offer to budget their finances. It was as close as Grover could get to saying "I'm sorry."

A few days after the death, a fireman brought Verna a message from VanDeventer, telling her that if she would meet him in the lobby of the Bliss Hotel, he would give her a hundred dollars toward the funeral expenses. She immediately went down to the hotel, took the envelope, and left, without a word. She was still traumatized.

Grover's brother Roy handled the funeral, which took place at the Immanuel Baptist Church, which Grover had attended a few times. The cortege to Rose Hill Cemetery was, as one witness put it, "three miles long": family, firemen, members of Saba Grotto, Shriners, and Masons. Grover had been a 32nd-degree Mason, high enough for his sons and grandsons to be admitted automatically to the order.

But the professional and fraternal organizations proved to be less than useless now. Verna applied for her widow's pension, but Dick Pitts, the fire chief, told her that suicide voided the pension. Pitts didn't like Grover, she later learned. Two months after her request was denied, a fireman shot himself, and *his* widow received a pension. Verna hired the same lawyer as the widow and filed a formal appeal at the state level, which was refused. She later learned that Pitts had sent three firemen to Oklahoma City to head off the appeal. The Masons offered her some old clothes and made the appalling suggestion that she put the boys in an orphanage in Guthrie, about one hundred miles away.

Each of the boys—Robert, nearly thirteen; Wayne, barely eleven; and Tommie, six and a half—had reacted differently to Grover's death. When one relative visited the house, Robert was behind the door, crying, and Wayne was repeating, "I'll kill 'em if I can find 'em."

Verna recalled that Wayne "was such a sweet kid and wanted to be helpful. He was half orphaned right at the time when he needed a father. He felt responsible for his younger brother and me, and it made it tough for him. If Robert felt the same way, he didn't show it as much as Wayne. Robert kept to his books a lot." Years later, Robert would, in typically male Padgett fashion, express his guilt obliquely, in a letter to Verna: "I've got the sweetest mother in the world who did the best she could for her unworthy son" (himself). His way of coping with his father's death was to withdraw into his books and his interior life. But Wayne, according to Verna, "took Grover's death harder than the other boys." Not only had it instilled a need for revenge, it had begun what was to be a lifelong distrust of institutions. "When my daddy died, those firemen and Masons didn't do a goddamned thing," he once told me.

Verna did receive the $1,600 Grover had amassed in the firemen's credit union, the sum of regular deductions from his paycheck. She used this money to pay off the mortgage on the house; with a roof over her head, she wouldn't have to "give the boys away." Then she paid off the car loan and funeral expenses, and bought a washing machine. She was out of debt, but near the bottom of an emotional abyss. The entire country was in the depths of the Great Depression and she was thirty-three, with three young boys and a couple of hundred dollars.

The family had a roof over their heads, but how were they going to eat? What was she to do? Verna was shattered. Roy Padgett, himself haunted by nightmares of the suicide for months, stayed nights with her and the boys. Some days, she could hardly get out of bed.

For a year she and the boys had a very tough time. Grover's veteran's pension of seventeen dollars per month didn't go very far. When the city cut off Verna's water for nonpayment, her father came down to Tulsa and paid the bill. But he, like everyone else Verna knew, was hurting financially.

The summer of 1933, only a few months after their father's death, Wayne and Robert started mowing lawns, scavenging for discarded pop bottles, old newspapers, and scrap metal—anything resalable. The panic to make money was one that Wayne and Robert would never be able to shake.

Sometime in 1934, Verna received a call from a woman who worked at Brown-Duncan, which described itself as "Tulsa's dominant retail store," located at Fourth and Main, the crossroads of downtown. Verna immediately accepted the woman's invitation to work there as a salesclerk.

The large department store offered a wide variety of goods and services, such as a series of free health and beauty lectures by a Madame Ida Chernoff. Customers could also sit in the tearoom and hear, live, the Singing Redheads at 11:30 and 1:30, or have a beauty consultation with Miss Bucholtz, described as Helena Rubinstein's personal representative. Ladies' sports hats were going for two dollars, and checked tablecloths were on sale for fifty-nine cents. Although standing for most of the nine-hour day was tiring, Verna was glad to be earning thirty-five cents an hour. She was glad to be earning *anything*.

Wayne's school records begin with his entering first grade on September 4, 1928. From then through sixth grade, his grade average turned out to be just a shade below B. His attendance was good and he was tardy only three times in six years. His marks for conduct could have been better, perhaps a reflection of his fisticuffs on the playground. But his fifth- and sixth-grade records show no effect of his father's death.

Robert's elementary school performance was sterling. His fourth-grade teacher told Verna, "We don't know quite what to do with Robert. He's reading tenth-grade books." He also had the leading roles in two sixth-grade plays and edited the school paper. His academic achievements continued in secondary school.

Probably around the ages of twelve and fourteen, respectively, Wayne and Robert had a momentous fistfight. They fought to a draw, as usual, but this one was different. For some reason, it engendered a mutual respect. It was as if they had realized that although they were different types of people, they could like each other anyway.

Wayne's relationship to his little brother was entirely different. Tommie was the baby of the family and Wayne played the big brother, a role that intensified sharply when they lost their father.

In 1934, Verna took in a young woman named Reba Carpenter, a carhop. In exchange for her room, Reba helped pay some of the bills and took care of the boys when Verna entered the hospital for treatment of a blood clot in her lung. It was about this time that Tommie came down with rickets and Wayne's teeth started to go bad—all, according to Verna, due to malnutrition. Robert was sent to Verna's parents in Claremore for a year. Reba moved on.

In September of 1934, at the age of twelve, Wayne entered the seventh grade at Grover Cleveland Junior High School. The leap from elementary to junior high school is sometimes difficult, but it seemed no problem for him. Every morning he would walk to the long, low, yellow brick building a half mile away.

In his three years at Cleveland, Wayne maintained a B/B- average, taking art, library, English, social studies, math, wood and metal shop, music, physical education, science, biology, and typing. His attendance was good, and on standardized tests he scored around the national average. In seventh grade he listed his hobby as playing marbles. In eighth grade, he belonged to Hands across the Sea, a school club, but in ninth grade switched to the News Club. For other extracurricular activities, he told his counselor that he played basketball. He lied when he listed reading as an extracurricular activity, going even so far as to claim, in the eighth grade, that he read for ten hours each week. There is little doubt that he was saying what the counselor wanted to hear, and he simply substituted his brother's reading habits.

It's possible that he also exaggerated his playing basketball, for although he was strong enough, aggressive, and well coordinated, he never took a shine to sports. He was too busy working. Other people played or watched sports: he sold popcorn and soda pop in the grandstands. He also worked concessions at horse shows. In the eighth grade he told his school counselor that he was earning three dollars a week working nine hours. He and Robert worked for the same concessionaire. "That man hired my two boys because they wanted to work and they could work. They'd work all evening for him, hard, and then clean up the trash," said Verna, ever the staunch defender of her children.

In the seventh grade Wayne listed his educational and vocational ambitions as "high school" and "scientist." The next year his educational plans rose to "college," but in the ninth grade dropped back to "high school," and his vocational aspiration changed to "farmer." Likewise, his home study conditions and hours per week fell from "good" and "two" to "fair" and "zero." But his grades held, his health seemed good, and he was a good-looking boy, so there was no cause for alarm. Nestled among the abbreviated and now cryptic names of various "objective" test scores on his school record is the notation "E.Q. 101," standing, perhaps, for Educational Quotient, with 100 being average. Such an interpretation jibes with his grade-level evaluation for language arts and mathematics at the end of ninth grade, which was 9.7.

Between seventh and eighth grades, there had been a major change at home. Verna had married Nick Miller, a man approximately her own age who lived across the street with his mother and sister. He worked as a butcher in a grocery store. Even with her and the two older boys working, she had been having a hard time making ends meet. Verna recalled, "One time, before I married Nick, I looked up at the shelf one day and all I had was a box of salt. When you don't have any money and you don't know where you're going to get it, you don't know what you're going to do." With a butcher as her husband, Verna wouldn't have to stare into an empty cupboard and feel a mounting panic.

Nick was a soft-hearted family man who went to work and came home and never mistreated anyone. Wayne accepted him on these terms. But

Robert, after spending a year with Verna's parents in Claremore and now entering high school, actively disliked him, refusing to allow him at the head of the table. Nick lacked Grover's manly authority, and was a constant reminder of the unspoken malaise that surrounded his death.

At home Wayne wasn't morose, but he wasn't visibly happy, either. According to Verna, it was as if he were carrying around a weight. But she saw him mostly at home, a place he now associated with violent death, loss, emotional stress, fraternal responsibility, and financial anxiety, as well as maternal love. Away from home, he was gregarious and adventurous. His friends consisted of other boys from the neighborhood, boys who, now propelled by hormonal changes, were becoming spunky. Wayne and his friends began to explore places you weren't expected to go. During one of these forays, they discovered an entrance to the city's storm sewer system, underground conduits six feet high, where they gigged frogs and then sold them. Occasionally they would get into some mischief—some hubcaps would disappear off a car or a bottle of milk off a doorstep. Such antics were not the kind you'd tell your mother about (unless she was Ma Barker).

The summer of 1937, Wayne, age fifteen, worked at nearby Archer Park, taking tickets for the softball games. The earnings went toward his first bicycle.

It was about this time that Tommie, age eleven, suffered his first major accident. Verna remembered that "Wayne felt like he was kind of responsible for him. It scared him to death when Tommie got hit by a car. It broke his back and gave him a concussion. Tom was blue all over from head to foot. Wayne was so worried about him. He acted like he was about to burst into tears he was so worried." To Wayne it must have seemed that the Padgett family was vulnerable to sudden, random onslaughts of destructive power.

On the first day of school in the fall of 1937, Wayne, now a tenth grader, rode his new bike all the way downtown to Central High School. The cornerstone for the school had been laid in 1916, in Masonic ceremonies. By 1937 its enrollment was around five thousand. Wayne's sophomore grades were straight S's—S stood for "satisfactory"— in English, machine shop, electricity, woodworking, physical education, and one other course, whose name is indecipherable on the school records. Back at Cleveland, all the students had been from similar socioeconomic backgrounds; that

OKLAHOMA TOUGH

is, from the East Side, a blue-collar neighborhood. At Central, Tulsa's only white high school, students from well-to-do South Side families rubbed elbows with kids from the wrong side of the tracks, the north and west sides of town. A product of working-class Cleveland, with only average grades and a record that stated his vocational ambition as "farmer," Wayne found himself much of the day some blocks away from the main school building, in the manual arts annex, a low-slung red brick structure that smelled of motor oil, acetylene, and sawdust. Many of the other manual arts students were boys on a blue-collar track.

With an IQ of 132, Robert had been steered into a white-collar course of study, finding himself among children from Tulsa's more affluent side of town, children who would go on to become doctors, lawyers, bankers, and businessmen. These students dressed in clothes from Tulsa's "better" stores. For the first time in his life, Robert felt embarrassed by the patches on his pants. The situation became so acute that he told his mother he was dropping out; he just couldn't go to school looking like that. Verna cashed in his insurance policy and bought him a suit, two shirts, two ties—Robert never went to school without a tie—as well as new shoes and a hat. But Robert's increasing problems with school were due to more than wardrobe. Verna's marriage to Nick had affected him deeply, as reflected in the sudden plunge in his grades, and eventually in his dropping out of school for three semesters and getting a job pumping gas.

Wayne's first year at Central—the year Robert dropped out—was otherwise uneventful. The school record lists his physical and mental health, social adjustment, home conditions, and study conditions as "good." He rode his bike to and from school, a total of around five miles. His interests were "softball and swimming," softball probably because of his work taking tickets at Archer Park, and swimming because by this time he was sneaking off to the "coal pits," large strip mining gouges filled with water near the community of Dawson on the northeast side of town. The coal pits were notorious for accidental drownings, but Wayne was a good swimmer and diver, undeterred by the danger.

After school and in the summer, he worked as a soda jerk at Larry Englert's neighborhood drugstore. Wayne was a local boy everybody knew and liked. In the front of the store was the pharmacy, a soda fountain, and a big magazine rack. In the back was a restricted area, with booths and a pool table. It was back there that adults could order beer. Wayne not only made cherry phosphates and banana splits, he also delivered prescriptions and beer. Occasionally, he also picked up some wine from a bootlegger and delivered it to preachers for use at communion. At least that's what they said they used it for.

At school, things went along pretty much the same during his junior year, except he started taking the bus to school with Robert, who had re-enrolled.

A blip appears on the screen: on September 19, 1938, Wayne was arrested on suspicion of the theft of fog lights from a car, but was not charged. Wayne denied any knowledge of the theft, and Verna believed him. The matter was dropped.

On the surface, things were improving. Tommie's broken spine was healing, though he still wore a brace. Robert was back in school. With both Verna and Nick working, and with Wayne bringing in some cash, the family was getting by. Passive and mild-mannered, Nick was doing his best to be a good stepfather. Although Wayne and Tommie liked him, Robert still deeply resented him, and underneath it all Nick sensed that Verna was not one bit in love with him. She had married him so her children could eat.

5   *Wayne and Lucille in High School*

AT SCHOOL IN THE SPRING OF 1939, Tommie had been telling his friend Lucille all about his big brother Wayne. Lucille was in the ninth grade at Cleveland, but she was a year older than her classmates. Wayne had just completed the eleventh grade at Central. Finally, at Tommie's urging, he came over to Cleveland to meet Lucille, at noon on her graduation day. She was all dressed up in a flowery graduation dress and new shoes. "Tommie had told me how good-looking Wayne was, and sure enough, he was," she recalled. "All the girls there went nuts over him." She wasn't so bad herself: petite, with long brown hair, big brown eyes, and a beautiful smile.

Shortly thereafter, he came to call on her. Lucille Huey lived with her parents, Noah and Daisy, and younger sister, Loraine, on a farm at the edge of town, a mile and a half east of Verna's, and only a block from Grover's grave. The Hueys were sharecroppers on the Stokes acreage. Mr. Stokes, both a farmer and the Tulsa county clerk, provided a two-room house (later he added two more rooms to accommodate the other relatives who piled in) and a small salary, in exchange for which Noah took care of his livestock, cornfields, and orchards. Noah and Daisy also had their own cow, some chickens, and a large vegetable garden. To the east and north was farmland. Daisy worked a few blocks south as a cook at the Buckhorn, a drive-in cafe, one of the few in Tulsa. The Hueys were poor—they didn't even have running water—but they were weathering the Great Depression, and their situation was better than it had been, back in Mountain Home, Arkansas, about thirteen years before, and considerably better than that of some other Oklahoma farmers. The Hueys were like the Joads in Steinbeck's *Grapes of Wrath*, except that they didn't own a farm to lose to Dust Bowl drought and bank foreclosure and they weren't forced to try their luck elsewhere by migrating to California. The Hueys were able to stay put and tough it out.

Wayne was unfazed by Lucille's background, which, after all, wasn't so different from his. That her uncle Leffel and aunt Elsie had spent time in a reformatory didn't matter to him. After all, hadn't his cousin Rena been convicted of robbery when she was still a young girl?

He and Lucille started dating. She recalled, "He'd come and pick me up in an old car he had, a Chevrolet that didn't have a body on it: four wheels, a steering wheel, and something to sit on," a contraption he had more or less put together himself. Verna also remembered this jalopy: "Four wheels and an engine. He took two-by-fours and boards and made the bed. Every time he went to school there was boys hanging on the sides, catching rides with him. He never went by himself anywhere, because he always got boys who wanted to ride with him. Kids didn't have cars then."

So it wasn't unusual for Wayne to come calling with friends. Lucille recalled: "It got to where all of them that could gather in would come out there. We didn't have a refrigerator, but we had an old wooden icebox. It was always full of good, cold milk. They'd stand there and drink that milk and drink it and drink it, to where I'd think, 'My, what's the matter with them people?' They didn't have any milk at home, but I didn't know it.

We had all kinds of cows, milk, and cream." Years later Wayne would remember going into the newly opened (1937) East Side Cafe on Admiral and ordering a glass of water and two slices of bread, to which he applied a generous amount of ketchup. Lunch: a ketchup sandwich. Cost: two cents.

Wayne and Lucille went to movies or to one of the few drive-in eating places, which were new in those days. At the Buckhorn, you could get a hamburger for ten cents and a bottle of pop for a nickel. "I worked out at the Buckhorn first, when I was thirteen," Lucille said. "Momma let me work there because she was the cook there and could take me home. I was a carhop. Grace Kruger, who ran the Buckhorn with her husband Ken, made us the cutest little uniforms, little satin sailor suits, red, white, and blue. There was this black jazz band, and a black boy who tapdanced and sang, outdoors on a stage with a little top over it. People would come and listen and order things to drink—we sold beer. I wasn't supposed to, but I did."

The Buckhorn was across the street from Grover's cemetery plot. Wayne took Lucille to the grave a few times and talked about his father, apparently something he did with no one else.

"Wayne and I would go down to the Circle Theater [in Whittier Square]. This was around 1939, 1940. On Saturday night, I'd go downtown to Macabees, a dance club run by the insurance company, over a billiard parlor. They had a big, beautiful dance floor, and tables where kids could sit down with soft drinks and all kinds of knickknacks to eat. The music was mostly jitterbug. But Wayne didn't dance. I finally taught him a little bit about it. I always had partners down there to dance with, just friends. Pretty soon here'd come Wayne. We'd go riding around, and get something to eat. Then he'd take me home."

Some months later, when Lucille's father accepted an offer to run a chicken farm, the Hueys moved out to what was called Turkey Mountain, an area on the far west side of Tulsa. Wayne was undeterred by the twelve-mile distance.

"He came out in that old car, the one with just wheels, a steering wheel, and seats," Lucille recalled. One time he took her and her mother to the grocery store, and on the way back, "he was driving as fast as it could go, seemed like we were flying, and a wheel came off. It jumped a fence and barely missed a horse. We never did wreck. He got it stopped and went way off down in that field and got the wheel, brought it back up and put

OKLAHOMA TOUGH

it back on, and we went on home. But Momma wouldn't get on that car anymore, and she wouldn't let me get on it."

After that, he borrowed his mother's Hudson for their dates. They'd usually end up at the Silver Castle diner in Whittier Square, where they'd sit and talk and hang out, mostly with his buddies. He avoided taking her to another diner, the one at the corner of Admiral and Peoria.

Admiral and Peoria had an aura all its own. It was at the corner service station there that Wayne had first met Lee Eller, who was pumping gas. Lee's family had moved into town from nearby Skiatook only a few years earlier. Eller reminisced: "I came up from the farm to Tulsa when I was about sixteen years old. That's when I got acquainted with Wayne. The city boys kind of educated me, out at Admiral and Peoria. That area was an escape hatch for a lot of these Eastern and other guys that needed to get out of town for a while—some of the big boys out of Chicago, bank robbers and so forth. There was gambling, too, in the apartment up over the drugstore, across the street, and in rooming houses. Yes, I knew a lot of those old tough boys. 'Burrhead' Cady, he was a tough-and-rough out of Chicago. Bank robber."

Not all the tough ones who hung out around there were hardened fugitives from out of town. A gang of local teenagers, known as the Dirty Dozen, could often be found between there and the corner of Pine and Utica, toward the north side of town. Among the Dirty Dozen was Bobby Wilson, who later got into professional boxing. Eller remembered: "Bobby Wilson was tough. I used to watch him and Wayne spar. They'd get hold of each other and wrestle, man, like two bulls. They liked each other—it wasn't a real fight. Bobby Wilson would come in going 'hm-hm-hm,' like a boxer [dodging and feinting], and he'd say, 'Hit me, hit me, hit me.' If he came in here today, he'd say, 'Hit me.'" One member of the gang became a deputy sheriff. And there was Bobby Bluejacket, who, with his brothers, had been part of Verna's home Sunday school group years before.

Bluejacket had a hot temper, and years later, one evening in May of 1948, as Wayne's old friend Howard Donahue put it, "Bluejacket blew that Kline's head off, out at that little hamburger stand in the parking lot across from the skating rink at Pine and Utica. Kline was a pretty tough boy— Billy Kline, I think it was—a hell of an athlete. One of the other boys had a sawed-off shotgun stashed in that restaurant. Hell, it blowed his head plumb off. Wayne had always known Bluejacket, but he didn't run with him." That was to come later.

The Hueys' stay at Turkey Mountain was brief, and after they moved back to the Stokes farm, Wayne finally took his girlfriend home to meet his mother. Lucille was well received: "I went there lots of times. Mom and Nick were always good to me." The Padgett boys called their mother "Mom," as if that were her given name, so everyone who met her through them called her "Mom."

Wayne and Tommie shared a room, but for several years Robert had had the luxury of his own room—part of the back porch, which had been enclosed—a private haven where he could read and dream and seclude himself from his stepfather. When the new Will Rogers High School opened in September of 1939, Robert jumped at the chance to go there. The pristine school offered him a fresh start. Wayne transferred simply because redistricting required it.

Both he and Robert entered Rogers at the same time, as seniors, the same year Lucille entered as a sophomore. Lucille said, "I was a year older than anyone in my class, because I had missed the second grade. We had lived way out at Shell Creek [a sparsely populated area west of Tulsa] and there wasn't any way for me to get to school. Then when we moved to town I was a year behind. Wayne and I had one or two classes together at Rogers. Every week we'd have a spelling test. Wayne had the most beautiful handwriting you'd ever seen, and he never missed a word, and I never missed a word. But we sat at each other's table and graded each other's papers. The teacher got suspicious, so she separated us. We never did cheat, we didn't have to. But he was always fighting, or out back smoking and pitching pennies. He didn't take part in athletics. He wasn't heavy enough!"

Wayne may not have been bulky, but he was nearly six feet tall, lightning fast, and utterly fearless. His biceps and shoulders were developing earlier than the rest of him, which made his punch more powerful than his antagonists expected. One of his opponents was an all-state wrestler named Manley Johnson (later a distinguished professor of English at Tulsa University). Johnson had gotten the better of Robert in a fight, so Wayne flattened Johnson. He won most of his fights, and the occasional loss didn't faze him.

OKLAHOMA TOUGH

Lucille remembered that "he wouldn't let nobody look at me. If they did, he'd give them a cussing and run them off. I started working after school as a curb hop at the Crown Drug Store. Wayne always picked me up and took me home. He came by one night and said, 'I won't be by to take you home tonight.' I said, 'Why?' He said, 'I've got something else I want to do.' I said, 'That suits me just fine.' So he left. About that time a boy named Chet Orchard came by. He was redheaded, the first good-looking redheaded person I'd ever met, but he was a goodlooking, muscular, nicely built boy, with big brown eyes and auburn red hair. He asked me for a date and I went out with him. Then he took me home and he left. And Wayne was waiting, to see who took me home. They got in a fight. Wayne thought he could whip anything that came along, but Chester whipped him good. In fact he broke his nose. About two or three o'clock in the morning, someone was pecking on my window. I raised up the curtain and looked out and there was Wayne with all these wooden things up his nose and all taped up, with both eyes swelled shut.

"Then I met another boy, Clifford Boyer. He had a nice car and everything. He was losing his hair. I didn't go with him too much, but Wayne found out about it. One night down there at the Crown, here come Wayne again and jumped on Cliff and like to beat him to death."

Meanwhile, Robert was finally on track to graduate. The principal told Verna that Bob's future was unlimited: tests rated his IQ as the highest in the school. Mary Margaret Fletcher, a Rogers student and later Bob's wife, recalled that "nobody would believe it, because he didn't act like a bookworm, not in the least. He liked to socialize." Lucille recalled that "one time Wayne got so mad because Robert was going to a dance, and Robert wanted a striped shirt with one of those white, detachable collars, and Mom took the last cent she had and went and bought it for him. It made Wayne so mad he like to died. But Robert was going to a fancy dance. He always was fancy: he ran with a higher class of people than we did, ha ha! They weren't any better than we were, but they were richer. I guess their parents were more educated." Bob's sociability is reflected in compositions he wrote during his senior year in English class. One of them, entitled "Character Sketch," is about his grandfather Jesse:

> When a man reaches the age of sixty-nine he is usually expected to
> be retired from active engagement in the tiresome business of

making a living. Not so my maternal grandfather, for at that supposedly ripe old age he is now an active Justice of the Peace. He is well known around the vicinity of Claremore as the "Marrying Justice" because of the numerous nuptial ceremonies he performs.

A little gesture he makes at the end of each ceremony is highly exemplary of the man. When the groom hands him the three dollars fee for services rendered he takes a fifty cent piece out of his pocket where he keeps a stock for this use and hands it to the blushing bride, telling her to keep it as a good luck token.

My grandfather is Irish in actuality as well as tradition and he shows it. He is a very tall man, six feet three inches to be exact. He is of ruddy complexion, with light grey eyes that throw soft kindly sparks from craggy eyebrows.

He is the typical small town politician but is very well informed on subjects of national and international consequence.

One would never guess that these words were written by a young man who in the past few years had flunked four out of five semesters of high school English.

In another piece—"College Ahead Then What?"—Bob wrote about himself and his future and, obliquely, his underachievement in high school:

I have hoped for many years that I would be able to attend a good college or university at the termination of my high school career. It seems right at the present that I will enjoy that privilege next fall if I graduate in the spring. But with the credits I need and my having to work all the time, it is going to be a pretty rough row to hoe.

My parents and next of kin (who seem to have quite a say in my affairs) want me to attend some good law school. They all believe my talents (?) lie that way. I have tried to tell them time and time again that I am not in the least interested in law and would much rather attend some good special school to prepare for a career in radio or . . . .

The rest is missing, but what remains is enough to demonstrate Bob's awareness of his audience—in this case, his teacher, who wrote in the margin, "College training in law would be valuable to you for any line of work."

No one urged Wayne to think of college. By today's standards, his grades and test scores were good enough, but in 1939 far fewer people went beyond high school. Besides, he just didn't look like "college material." His first two years of high school had been heavily slanted toward the manual arts. Maybe he could just keep driving a delivery truck for the Dr. Pepper distributor, as he had for the past year. After all, lifting those cases of soda pop had enlarged his biceps and broadened his back.

During his senior year, his academic career staggered. He was more interested in making money for his family, hanging out with his buddies, and going out with his girlfriend, Lucille. For his photo in *The Lariat*, the school yearbook, he refused to wear a tie. Actually, he did well in his final semester, with satisfactory grades in all his subjects: English, woodworking, typing, sales, and penmanship/spelling. The first semester, he had received satisfactory grades in English and arithmetic, but failed three other courses: law, woodworking, and the dread auto mechanics. It is odd that a young man who could assemble and maintain a jalopy would flunk auto mechanics. But flunking woodworking turned out to be far more serious.

The explanation he once gave me went as follows. Near the end of the semester, he was on the verge of completing the course's final project, a mahogany end table, when the instructor walked by and issued an order to him in a contemptuous tone. Ultra-sensitive to insult and backing down from no one, Wayne refused to comply. Tempers rose. The teacher threatened him with a visit to the dean of boys. Wayne held up one of the table legs and said, "For all I care, you can just stick this up your ass," and stormed out.

The next day the dean of boys summoned Wayne to his office and told him that unless he apologized to the teacher and completed his table, he would receive a failing grade. Wayne countered that it was the teacher who should be apologizing. The matter was left at that, and the failing grade went into the record.

There were 350 seniors in the class of 1940, of which 332 received diplomas, but Wayne was not one of them. After all those years in school, he needed only one more credit. One credit in woodworking. And to get that credit, all he had to do was to say I'm sorry and to glue the legs on the table. But he was stubborn and hot-headed, he had no father figure to keep him in line, and the threats of school officials had lost their power over him.

Will Rogers High School's First Annual Junior-Senior Prom was held in the Crystal Ballroom of the Mayo Hotel, one of Tulsa's biggest and best hotels, on May 29, 1940. In a photograph of the gala event, Robert and his date can be seen in the foreground, dressed to the nines. Commencement was held two days later. Of course, Wayne attended neither event. To hell with school.

Officially, his shearing off from the "straight" world had begun.

6   *Wayne and Lucille Get Married*

SCHOOL OFFICIALS EXPECTED Wayne to return to school in the fall to complete his degree, but when he didn't they suspended him, on November 4, 1940, for "failure to abide by rules, poor attitude, and truancy," the final words on his school record. To him, the suspension notice must have come as a joke.

But what was he going to do now? He had to get a job. The national unemployment rate, after having gradually declined since its all-time high of 25 percent in 1930, had jumped back up to 19 percent in 1940. Still living at home, Wayne took what he found: a job guarding buried Bell Telephone cables near construction sites. It paid an uninspiring sixteen dollars a week—better than nothing. The year went by.

After Lucille finished her second year at Rogers, the Hueys moved five miles west of Tulsa to the small town of Sand Springs, where they rented a small house, their first with indoor plumbing. Lucille and her mother got jobs at Commander Mills, a textile mill. Beginning in September, she divided her time between work and school, at Charles Page High School in Sand Springs. With a large number of credits from Rogers, she was able, with minimal course work at Page, to earn her diploma in the late fall of 1941.

That same year an incident had taken place that has never been adequately explained. Wayne and a buddy were arrested on April 10 in Houston, Texas, for a check investigation. The police stated their suspicion that the hubcaps on the boys' Ford sedan were stolen or that Wayne's friend was a runaway. Take your pick. Among the background information on Wayne Merriott Padgett was: eyes, blue; height, 5' 10½"; weight, 154; complexion, ruddy; build, slender; occupation, laborer; residence, 153 North Florence, Tulsa, Oklahoma; identifying marks, gold crown on left upper front tooth. (Had the original tooth been knocked out in a fight?) The full-face mug shot shows a cocky young man with his head tilted slightly to one side, with a kind of go-ahead-and-try-me look on his face. After two days, Wayne and his "accomplice" were released.

Oddly, neither Verna nor Lucille recalled the incident. Many years later, Wayne was to dismiss it as simply a matter of two little boys running away from home. But he was hardly a little boy, and his home was hardly a place to run away from. His evasive explanation doesn't ring true. He was up to something nefarious. But what?

When Wayne got back to Tulsa, Lucille's uncle, Wesley Pilkington, said that if she and Wayne got married, he'd get Wayne a job as an iron worker. Lucille tells the story: "Wes took it for granted that we'd eventually get married. Mother always told me that if I got married before I was eighteen, she'd have it annulled. I told her it wouldn't do any good, I'd just get married again. Anyway, we slipped off one day, November 29, 1941. Bill Adams loaned us his car, a little '36 Ford coupe. We went to Bentonville, Arkansas, to get married, so nobody would know it. You didn't have to have a blood test or ID or nothing. We went to the court house and got the license, and then found a justice of the peace. He asked Wayne if he was twenty-one—and he wasn't, he was nineteen, and I was eighteen. We told him we were twenty-one and eighteen and he married us. Then we stopped at a grocery store and bought some baloney and cheese and crackers and pop, and pulled off the road down into a shady place to have lunch. Then he took me back to Sand Springs. I didn't tell Momma nothing. I went on to work at the cotton mill, and after two or three days, I told her."

Lucille told her that they had been married back on June 20. What she didn't tell her—or anyone else—was that she was already two months pregnant.

When Wayne had first heard about the pregnancy, "he didn't act concerned, or worried—it didn't bother him," according to Lucille. After briefly considering an abortion, he dismissed the idea. Instead, he suggested marriage.

The newlyweds needed their own place. "We moved down on Seventh Street just off Lewis, where old Dr. Roberts owned a big house. Nine people shared the bathroom. We had one big room, in which we cooked, slept, everything. I had to quit Commander Mills, because they had that

Vigo [dogfood] place back there, and because I was pregnant the smell made me sick," and Lucille.

"One morning we got up—oh cold, coldest time I ever saw in my life! It was a Sunday, and what woke us up was newsboys coming down the street hollering 'Extra! Extra! Pearl Harbor's been attacked!' I jumped up and ran downstairs and got a newspaper and that's when we found out about it. I was about three months pregnant."

Shortly after that they moved in with Mom, and Wesley got Wayne into Local Union No. 584, the International Brotherhood of Bridge, Structural, and Ornamental Iron Workers. He went to work at building Air Force Plant No. 2, which everyone called "the bomber plant," out by the airport. Lucille continued: "It's McDonnell-Douglas now. The other guys talked about how daring Wayne was. They didn't see how he kept from getting killed. Instead of walking and holding onto something, he'd just take a flying leap, with nothing under him, hundreds of feet up in the air." Wesley once commented on how Wayne, unlike the other workers, never hitched himself to a post when he was catching the red-hot rivets that were thrown to him.

His taste for risk extended into his time off. According to Lucille, "He played poker up there at the union hall in Whittier Square. He came home one night—we were over there at Momma's in Sand Springs—out of breath. He ran in and said, 'Lock the doors. I won a lot of money and somebody's following me.' He gave me and Loraine a lot of money—two or three hundred dollars apiece—and a solid gold pocketwatch to Daddy. He told us to go to Tulsa and buy whatever we wanted. Boy, we had the best time: we bought snazzy kimonos and lounging stuff, makeup, everything." Apparently, his pursuers never caught him.

Wayne worked on the mile-long bomber plant until his part was finished, in the spring of 1942. The next job was waiting for him in Kansas. The baby could come at any time. But it didn't. Finally, on the morning of the 16th of June, Lucille said, "Wayne, if you don't leave town, I don't think I'm ever going to have this baby." She and Wayne went to J. C. Penney's to buy khakis and work shoes.

In the car on the way back, a bus behind them honked aggressively. Wayne slammed on the brakes, jumped out of the car, and approached the bus. The driver emerged. "They had the damndest fight you ever saw. The law came, but they just told Wayne to settle down. He said, 'Well, tell that son of a bitch to quit honking at me.'"

Later that day he drove the 110 miles up to Baxter Springs, Kansas, "to work on the Jayhawk Ordinance Works up there—some other kind of defense plant. I went to Momma's in Sand Springs the day he left. I got up the next morning and went to the bathroom, and I knew I was starting. I did a big ironing and listened to Bob Wills—we listened to Bob Wills at 12:30 every day on the radio. After Momma came home from work, I told her, 'I think I'm going to have the baby pretty soon.' We waited until about ten o'clock that night, and finally I said, 'OK, let's go.' I got to the hospital at eleven o'clock and the baby was born at five minutes until twelve.

"As soon as they found out I was going to deliver, they called Wayne. He said, 'I'll be right there.'

"I didn't have a hard delivery at all. I felt something on me and I heard somebody say, 'Somebody's going to be awfully disappointed.' I was the only one who wanted a boy. Pretty soon Nick called the hospital and said, 'I hear Wayne passing down here at Third and Florence at ninety miles an hour.' His car didn't have a muffler. It was late when he got to the hospital, but they let him in."

Verna recalled, "He went in to see the baby and he looked at it and— I think he thought the baby was going to be sitting up and laughing—he never said one word." But when he went in to see Lucille, he said, "He's awfully scrawny. What makes him so red?" And she said, "He was just born!"

"He" being the author of this book.

Wayne was twenty, Lucille almost nineteen.

She wanted to name the child Wayne, but he preferred Ronald, after one of his favorite actors, Ronald Reagan. They compromised on Ronald Wayne Padgett.

The next day, Wayne went back to Baxter Springs. Verna recalled: "Lucille stayed in the hospital three or four days. I cleaned up the front bedroom of my house, had all clean linens, and of course Tommie was the only boy at home—Bob was in the service. I had some gladiolas blooming in the yard. I went and cut them and put them in a vase by the bed, and Lucille thought that was the nicest thing, that she had that big bedroom and those flowers."

Wayne came home every weekend. Then around February of 1943, Mother and I moved up to be with him. The three of us shared a large house with the Pilkingtons: Wesley, who was also working on the munitions factory, and his wife Gladys and son Jimmy. But Wayne drove Mother and me the hundred or so miles down to Tulsa to spend most weekends, and after six or eight months, when the job was finished, we all moved back to "T-Town." That's when Wayne started pumping gas, an ordinary job that would quickly lead him to one of the most momentous decisions of his life.

7 *Higher Octane*

"WHEN WE MOVED BACK FROM Baxter Springs, we got an apartment a few blocks from Verna's. People wouldn't hardly let you in with a kid. Wayne said to the landlady, Mrs. Coleman, 'What do you want us to do, send the baby back?' She saw that we looked pretty respectable and clean, so she rented it to us, a little shotgun three-room place with a bedroom, living room, and kitchen. We shared the bath with her—she lived up front, her and her husband."

Wayne got a job at Earl Montgomery's service station, on the corner of Admiral and Lewis Place. He had been buying gas there since he was sixteen. Verna recalled: "Earl Montgomery told me that Wayne was the most honest kid he ever saw. He said, 'If Wayne buys fifteen cents worth of gas on credit from me, he comes back the next day and pays it. He don't try to cheat anybody.'"

Wayne's promptness in repaying loans was noticed also by Carl Weideman, the vice president of the National Bank of Commerce. Weideman gave Wayne a loan for his first real car. According to Verna, "Mr. Weideman said that Wayne kept his payments up real good and was really an honest kid. After that Mr. Weideman would loan him any money he wanted." Weideman was an old-fashioned banker who lent money on character, not just collateral.

The house directly across the street from the gas station became vacant when the woman who owned it suddenly moved out, leaving linens, furniture, silverware, and dishes. Wayne and Lucille moved in.

Pumping gas wasn't all that lucrative. Maybe he could sell other liquids too. Like a few years ago, when he had delivered communion wine. Oklahoma was still a "dry" state, but with all the bootleggers around, it was easy to buy alcohol. People did it all the time. It was no big deal. It wasn't even that risky. In 1944 the Tulsa Police Department had a grand total of three cars, and because of the war, tires were virtually unobtainable. Because so many police officers had gone off to war, the force had dwindled to fewer than two hundred. It was a great time to break into bootlegging.

Wayne started modestly, buying a case or two locally and reselling it by the pint. He kept his stash off the premises, either in his car or in the field behind the station. The arrangement was convenient: the customers could drive in, buy some gas and a bottle of hooch, and drive off happy. Wayne's friend Bill Martin, whom he had met back in the 1930s, told me: "He had that filling station when I come back out of the Navy, in December of '44, after a year in the hospital. He had that walk-in joint down there, selling whiskey. When I went to work at a gas station downtown, we more or less had a deal: I started selling whiskey for him down there too."

Wayne put new meaning into the expression "to wheel and deal." Martin recalled: "One day Wayne came by the gas station downtown in a souped-up Ford, wanted to take me riding. I said, 'I can't leave right now.' He said, 'Aw hell, everything'll be all right.' And he said to some guy standing there, 'Hey, you watch the station for us.' Hell, I'd never seen the guy before! The guy said, 'Yeah, I'll watch it.' We went down Sixth Street going east under that viaduct where the Coliseum used to be. We went down underneath that sonofabitch doing eighty or ninety miles an hour and up the side and around that curve and down, went up to Sixth and Peoria—he had that thing leaned so bad it drug the fender skirt off one side. Went around the block just laughing. He thought it was funnier than hell, but I was about to wet my drawers. I was holding onto anything I could get hold of." The car may have been his "Fordillac"—a lightweight Ford body with a powerful Cadillac engine.

At his own station, he was freewheeling in other ways, as well. During the war, gasoline was rationed, usually three gallons per family per week. You couldn't buy gas unless you presented your allotted government ration stamps. Wayne illegally resold or give away some of the stamps that he had collected at the station. Many people couldn't afford extras, but if he thought they were good people, he would just gave them the stamps, asking nothing in return. He then replaced the stamps with those he got from various preachers. The preachers had been given the extra stamps by their "flocks," stamps they then exchanged for Wayne's whiskey. At some point he was called up before the rationing board, but he came out unscathed.

Meanwhile Wayne had to deal with another board—the draft board. Robert had received his draft notice the day after Pearl Harbor and was now in the Army Air Corps, and many other boys from the neighborhood had been called up. Wayne was willing to serve his country, which he felt was his duty, but he had originally been classified 4-F. When his draft notice arrived, he had been reclassified 1-A, and was ordered to report immediately for a physical at the induction center in Oklahoma City. Lucille sold the car and furniture, all in a few hours, and moved to her parents' house in Sand Springs.

When Wayne came back from Oklahoma City two days later, she asked him, "When do you leave?"

Wayne's friend Clemens, standing next to him, replied, "He don't."

"What's wrong?" she asked.

Wayne said, "They classified me 4-F."

"What for?"

"They said I have an unstable nervous condition."

She never did know what that meant, and the army records no longer exist. Daddy must have been embarrassed by the classification, for, as will be seen, another explanation quickly took the place of the true one. As with his father's death, he substituted a more acceptable version of a painful event.

The three of us stayed at the Hueys' a few days, then Daddy found an apartment on the Sand Springs Line—a highway with a parallel trolley line that connected downtown Tulsa to Sand Springs. The apartment was in a converted motel, with concrete floors and linoleum, but, according to Lucille, it wasn't bad. "We had a baby bed—of course we couldn't get anything made of metal, because of the war—and you were jumping up and down in that baby bed and it all fell in on you. It didn't hurt you." Taking it back for a refund wasn't sufficient. My father smashed it to smithereens.

"It flooded out there, and that's when we moved back to Mrs. Coleman's. Wayne was still working at Montgomery Oil, pumping gas and selling gas stamps and whiskey. He worked all night long, came in at daylight. Not many things stayed open all night. He slept all day, or the biggest part

OKLAHOMA TOUGH

of the day. And he had to have a clean kakhi shirt and pair of pants every day, and they had to be starched and ironed to a gnat's bristle.

"I don't know how he started selling whiskey. In fact, I didn't know he was doing it, for a long time. The police never did bother him. They'd come in there in their own private cars and he'd give them gas stamps. And that's why he never did like preachers—they took stamps from their congregations—and by the time I knew him, he never went to church, not one time."

Instead he sold gas and whiskey all night. In cold weather, he and his buddies would gather inside the little office, which was heated by a gas stove. In hot weather they'd turn on a fan or move the chairs outside, talking and joking and making deals into the wee hours, while the crickets crackled away in the dark. At the gas station, Wayne discovered a good way to live: by fusing friendship and livelihood. You couldn't count on big organizations or official bureaucracies, but you *could* count on your friends. And besides, in Tulsa the whiskey laws didn't mean all that much. They never had.*

8   *King Street*

THINGS WERE GOING WELL. Daddy's whiskey business at the gas station kept getting bigger and bigger, until one day he came home and announced that he had bought a house, for $4,500 cash. The one-story house at 2742 East King Street was made of fieldstone painted white and had two big cedar trees in the front yard and evergreen shrubs around the foundation. In the backyard was a well-kept lawn and a large cherry tree. Lucille remembered: "It was a nice house. It had two bedrooms, and a nice bathroom between, all tile, a huge kitchen and a big breakfast room and living room and dining room. We were living there when the war ended. By then we were selling whiskey by the case and delivering it. I don't know how we got into that. Wayne handled all that. I answered the phones and took orders." Wayne was twenty-three, and he had taken a decisive step into a criminal profession.

---

* See Appendix A.

There were two types of whiskey dealers: wholesalers, who sold by the case, and retailers, who sold by the bottle. Among Daddy's customers were retailers, businesses, civic groups, and individuals. Retailers (also known as "pint pitchers") were free to buy from any of the numerous wholesalers in town. There was no formal structure to the business, no territories or hierarchy.

One of Daddy's "delivery boys" was Clemens Laurrell, his childhood friend, who had come back from the war early. Clemens had been a paratrooper. When, on a training jump, his chute didn't open, he plummeted toward the earth and hit a large tree, which broke his fall. It also broke his legs, back, and assorted other bones. When he healed, his commanding officer told him he was fit for jumping again. Clemens replied, "Oh no I ain't! I'm finished with this whole deal." Confronted by medical records, the army gave him an honorable discharge.

Clemens was a funny, good-natured guy. One friend remembered: "Clemens was a character. We'd get through eating and that boy'd sit there and take everything that was left over and mix it up in one bowl and eat it!"

He was around twenty years old when he went to work for Daddy. From time to time, Clemens's sister Eileen helped answer the phones. Eileen was a little goofy, but sweet and dependable, a Seventh-Day Adventist. Even Verna helped from time to time.

"Wayne bought the whiskey in Joplin, off in some liquor store somewhere," Lucille said. "He'd drive up in a car or truck. At first he'd pile it in a back seat and cover it up. Then he got a car that had a 'plant' built into it, where you couldn't see nothing."

How could they get that many cases in a car? They "lugged" it; that is, they took it out and stacked it by the lug, with three fifths or six pints wrapped in brown paper to form a lug. Stacked properly, forty or fifty cases would fit in the car, which had overload springs to support the extra weight.

Lucille recalled: "We kept the whiskey there in the garage on King Street. The police never really did bother us. Jack and Jim Gott, they were on the vice squad, and they were drunk all the time. They were 'friends': they came by and got free whiskey. Meanwhile we had bought the house next door. At first the Vardemans—Tommy, old lady Vardeman, and old lady Vardeman's sister—lived there, and Tommy delivered whiskey for us. Then Wayne's brother Tommie and [his new wife] Elda moved in there. By this time Tommie was selling whiskey too, but by the bottle. We kept whiskey over there and we'd bring it across the driveway and through the window. You couldn't see anything for the cedar trees and bushes." There were only these two houses on the block, which dead-ended just past Tommie's house. Across the street was a big untended field that went all the way to the Frisco railroad tracks. You could hear the train whistle in the distance.

Mother told me that "one day we had a couple of cases of gin that somebody was supposed to come by and get. The police came to raid us and everything was all right, but you ran in there and sat on those two cases of gin and said, 'You can't have my daddy's hooch!'" The cops gently lifted me down and carried the cases out the door.

If Daddy had police protection, why did he get raided? "Oh, because the police had to do something. Every once in a while they'd call up and say, 'Get all your old cheap rum and cheap wine out and leave it somewhere, so we can say we caught you.' Then there'd be a big write-up in the paper: people *thought* he was getting caught."

It was in the garage of the house on King Street that Daddy did some dental work on me, when I was around three years old. He was unloading lugs from a car as I silently toddled up behind him. When he swung around, the lug in his hand smacked me right in the mouth, bending my two front teeth straight back. He put down the lug, grasped the teeth between his thumb and index finger, and pulled them back into their original positions.

He had a magic touch. A few years before, he had been pumping gas. Now he owned a nice home free and clear, a sparkling new car, and a thriving business that was practically running itself.

Around this time, Daddy did have one bit of bad luck. It was in 1944 or '45 that he had his first motorcycle accident. "He was riding on the back with [bootlegger] Martin Edwards and they were coming to pick me up to go to the show," Lucille said. "Somebody made a left turn in front of them, and Martin Edwards swerved to try to miss him and when they wrecked, it threw Wayne's leg over backwards and broke it. He laid around three or four days and finally that old Dr. Childs came over and put a cast on it. He was in bed with it a long time. It got to itching so bad he took a wooden stick out of a windowshade and run it down in there and scratched. Finally, before the time was up, he cut the cast off. He couldn't stand it no longer."

Mother doesn't recall his being hospitalized by the accident, but I have a clear memory of going to visit him in the hospital when I was very young and seeing his leg in a cast. I vividly remember his big smile as I handed him a carton of Luckies.

"His leg was stiff for a long time. Howard Donahue had a big welding shop on North Lewis. Everybody hung out at Howard's. Wayne was in there one day. There was a broom handle laying on the floor, and as he was walking backward to go out and get in his car, he slipped on that broom handle and fell, and that stiff leg went down and bent. And it never was stiff any more." But for the rest of his life his left knee would periodically cause him problems, by "going out." Sometimes when he knew he was going to be walking a lot, he wrapped an elastic bandage around it. Unlike his father, though, he never limped.

Forever after, he put the motorcycle accident to good use. Growing up, I heard it described many times as the reason for his not going to war. According to this fictionalized version, he had the wreck the day he was to report for his physical. All of his acquaintances, friends, and relatives I have asked still believe this cosmetic version, the only one they ever heard. My mother maintained his charade for fifty years, just as she maintained the fiction of Grover's "murder."

In the summer of 1947, my parents took what amounted to a belated honeymoon. Leaving the whiskey business and me in the hands of friends and family, they drove to California to visit his brother Bob and Bob's wife, Mary Margaret. Out of the service, Bob was working mornings 4:30 to 7:30 at the post office and going to school full time at the University of Southern California, majoring in education. Since Mary Margaret needed their car for her job, he hitchhiked the twelve or so miles to school each day.

From Mission San Juan Capistrano, Mother and Daddy sent a postcard to Verna at our house on King Street, where she was running the business and watching after me: "Hi Mom, Wish you could see the pretty flowers

OKLAHOMA TOUGH

and birds, this is really a beautiful place. Wayne." According to Mother, she wrote the message, he signed it. An August 9th postcard to me, with its one-cent stamp, read: "Hello, Ronnie, This is a picture of Capistrano. Keep it and I'll be home in four or five days. Daddy." He wrote this card, but the handwriting was similar to Mother's, a result of the penmanship classes they had taken together. Lucille recalled: "We also went to Tijuana to buy a bunch of stuff—gifts, belts, purses—you name it, we bought it!" They had plenty of money.

Three years later, in June of 1950, they took a second trip to visit Robert and Mary Margaret and to stop off at Laguna Beach. It turned out to be the last big trip they would take together.

Such trips weren't adventuresome enough for him. He preferred the thrills of speed and risk. According to Lucille, "He and Clemens were going out Admiral to Jimmy Leach's"—Leach was a bootlegger and later the owner of various nightspots around Tulsa—"to deliver two lugs of whiskey they had in the saddlebags of Wayne's big Harley Davidson. They had a wreck. It knocked Clemens off and didn't hurt him, and he had sense enough to hide the whiskey before the police got there. But it cut Wayne's head open, across the forehead, and knocked him unconscious. He came to pretty soon and called me, and told me where to pick up the whiskey and go meet Jimmy." And of course he didn't stop riding his Harley.

It was sometime in the late 1940s that Daddy got into auto racing. There was a regular circuit in the area—Tulsa, Oklahoma City, Kansas City, etc.—for what are called midgets, or midget cars. Midgets were similar to the cars that raced at Indianapolis, only smaller. Most of them had Offenhauser engines, but a few had Ford motors. According to Howard Donahue, who raced cars and who had known Wayne since the late 1930s, "Wayne owned two of the best midget race cars in the business. One was an Offy—an Offenhauser—one was a Ford, one of the hottest Fords to hit this part of the country." Jimmy Hicks drove the Offy in races in St. Louis and Chicago. "Jimmy was a hard driver," Howard recalled. "I saw him drive with his back broken, in a cast. At St. Louis, if he was running that night, they wouldn't even sell the first three or four rows of box seats, because he was liable to end up in them." Howard himself was driving in a car owned by "Peaches" Campbell, a Tulsa motorcycle cop who lived a few blocks down the street from where Daddy had grown up.

The Ford, with its black and white color scheme and the number 33 painted on its sides, raced on the local circuit two or three nights a week. During the season, the races in Tulsa were held at the Tulsa State Fairgrounds every Saturday night. The midget track was one-fifth of a mile, made of red clay. At first Clemens drove the car, but he didn't have much success, so Tommy Vardeman took over.

According to Donahue, "If the track was just a tiny bit slick, the Fords would run just as good as the Offys, because the horsepower didn't mean all that much, see? Tom was a good driver. I saw him sweep the card one night: the heat, the trophy dash, and the main. But I won the championship three years in a row. Tom told me, 'I could stick a spark plug up my ass and run faster than you can.' I said, 'Tom, you might outrun me part of the time, but I'll outrun you more times than you'll outrun me.' And I did. Tom's biggest fault was he'd get drunk and try to drive with a hangover. I've tried it, and it don't work!"

Mother and I watched the races in our box seats, cheering amidst the roar and whine of the engines, but Daddy spent the entire evening down in the pits, looking after the car and hanging out with friends. It was macho down there. When the last race concluded, Mother and I would go down into the pits to talk with Tommy Vardeman and some of the other drivers we knew, friends of Daddy's: Howard Donahue, Angelo Howerton, Chick Ciccoletto. The smell of the moist clay track mingled with the smoke of Luckies and Camels and the lingering odor of spent fuel, a heady mixture of methanol and nitroglycerine. I remember staring into the cockpits of the cars and feeling pure power radiating out of them.

Howard Donahue reminisced: "Wayne and I knew the old boy who took care of the race track. On one occasion, Wayne and Clemens and I took the Ford out to the track, and Wayne could get it around there as good as anyone that ever drove it. But he didn't want to race." He preferred to be the silent partner.

For the more successful cars, the prize money made it more than worthwhile. Donahue continued: "I made some good money, never less than $350-375 a night, and see, you're running three nights a week. Back then you couldn't make that kind of money welding! And you *enjoyed* it." Donahue stopped welding and started racing full time. But around 1949–50, a new kind of racing car caught the public's fancy—the stock car—and midget racing waned.

In those days, some of Daddy's acquaintances were young and irresponsible. Some, like Tommy Vardeman, also had a devilish sense of humor. When I was learning to talk, Vardeman would coax me, "Go tell your daddy he's a sonofabitch." The other guys would all crack up. But Vardeman's big mouth, loosened by alcohol, eventually caused him to run afoul of Daddy.

Donahue explained: "See, Tom just owed him and owed him and owed him, and you'd help him and he'd put the badmouth on you. Raymond Cates was instigating a damned deal, that Tom could whip Wayne. I told Raymond, 'Goddamn, Tom couldn't whip the lazy side of Wayne. You're gonna mess around until you get Tom hurt.' But Raymond was wanting to get someone to whip Wayne because he knew *he* couldn't. One night after the races, Wayne jumped Tom about it. Wayne stood there and told him, 'Tom, just hit me as hard as you can and then I'll be mad enough to whip the shit out of you. Go ahead, hit me.'" Vardeman declined the invitation.

Howard Donahue's welding shop was a popular hangout. "Even police officers would hang around. In fact they were Wayne's friends. I never will forget one time. Wayne had a brand new '46 Plymouth. A policeman was bird hunting with him and accidentally shot a hole through the roof of that Plymouth. I asked Wayne how it happened. 'That ignorant son of a bitch, he was wondering if his gun was on safety, so he reached over and pushed the trigger down.'

"[Wayne's delivery boy] Clemens hung around the shop too. To make his work easy, he'd have the pint pitchers meet him at my shop. They'd come in the front door—Clemens had his car parked inside my shop, a 40 X 80 building—and they'd load up and go out the back door. One day Roy Rains, with the Sheriff's office, pulled up across the street and started watching the place, and, man, the bottleggers scattered like a covey of quail.

"But I didn't care, because Wayne was a good friend of mine. My mother even liked Wayne. She was a religious woman, but. . . . One time we had to get the whiskey out of one of his stashes, because the police had gone to get a search warrant. I went in one car, a Buick Roadmaster, but

I had to sit sidesaddle in it, because we had so much whiskey in it. It was out at the edge of town, and I wondered, Where am I going with this thing? So I just brought it over to my mother's house. Mother knew Wayne. She said, 'Bless his heart, I don't care if it is whiskey, put it in the back yard, where nobody'll see it.'"

People such as Howard's mother liked Wayne because he was polite and congenial with them, especially with older people, and he was handsome and well groomed, a man of his word. The fact that he sold whiskey didn't matter. Donahue observed: "If Wayne heard of somebody having a bad time, he was real free-hearted. A lot of people think of nothing but money, and if Wayne had been that way, there's no telling how much money he would have made. But he helped a lot of people along the way, gave a lot of money away."

One day in 1948 he gave away some of his money unwillingly. A February 9 article in the *Tulsa Daily World* described how Daddy and a grocer had been arrested for liquor possession. At the end of the article came the interesting part:

> This was the second case in which Padgett had figured in less than three days.
>
> Joe C. Crow, 53, held in jail on suspicion of robbing Padgett and [Jack] McLane of $1,035 Friday night, still was being questioned today and firmly denied the 'trap' highjacking. . . . Padgett identified Crow, an ex-convict, as one of four persons, at least one a woman, who met he [*sic*] and McLane on North Peoria Avenue purportedly to deliver 19 cases of whiskey but instead covered them with guns, tied them in their car, and fled with their money.

Lucille recalled the incident: "We still lived on King Street—I remember because Wayne left a big old bundle of money on the dining room table. These people had ordered whiskey, and it was in some sort of a van. When he got up there, they tied him up and made him get down on his knees and wanted his money. He was scared as hell. They had a gun on each side of his head. They thought he'd have a lot more money on him than he had. Somehow they left him and either he got loose or the law came, and the police took the truck of whiskey and him to jail. He called me and told me where to meet somebody who would be driving the truck, and to leave my car, and to get in the truck and don't look back until I hit home. I went and got it. Somebody in that jail made a deal with him—you know how he was, making deals." The "somebody" was, of course, a police officer.

But clearly the ante had been upped and the players weren't just guys from the neighborhood anymore. These unknown outsiders played rough. Challenging them to a good old-fashioned fistfight would no longer suffice. From then on, Daddy kept a loaded revolver in his glove compartment.

However, he had little to fear from the police. On the federal level, the FBI wasn't at all interested—not yet, anyway. City authorities posed no threat. He got an advance call from the police station anytime the city's vice squad—headed up by his friends the Gott brothers—was headed his way. Between 1944 and 1947, he was raided five times. In every case, the disposition is listed on police records either as "Nothing found" or "No disposition available." Every once in a while a patrol car would stop him or a delivery boy on suspicion and discover hooch in the back of the car. He would pay the fine (in the 1940s it varied from five to sixty-five dollars) and go on about his business.

The only really troublesome policeman was Roy Rains, the county sheriff. Rains was an incorruptible cop, single-minded in his pursuit of criminals. He was particularly keen on surveillance: one time he even watched a suspect while hiding in a garbage can. Bootleggers feared him not only because he might arrest and fine them, but also because he might confiscate their hooch, or worse yet for the wholesalers, discover their secret warehouse (which they called their "plant"). Depending on the inventory, that could mean a serious financial blow, and require a different plant.

Thus the location of the plant was top secret. Daddy never even told Mother its location. Only the trusted delivery boy knew, along with the owner of the location. Most of the larger plants were in remote areas outside of town. Bill Martin, who succeeded Clemens as delivery boy, recalled, "We had them around here and there. We'd use one until we thought it was getting hot, from thieves or the law. We'd change them, go to a different location." For example, in March of 1953, the sheriff's office raided Daddy's plant on a horse farm at 6901 South Garnett Road, which in those days was quite a ways out of town. Martin remembered: "We had about 500 cases in there, but we got it all out except 75. We knew they were coming. We had a lot of friends down there [at the police station], guys we had grown up with. There was a highway patrolman I used to hunt with, he'd do just about anything for you. Guys we'd gone to school with." Guys you could trust.

9
Fourth Street

IN 1948, DADDY DECIDED TO MOVE again. He sold the house on King Street to—surprise!—a policeman, Nofel C. Sturgeon, who had been on the force since 1924. Elda Padgett, who alongside Tommie continued selling whiskey right next door, recalled "Sturge" and his wife Liz as sweet, nice neighbors. Sturgeon was not an officer who came around with his hand out. He was a paying customer.

Daddy bought a brand new house at 2724 East Fourth Street, in an area known as the Daniel Addition. In the 1930s a man named R. T. Daniel had bought a large tract of land and prepared it for a housing development. He paved the streets and installed water, sewer, and gas lines. Daniel even planted trees in what would become the front yards. Launching such an optimistic project during the Great Depression was considered foolhardy, but the speculator's gamble paid off. After the war, with an upswing in prosperity and the advent of the baby boom, he began building the houses, which sold quickly. Fourth Street became a quiet, clean, middle-class group of one-story brick houses, solidly built, with front lawns, ample backyards, and twenty-year-old elm trees. Children played up and down the block. Like much of the rest of Tulsa, it was a safe neighborhood. Most folks didn't bother to lock their doors, except at night.

Wayne had second thoughts about the new house. The garage was too small, and there were only two bedrooms. So he sold it for what he had paid for it—we hadn't even moved in—and arranged for a new house to be built across the street, on a plot that originally had been intended as an open area for block residents. Daddy paid $10,200 cash, and in the fall of 1948 we moved in.

The new red brick house had three bedrooms, a bath, living room, dining room, and kitchen. Connecting the house and garage was a breezeway (a porch screened on the front and back sides) that he soon enclosed and converted into a combined breakfast room-office. Mother went about decorating and taking care of her new house. From magazines such as *Ladies*

Home Companion, House Beautiful, and *Better Homes and Gardens,* she knew all about the most up-to-date designs and appliances. She bought new furnishings, all from friends of Daddy's at discount prices—he paid retail only when he had no other choice. She bought a mahogany Duncan Phyfe dining room set: a table, a china closet, and a sideboard. For the living room, she chose a new couch, armchairs, coffee table, end tables, lamps, drapes, and curtains, but she brought the old combination radio hi-fi from King Street, along with her collection of 78 rpm records: Glenn Miller, Tommy Dorsey, the Andrews Sisters, Bunny Berrigan, Nat "King" Cole, Benny Goodman, the Mills Brothers, and others. For the fireplace in the living room, she bought a gas stove designed to resemble a small pile of firewood.

It was as though she were saying goodbye to her past: she had been born twenty-five years before in a log house that had a dirt floor. Like her mother, she was a fastidious housekeeper, but the pristine new house gave her a chance to show what she could really do. She was so proud of her new living room carpet that she made me and my friends—and any other potential carpet smudger, child or adult—remove our shoes at the front door. After taking me to school, she came home and made the beds straightway. She dusted and vacuumed daily, using her new Electrolux. She waxed the kitchen linoleum and breakfast room floor tiles. Immediately after dinner, she washed and dried the dishes and put them away. When someone finished a cigarette, she would discreetly whisk away the ashtray and return it moments later, its contents expunged by a fresh Kleenex. She had an encyclopedic knowledge of household products, from Ronson lighter fluid to Tide to Jello. Her house was a sparkling gem. Bobbie Hood, a friend and former bootlegger, remembered her as "the cleanest woman in Tulsa." At one point, Daddy told Mother, "One thing I'll never have to be ashamed of, is to bring anybody in this house, or to sit them down to anything you've cooked." He meant that as a compliment.

Shortly after the move to Fourth Street, Daddy abruptly stopped selling whiskey. Lucille remembered: "And we didn't have any money. I told him, 'You either better get a job or I'll get a job, or we'll sell whiskey. We got to get some money.' So we started selling whiskey again. I don't know why he stopped. We had moved in before my birthday [September 21] in '48, and we hadn't lived there six weeks until we started again. While he laid off, he was buying and selling cars, anything else he could get hold of. If he had a chance to pick up something worth any money—'hot' stuff—he'd sell it."

Was he thinking of going respectable? "Nah. I guess he was just tired of selling whiskey. Clemens was working for us there on Fourth Street, him and for a while a boy named Junior VanDeventer." (Apparently Junior was no relation to Ned, the card player Grover lost to the last night of his life.) "Wayne would have to go hunt Clemens up every morning before it was time to make deliveries. Clemens was always in some motel somewhere with a different old girl every night. Wayne'd jerk him out of bed and bring him over to the house and say, 'Now, Clemens'—I remember one white shirt Clemens had with lipstick and stuff he'd spilled all over it, his hair sticking right straight up—'Clemens, you're going to have to go home and clean up. You can not make deliveries looking like that.' Clemens was still half drunk, leaning up against the wall, and he said, 'Now, Wayne, I don't know why you want to talk to me like that. You know I'm always teat and nidy.'" In general, Clemens was a mild-mannered, soft-hearted guy, and when he went into another line of work, he and Wayne remained close friends.

Bill Martin took his place. Bill was a modest fellow, part Indian. He had grown up in Wayne's old neighborhood, and had attended junior high at Cleveland, where he had known Lucille. He then went to Marquette, one of Tulsa's two Catholic high schools. "I went to Marquette to play football and basketball, working and trying to go to school, but my mom and two younger sisters were having kind of a hard go, so I dropped out and went to work. Then I joined the Navy, in World War II. And I paid for it, too. I got my back all busted up, spent a year in a naval hospital." Honorably discharged, Bill got a job at the gas station downtown, selling a little hooch on the side for Wayne. He had gotten married, and was looking to change jobs, so in 1949 or 1950, he replaced Clemens as delivery boy.

Talking with me, Bill said, "First time I saw you, you were real young, you all still lived up there on King. I used to come up there and tease you. I'd say, 'Your daddy's a bootlegger' and you'd say, 'No he's not, either. My momma is, but my daddy ain't.' Ha ha!" Bill confirmed that Daddy's whiskey came from Bud Allen in Joplin. Bud Allen was a nondescript, quiet gentleman who would come to Tulsa occasionally with his girlfriend to visit my father. Bud never married her because his wife, a devout

Catholic, did not believe in divorce. So he lived with his girlfriend but supported his wife and children. Every once in a while Daddy would make a run up Route 66 to Joplin, to go out to dinner at Wilder's Restaurant with Bud, maybe play cards or shoot dice in the gambling club on the floor above Wilder's. Daddy left most of the whiskey hauling to others.

The loads were stashed at the plant. Before dusk, Bill would come by our house, knock on the breezeway door, come in, and pick up the day's orders from my mother. Then, as darkness set in, he'd go out to the plant, load up the car, and make the deliveries. "We run quite a few cases. Some nights we'd have 35, 40, or 50 cases. Some nights would be light, 20 or 25. We had good volume. A lot of the customers were on the South Side [Tulsa's wealthy residential area], but we had a few of what we called pint pitchers," who sold by the bottle. "Of course we supplied Tommie." At some point in the 1950s Tommie and his wife Elda had moved into the house next door to us on Fourth Street, which Daddy had bought. Tommie made good use of the elaborate plant that the previous tenant, Neal Allen, had installed. Neal, also a bootlegger, was a relative of Bud Allen. Neal had excavated a large area under the front bedroom and installed a delicate latch system that could be activated by inserting hatpins in very small holes, springing loose a section of the bedroom's wooden floor. Of course, Neal was a customer of Daddy's.

Even the mayor was a customer. "Yeah, and a preacher. The preacher would always leave the money in the garage, under a washtub, and we'd put the cache of whiskey under the tub," said Bill Martin. Other customers included Oklahoma Natural Gas, First National Bank, Public Service Company, Barker, Grimm & Company, and Wheatley Manufacturing Company—all highly respectable businesses. "On Christmas, down at Oklahoma Natural Gas, sometimes they'd buy 150 cases, sometimes 200. I'm not lying! I'd take a great big old long dolly, just wheel it out there in the alley and stack it and take it up on the elevator. They had parties and they gave it away to different customers." Another good customer was Irene Herbert's, a store that sold fine furs and catered to Tulsa's elite.

From time to time Daddy would also make a contribution to a good cause, "like a policeman's ball or something like that. He'd send them ten or fifteen cases, so they wouldn't have to buy no booze. If we found out that a policeman was getting married, we'd go down there, kind of keep everything running smooth. You know, you can catch more flies with honey than with sour apples. That was Wayne's motto, and mine too. But hell, he did all the thinking. You know, he had a mind."

But sometimes the honey didn't spread far enough. From time to time, Martin got arrested. "Yeah, I got busted. There was a couple of guys on that raiding squad, they had another friend that was a bootlegger, so they kind of whomped on us every chance they got. I was loaded one night, and goddurned, I went straight across on Thirty-first Street, and it just so happened that I crossed right in front of them. They fell in behind me and turned on the siren. So I tried to outrun them. They pulled up beside me and turned on the red light and yelled, 'Pull over, pull over!' One guy pulled out a gun and said, 'We're going to shoot you if you don't pull over!' About that time we came up to this intersection, so I just made a sharp right and they went straight ahead. Boy, that really made them mad! God damn, they turned around and here they came. We came back across Thirty-first and turned the corner, but they'd already called in another car and had me blocked off. I knew I couldn't outrun them loaded. Finally they got me out and told me they was going to do this to me and that to me. Hell, they never did nothing. Took me down and booked me. Your dad sent somebody down and got me out in thirty minutes. They just confiscated the whiskey, they couldn't prosecute." They couldn't prosecute because the officers had made what was called a rough raid—a raid without a warrant. The event was a virtual carbon copy of one the previous night. Police estimated the value of the two nights' confiscated liquor at $5,500.

There was also the danger of losing product to hijackers. Martin recalled: "I came close to it once. If we'd run short on whiskey I'd have to go up to Joplin and get a load. One time I was coming back and some guys started to highjack me, and I saw them coming and went back up to Missouri and got Bud Allen and his buddy. Bud had a Thompson submachinegun and his colleague an M-1 carbine. They stayed on my tail all the way into Tulsa." The return trip was along back roads, of which there were many. Twice, though, the haulers lost their loads to the Highway Patrol.

Sometimes Daddy kept the whiskey right in the house, in the third bedroom. But he always had a plant. Lucille remembered: "Homer Gafford's brother lived way out on a farm down there in the weeds, and we kept it in his barn. They had another one out here somewhere in West Tulsa, a

OKLAHOMA TOUGH

rundown kind of place. There were three thieves, and one of them liked to break into stashes and steal whiskey. But one of them was a friend of Wayne's, so he told him that the guy was going to break in. When the whiskey thief did break in, Wayne and Homer were waiting for him. They like to beat that man to death. Homer said, 'I'm just gonna kill him.' Wayne said, 'No, it ain't worth killing him.'"

One ingenious plant was the two-car garage at his brother Tommie's house. One wall was paneled, and if you stuck a nail in a certain spot between two of the panels, a large section of the garage floor—a cement slab—would rise on one end, exposing a stairway that led down to a underground storage space.

At one point Daddy stashed whiskey in a motel room, but somebody broke in and stole it, leaving a pint of Seagram's on the table. That was the only time he ever lost any whiskey to thieves.

When making deliveries, Bill went in for disguises. "I wore a bunch of different hats and colors." Sometimes he'd hang up a jacket or suit coat on one of the hooks that all cars used to have in the back seat, to give the impression that he was a traveling salesman. Apparently, this was a standard ploy. According to Esther Kellner, author of *Moonshine, Its History and Folklore,* "One of the [transporter's] most successful moves was to travel after dark, posing as a weary young salesman. . . . [He] wore a business suit, white shirt, and tie. He had an extra suit and raincoat hanging in the back. . . ."[1]

Kellner describes the moonshiners' favorite tanker-car as a 1940 Ford coupe, "because of its even distribution of weight."[2] These cars had built-in tanks for the moonshine, with supercharged motors sporting four-barrel carburetors. Martin explained: "Our cars were different [from regular cars], but they looked like plain, everyday cars. They had heavy-duty springs. We had switches to turn the taillights off any time we wanted to. The brakelights too." But, unlike the specially equipped cars in movies such as *Thunder Road,* in which Robert Mitchum plays a moonshine transporter, Daddy's did not spray oil out the back in order to slicken the road for pursuing cars. To load the car, Martin simply removed the bottom part of the back seat, stacked the whiskey lugs, and covered them with a blanket.

Bill got to know the idiosyncracies of his customers, such as Edith Martin (no relation to him). "The first time I saw Edith I thought, 'Man, that's the prettiest thing I ever seen.'" In an unusual role reversal, Edith's husband, Brad, answered the phones and she did all the delivering. "He was supposed to have been a highly educated some kind of something. I went down there to Edith's to deliver one time. She was there with two girlfriends, and they damned near took every piece of clothes I had off me. And there I had four damned orders to make! Hey, let me tell you something: every time I went down there I always looked her over pretty good, and if she was drinking I just sat the order down and run!"

Around 1951, Alma, Daddy's first cousin, and her husband, Tom Montgomery, bought the Fourth Street house that had been Daddy's first choice, and Alma went to work for us. She was highly qualified. When Tom had gotten out of the service after the war, he had had trouble finding a job, as did many others. So he got into retail bootlegging. Like my parents, Tom and Alma were able to pay cash for their first home, and then move on to a better place, a ranch-style house up on Reservoir Hill, a nice residential area and the highest point in Tulsa. Among their acquaintances were any number of policemen. Alma recalled: "The police was our friends. In fact they socialized with us. Billy and Jimmy Lang practically lived at our house. They'd come up and have dinner and play cards. They were detectives with the City."

Like my parents, Tom and Alma had no moral compunctions about selling whiskey. "Why would we? It was legal everywhere but Oklahoma! I don't know what the big deal was. I never felt bad about it. I never felt that people ought to look down their noses at me because we were doing it. Of course they did. As if we was villains of some kind. We really wasn't."

But the business did have its hairy moments. "Tom bought one load wholesale, in Kentucky, and on Route 20 outside of Claremore, at 3 A.M., he turned it over. He thought somebody was chasing him. You never saw so much broken whiskey in your life." Another time, Tom got hijacked, up in Kansas: "They put him in the trunk of his brand-new Ford, and it was winter and he had on a wool suit and it was wet and it started shrinking on him. They drove him down in a bunch of trees and cut the tires." Then they let him out. It must have been pretty tight in the trunk for a man his size: six-two and 220 pounds.

According to Alma, Tom also "hauled whiskey in for Wayne from Kentucky for quite a while. I went with him, but I got so nervous I had to quit. Every time I seen a car I like to went into hysterics. Tom hauled it to

Wayne's plant." Alma never knew where the plants were, even her husband's. The women were told as little as possible.

One night when Daddy was out of town, Bill needed help delivering. So my mother and Alma took me and Alma's daughter Sharon along to make a few deliveries. Sharon and I were around nine years old. What policeman would pay the slightest attention to two ordinary women driving down the street with their children? Sharon and I sat on top of the Indian blanket that covered the merchandise as we cruised quietly up and down the tree-lined streets of the wealthy South Side, stopping here and there to drop off orders. It was fun.

10   *Nice People among the Pint Pitchers*

FOR SOME WHISKEY DEALERS, bootlegging was a normal business, even a family tradition. Sometime before World War I, a man named Bob Hood had come to Tulsa in a covered wagon with his wife Bessie, father, mother, and four brothers. Back in Arkansas, his parents had been bootleggers, as had his wife's parents. In Tulsa, Bob and Bessie had three girls, Jacqueline (Jackie), Dorothy Aline (Dot), and Bobbie Aline (sometimes called Jo). Bob and Bessie set up shop selling moonshine right out of their little shotgun house.

Eventually everybody in the block was either a bootlegger or knew about the business. It was one big extended family. If the Hoods had to go somewhere, they'd have a neighbor or two babysit the business.

Bobbie Hood recalled: "Customers just walked to the back door, bought the whiskey, and left. And right across the street, my Uncle Fred had a bootlegging place. Around the corner my Aunt Dora had one of the biggest bootlegging places in Tulsa. It was all aunts and uncles and sisters and brothers—*all* of them were bootleggers. It was the whole block. As far as us girls selling whiskey, it was just like running a grocery store."

Like other bootleggers, the Hoods had secret stashes. The most ingenious one was in the back alley beneath a trash burner made from a fifty-gallon oil drum. The can was hinged to a base: set in the ground below was a padlocked cement vault big enough for three or four cases of whiskey. "When the law was coming, we'd tell the kids to go out and set the trash on fire," Bobbie said. The Hoods needed such stashes to protect the hooch from the occasional police raid. In all the years the Hoods ran the business, they were robbed only once.

Violent criminal behavior such as armed robbery scared the Hood girls. Jackie was kind and generous, Bobbie was gregarious and innocent. They weren't tough, and the only law they broke was the liquor law.

And so the police rarely interfered with the Hoods. Besides, after Jackie and Bobbie took over the family business, around 1948, they routinely paid the city police $200 a month for protection. According to the ex-bootleggers I've talked with, virtually every cop could be bought. Occasionally, of course, the police had to stage a raid for the sake of appearances. The county cops were always dressed in suits, ties, overcoats, and fedoras, and they were polite, even friendly. One time they raided Bobbie just after the birth of her first child: "I was laying in bed and the baby was besides me in the bassinet and the county men came in. They said, 'Bobbie, we didn't know you had this baby! We don't have to do this today, we can come back anytime.' Then they went over and looked at the baby and said, 'My goodness! We'll come back and raid you in a couple of days,' put their hats on, and took off. They were *real* nice men. They didn't really want to raid us, but they had to put in an appearance." The principal exception was the assiduous county cop Roy Rains, who could not be bought.

After the war, the Hoods complied with federal law by abandoning moonshine and selling brand-name whiskey, for which an excise tax was paid. They bought their federal tax stamp every year and displayed it on the kitchen wall. Their whiskey was now supplied by local wholesalers. "Wayne Padgett and Sam Bryson were the only two bootleggers we ever bought from during all those years. Sam was our cousin and Wayne was just a good friend."

Bobbie's parents were an interesting combination of the usual and the unusual. Her dad, Bob, sort of kept an eye on things around the house, you might say. He whiled away the hours sitting on the porch and looking after his private zoo, which at one time consisted of a red monkey, three Shetland ponies, a big horse, a goat, and an assortment of squirrels. "He liked animals. He was a real sweet man. But he drank. All the Hood boys drank."

Bobbie's mother, Bessie, was the hard worker. She did all the cooking, cleaned the house, took care of the girls, and ran the whiskey business, from which she saved her money, gradually buying up most of the property on the block. She loved her daughters but was strict with them. Smoking and drinking were absolutely forbidden. A strong believer in education, Bessie saw to it that her daughters took going to school seriously. Bobbie went all the way through the eighth grade without being absent or tardy once! Bobbie said: "I graduated from high school, barely, but I graduated! Momma told my girlfriend Betty Collins that if she would go to college and take me with her, that she would pay for Betty's education too." Bessie also promised Bobbie a new red convertible.

Bessie didn't worry much about Dot, who was quiet and bookish, and who refused to have anything to do with the whiskey business. Bobbie described Dot as "more refined, more polished" than herself and Jackie. Dot went to business college and eventually ran her own home construction business.

Bessie kept an eye on Jackie and Bobbie. The two sisters loved to go down to Cain's Academy, the now legendary dance hall, on Saturday night. They'd pool their money and take a cab down to 423 North Main, pay the admission, and have a dime or fifteen cents left over for a Coke. Alcohol was forbidden at Cain's, though the guys might have a bottle stashed out in the parking lot. Jackie and Bobbie—like Wayne and Lucille and so many others—went to hear Bob Wills and his Texas Playboys. They weren't there to get picked up, and they weren't there to get drunk. They were there to meet their friends and dance. They loved to dance, as did many of the guys. Howard Donahue recalled, "I wouldn't have missed it for nothing. Back in the men's room, they had shoeshine boys. We even paid 'em to polish the bottoms, so we could dance a little better, ha ha! A man would have to be about half drunk to have the *bottoms* of his shoes shined! I wore out many pairs of shoes there." There were no tables, just a huge dance floor, at the far end of which was the stage. Along the sides were low benches, and back near the door an area where you could buy Cokes, 7 Ups, potato chips, and popcorn. There was an innocence to it that is hard to comprehend now.

Of course, boys will be boys. Whenever anyone got a little rowdy, the bouncers—four off-duty police officers—took care of things quickly. After Cain's closed (around midnight), some of the faster kids would go to after-hours clubs. But Bobbie's mother wouldn't allow her to stay out late.

"Mother was very strict," Bobbie said. "She almost fainted when she found out I was going out dancing with Homer Gafford. He was ten years older than me. That's why she wanted to get me out of town to college. But he liked her and she liked him. Homer was a handsome Casanova, a handsome, handsome man! The most immaculate man I ever seen. Fancy suits—I never saw him in a pair of jeans or khakis but once, and they was ironed! To go fishing with Wayne. And I never saw Homer perspire in my life. The most gorgeous hair. He'd walk into a place and everybody'd look at him. Of course they all knew he was no good, but they looked at him! Like the way people today look at gangsters. But he wasn't but a little local bootlegger from the backwoods of Tennessee."

Bessie's protectiveness vanished when she died suddenly of a massive coronary at the age of forty-seven. Jackie, twenty-three, and Bobbie, nineteen, inherited the business. Jackie became the mother figure: she cooked and ran the household. Bobbie took up with Homer, and two years after her mother's death, married him. During the four years of their marriage, all he did, according to her, was go to clubs and go hunting—which in varying degrees was typical of quite a few other bootlegging men.

Bessie had been generous with her girls. "My mother would give you anything in the world. When I was fifteen I had the prettiest fur coat you had ever seen in your life. My sister had a red fox fur coat. We dressed like you'd think we was the Queen of England. She thought we was the prettiest girls in the world, wanted us to be beautiful and all that, but she didn't believe in freeloading. She wanted you to work." The Hood girls continued their mother's traditions of working hard and supporting husbands, but unlike her they treated themselves well. They liked jewelry and high-class clothes and furs. Bobbie recalled: "When we went downtown and walked in the door to Seidenbach's [clothing store], those sales clerks would jump, they would light up and start vibrating." Bobbie, a platinum blond, had a full-length white ermine coat, while Jackie, with her hair dyed coal-black, had a matching black mink. The Hood girls created a larger-than-life impression purring along in their new bright red Cadillac convertible with the white top down.

After four years of marriage to Homer, Bobbie divorced him. She bore him no hard feelings, even when he married Jackie. The next year Bobbie married a handsome fellow named Ricky Mitchell.

"Ricky's father Buck was a bootlegger too. He got five years in the penitentiary for selling a pint of whiskey to an Indian. When I married Ricky, I'd only known him thirty days, and I was kind of ashamed of my family. So when I heard about his daddy, I said, 'Hell, Ricky, I thought *you* had married into a family of gangsters!' And it turned out that years ago Ricky's grandmother had killed somebody, over in Claremore!" But I decided that Ricky was a good old boy, a nice fellow. Ricky was a nice-looking fellow, a *good* boy."

My father liked Ricky too. As with Homer, the two of them would frequently go on hunting or fishing trips together.

But Daddy wasn't just a man's man, he was a family man, a friend. Bobbie said, "I really liked Wayne. He was one of these men that come in the house and laughed and talked, and Jackie's two kids just loved him. He'd take the kids and throw them up in the air. Really a nice man. You couldn't keep from liking Wayne. I couldn't say a bad word about him if I wanted to. He went to everybody's funeral. He went to Jackie's, and Jackie's son's, and to Dot's, and he didn't even know her that well. And he was at my mother's. He went to everybody's funeral—he was nice like that."

He *was* considerate, but perhaps his attendance at funerals was also an unconscious attempt to come to terms with what for him was the primal funeral—his father's. Deep down, he knew how much the bereaved needed consolation. He himself had never gotten enough.

11 *Out and About*

DADDY'S ENERGY AND RESTLESSNESS, his thirst for making a deal, his freedom and mobility—all enabled him to handle a wide variety of activities in the course of a single day. He was far more than just a bootlegger. After an early breakfast at home, he might join some of his buddies for coffee at a diner, then go "see about a car" or some other deal he had working, take his bird dog out for a run in the country, drop by to see his mother, help someone transport a load of lumber or cement, spend an hour shooting the breeze with friends at a used car lot, go fishing or

Grover Padgett in the cavalry,
probably in Mississippi during
or shortly after World War I.

*Grover, baby Robert, and
Verna Padgett, probably in
Claremore, Okla., 1920.*

Verna, Wayne, Tommie, Grover,
and Robert Padgett, 1930.

Lucille Huey (far right,
not far left), *age sixteen,*
at the Buckhorn Drive
Inn, Tulsa, June 1940.

Wayne Padgett, senior year school photo, for which he refused to wear a tie, 1940.

Wayne and Lucille
at Mohawk Park,
Tulsa, 1940 or 1941.

(From left to right) *Robert, Verna, and Wayne Padgett at Verna's on North Florence, Tulsa, August 1942. Robert was home on leave from the Army Air Corps.*

My mother (second from left) *with her father Noah, sister Loraine, and mother Daisy Huey, at the Hueys' in Sand Springs, Okla., 1943.*

My father and I on
King St., Tulsa,
probably 1944.

*My father and I on
King St., Tulsa, 1947.
Both of us are wearing
custom-made cowboy
boots.*

My mother, my father,
and I, Tulsa, June 17,
1947. My mother's dress
was lime green and black.

(From left to right) *Norma Young, a Tulsa pop singer; Wesley Pilkington; Wes's sister Dolly Young, who played the piano and, with her husband, owned the supper club depicted; Dolly's son and Norma's husband Toby "Billy" Young, Jr., band leader who later was secretary to chief of police Jack Purdy; my father; my mother; Tommie Padgett; Elda Padgett; Gladys "Happy" Pilkington, my mother's aunt; Doris and her house painter husband E. L. Keltner, who rented the Pilkingtons' garage apartment, at the Casa-Del supper club, Tulsa, January 9, 1948.*

My father in the dining room of our house on King St., Tulsa, probably early 1948. One phone was for personal use, the other for the whiskey business. A spiral notebook and a ledger completed the business paraphernalia: a very low-overhead office. Note the pulled windowshades on both sides of the wall lamp.

(From left to right)
Tommy Warren
(employee of the sherrif's
department and former
Tulsa Oilers baseball
player) and his wife, my
father, my mother, and
Dolly Young, probably
at the Casa-Del supper
club, Tulsa, ca. 1949.

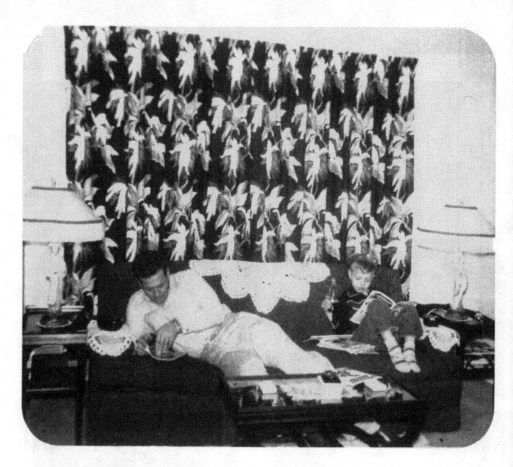

My father and I, in an unguarded moment at home at 2733 East 4th St., Tulsa, around 1950 (pre-TV). He occasionally read Argosy *or* Field and Stream. *On the shelf in the endtable at left, a Bible. On the coffee table, a* Straight Arrow *comic book.*

Tommie Padgett (far left with cigarette, steadying the driver) *at the Saturday night stock car races, Tulsa, early 1950s.*

My father and Homer Gafford,
Hot Springs, Ark., April 21,
1959, possibly carrying pro-
grams for Oak Lawn race track.

My father and Louise "Kam" Thompson, probably at the Tropicana Hotel, Las Vegas, July, 1963. Kam's green dress had white polka dots.

My father under arrest, Tucson, Ariz., January 1968. FBI mug shots.

My father, Wayne Jr.,
and Kam Padgett,
Tulsa, July 1978.
The bookshelves were
two dimensional.

My father and
Nancy Mann, Tulsa,
probably 1990, the
year before he died.

hunting, drive out to see a piece of property, unload and reload fifty cases of whiskey, drop off a loan at a friend's house, or suddenly take off for Kansas or Florida or California. As Bill Martin put it, "He'd turn up in the most unexpected places."

At various periods he had special buddies, such as Homer Gafford in the late forties and early fifties. In his late teens and early twenties, around 1940, Homer had earned a local reputation as a tough kid, hanging around clubs and dance halls and doing a little bootlegging. No stranger to self-esteem, he called himself "The Iron Fist." Soon he was hired as the bouncer at a tough joint called The Music Box.

The Music Box operated during and after hours. Located next door to the Buckhorn Drive Inn, where Lucille and her mother worked, it was owned by the colorful Willis Newton. Back in 1924, he and his brothers had pulled off the greatest train robbery in history, at Roundout, Illinois, temporarily netting them more than three million dollars. Newton's police record went back to 1912: burglary, escape from jail, bank and post office robbery, and the 1924 train robbery, for which he was sent to Leavenworth. In the early 1930s he settled in Tulsa, going into the wholesale gasoline business and opening the Buckhorn. Next door to it he built The Music Box. (The building still stands, with "Newton 1934" cut into the stone above the door.) But he was immediately charged with robbing a bank earlier in the year, tried, and given a twenty-year sentence. In 1942 he was paroled, but the next year he got a one-year stretch for transporting whiskey from Joplin into Oklahoma. Released in 1944, Newton resumed his career as a night club operator. He openly carried a loaded gun in his hip pocket and everyone knew he would use it—either end of it. In 1945 he was charged with pistol-whipping a customer, who reported that Newton knocked him unconscious: "When I came to, Newton had my brother down and someone was trying to stomp him in the face." (Homer Gafford may well have been the "someone.") The victim decided not to press charges when he read in the newspaper that Newton was "the roughest, toughest gambler that ever operated in the Tulsa area." Newton's philosophy was simple; he once told a *Life* magazine interviewer, "The whole trouble with this world is all these —————— laws, and that is a plain fack (*sic*)."[1]

Although Newton was in some ways a role model for both Wayne and Homer, neither of them was into bank robbery. Homer was just a fighter and a ladies' man. Homer and Wayne—both handsome, fearless, and living just on the far side of legality—became like brothers. They palled around, they went to clubs, they went hunting and fishing together.

They had other joint pursuits, as well. According to Lucille, "Wayne and Homer set up a scheme. They'd go down to the Easleys to play poker two or three nights a week. Homer and Wayne had a signal worked out, and they took the Easleys for a cleaning every time." The Easleys had money, partly from bootlegging. They also had quite a wild streak themselves.

The head of the family was Claude Easley, also known as "Old Man Easley," a bootlegger client of Daddy's. One of Claude's daughters, Priscilla, had married a bootlegger named Fred ("Little Griff" or "Griff") Griffing. At one point, after a fight with Griff, she had gone home to her parents. In a drunken rage, Griff stormed after her. Bill Martin recalled the incident: "I was fixing to deliver an order up there at Easley's and I'd just turned a corner and I heard a gun firing—I'd delivered whiskey down there, and every time that old man would come out he'd have a shotgun or a rifle or a submachine gun. That old man was meaner than hell! Old Claude Easley. When I heard those gunshots, I pulled in a driveway and backed up. That was the last order, so I just took it on back to Wayne's. I told him, 'There's something going on over at Easley's. I heard the damndest gunshots.' About that time it came over the radio. Old Man Easley had shot Griff and damn near killed him."

Lucille confirmed the incident: "That happened on New Year's Eve. We were all going out that night. Griff found out about it—he and Priscilla were separated or divorced—and he went down there and broke in to get her and knock her around, but that old man came down the stairs and started shooting."

Also in the family were Priscilla's brothers, Thurmond Easley and "Pretty Boy" Jim Easley, and Homer Brown, a cousin. During a drinking and gambling party, Brown shot and killed Priscilla's first husband. Daddy's delivery boy, Bill Martin, who had an uncanny knack for being within earshot of the action, recalled: "I was up at Bill Rudolph's motorcycle shop, just about two blocks down from where they had that shooting match. You could hear those shots just as plain as day."

"Pretty Boy" Jim Easley was a chip off the old block. After an argument with him, his young wife had stormed out of the house. He followed her out and shouted that he'd shoot her if she didn't come back. She kept walking, through an opening of a tall hedgerow, and headed down the other side, barely visible. He raised the pistol and fired one shot. Her body slumped to the ground, a bullet in her brain.

This was the kind of people Daddy and Homer Gafford were fleecing at the Easleys.

Eventually, Daddy and Homer had a falling out, and there was bad blood, probably over money. (Homer was as tight as Wayne was generous.) Thereafter, every time Homer would drive by a place where Wayne was, he would cuss Wayne out, according to Lucille. So Wayne issued a challenge to Homer to meet him at a car lot where both had hung out.

Wayne was there when Homer drove up and got out of his car with a .357 Magnum. Wayne brought out his bird-hunting shotgun, sawed off right at the legal limit, and racked the pump. Homer heard the unmistakable sound, crouched down behind the cars, and beat a hasty retreat. The story of a big shootout spread, but actually no shots were ever fired.

Sometime in the early 1950s I accompanied Daddy to the skeet field near Tulsa's exclusive Southern Hills Country Club. That day he put on something of an exhibition, breaking ninety-nine out of a hundred clay pigeons. I was impressed. So were those in attendance, including a tall, slender gentleman dressed in a gray double-breasted suit and fedora. He was probably around sixty, but he looked younger.

"That's fine shooting," he said. "My specialty, however, is the pistol. I can hit a dime at a distance of—" and here he gave what sounded like an outrageous distance.

The next step was for Daddy to bet him he couldn't. Daddy didn't bite.

The man started to smile, but instead he said, "Well, OK, I'll just show you."

He took out a dime, walked over to a telephone pole, and lodged the coin flat against it, beneath the nib of a splinter. He then paced off the distance he had mentioned before, drew a nickel-plated revolver from his shoulder holster, aimed, and fired. Daddy had me retrieve the dime.

It was mangled.

We gave the gentleman a ride back to his downtown hotel. I watched and listened from the back seat.

"What's your line of work?" he asked Daddy.

"I sell whiskey."

Daddy's openness surprised me.

"By the way, my name is Titanic Thompson. What's yours?"

Daddy paused. "You're not *the* Titanic Thompson, are you?"

"The same. And you?"

"Wayne Padgett."

After we dropped him off, Daddy turned to me and said, "Ronnie, that was *Titanic Thompson*!" Thompson was a legendary figure who, by the age of forty, had won more than a million dollars playing poker, shooting craps, and fleecing unsuspecting sportsmen by challenging them at golf, bowling, pool, and marksmanship, and by arranging various cons. He worked all over the country (in New York, Damon Runyon based the character of Sly Masterson, the gambler in "The Idyll of Miss Sarah Brown," on him), but his favorite haunts tended to be in places like Joplin, Springfield, Hot Springs, Kansas City, Lubbock, and Tulsa—not too far from the Ozarks, where he had grown up.

I have no doubt that Daddy and Titanic's paths crossed again, but I have no information. The next time I heard about Thompson was in Red Smith's column in the *New York Times*, just after Thompson died.

In addition to Homer Gafford, one of Daddy's hunting buddies was Lee Eller, who had originally pumped gas in a station at Admiral and Peoria. After a European tour of duty in World War II, in which he rose to the rank of battalion commander and oversaw the construction of General Eisenhower's headquarters, he opened his own car lot. Eller recalled: "Wayne and I was like brothers. We had a *lot* of fun. We started going to Canada probably around '47, '48, that area. We fished and hunted, just played around. We went to Lake of the Woods, near Winnipeg. There was a nice camp we liked to go to. We drove up. We flew up too, with B. K. Daniels, who was a good friend, in B. K.'s plane. But it was frustrating to hunt quail with Wayne, because you never got to shoot any: as soon as you brought the gun to shoulder, the quail were already down!

"We also went to Colorado, deer hunting, and to Kansas, pheasant hunting, and to Dakota. Just anything either one of us decided we wanted to do—wham!—we'd load up and go. Wayne enjoyed life."

But he especially enjoyed hunting, so much that from time to time he'd even go hunting with Mother, usually for quail. Lucille remembered: "We also went rabbit hunting several times. There was snow on the ground, and Wayne and his friend would get out on the fenders and I'd drive and they'd shoot these rabbits, while I was driving through these snowy fields. It was at night, but I had the headlights on."

But Daddy's best bird-hunting buddy was Al Haddock. This relationship casts light on both men, and to some degree on others of their time and place.

Haddock met Daddy under unusual circumstances. Haddock, a Tulsa city policeman, recalled: "I was coming down Admiral Place, coming west, and I looked up and saw him run a stop sign at Admiral, in a little convertible. I dropped in behind him and he also run one at First Street, Second, Third, and Fourth, and when I caught him at Fifth Street, I said, 'Do you know how many stop signs you've run?' And he said, 'All of 'em.' And I said, 'That's right, you didn't miss any of them.' I gave him a ticket. And I got acquainted with him."

This instant bonding might sound unbelievable, but it isn't. In the first place, it is quite possible that Haddock had heard good things about my father from other police officers. As for the traffic violation, it might have consisted of my father's coming to a rolling—not a complete—stop. Neither my father nor Haddock would have considered such an offense to be serious. Also, in those days the general attitude toward traffic safety was far more casual than it is today. Finally, Haddock was a quiet, easygoing man who would have appreciated my father's open admission of guilt and his good humor. In any case, the two men found that they had something in common: a love of bird hunting.

Parenthetically and ironically, the world's first yield sign—invented by Tulsa policeman Clinton Riggs—was installed about this time at the corner of First and Columbia, near where Daddy had run the stop signs and only two blocks from where Haddock himself lived.

Haddock recalled one day of hunting with Daddy: "We went out to Hassell Ranch, with a policeman, and we got out of the car and was in birds you wouldn't believe. Wayne and I both were hunting a lot and we were both good shots—he was one of the best shots I ever hunted with. I saw him kill birds as they come up off the ground. Three or four feet up, time they got that far he was knocking down birds. I used a twenty-gauge Browning automatic and Wayne shot a twelve-gauge pump gun. He could shoot it faster than I could an automatic!

"And he didn't have a nerve in his body. Hell, he'd come up to a fence and go over, with signs telling him not to, and he'd go in there and go to bird hunting.

"Anyway, this old policeman said, 'I'm gonna watch you guys for a little bit. You go ahead.' After a while I told Wayne, 'We'd better count up our birds.' We had around twenty-seven birds. So we came back to the car and told him, 'You take these birds home with you and come back and we'll go on hunting.' When he got back, he asked us, 'Don't you SOBs ever miss a bird?' We had killed just about every bird we shot at. We ended up that day with fifty-four, I think it was, and we'd shot fifty-eight times."

Daddy and Al had a good relationship based on mutual respect. Haddock recalled: "He and I hunted together for thirty years, at least, and you know, I never hunted with a more congenial guy. We never had one cross word. The only problem we ever had was getting down to see who would pay the check—he was hard to beat. We'd stop in a restaurant to eat, he'd say, 'I've got to go to the bathroom,' and hell, he'd go by and pay the bill. He was that kind of a guy. They don't come any better."

In all this, the question naturally arises, how did Al reconcile being both a policeman and a friend of a known criminal?

"You know, it was a funny thing: I was a policeman and he was on the other side, but it never made any difference. All our dealings were on the up and up."

Mother confirmed this: "Al and Wayne didn't do no business at all."

Haddock recalled, "Wayne didn't try to change nobody. He knew his side and he knew mine. I had my principles and he had his. He respected my feelings and I his, and we got along swell. Never had any problems. I knew Wayne liked me.

"I didn't go with him anywhere, only just hunting. My wife and I'd be sitting out on the porch in the summertime. He'd drive by and pull in and talk a little bit, but I really never did know too much about what Wayne done. I didn't *want* to know. But it caused me no trouble. He had a lot of friends down at the station. You know, he had a reputation for being a little bit wild. Some of the policemen didn't like him, but I'd say that ninety per cent of them liked Wayne Padgett. He was a good friend of [policeman, and later chief of police] Jack Purdy's! Wayne never said a bad word about Jack Purdy. He always said the same thing that I did, that Purdy was straight, and Wayne *appreciated* it. Like Wayne, his word was his bond. Wayne was just ornery, heh heh.

"But there wasn't nothing he wouldn't do for you. Hell, I've seen him take stuff to people that was sick. He had a heart of gold. I know one of the policeman's widows who moved over to Arkansas, and he'd go over to see if she was getting along all right, give her money.

"Wayne made a lot of money in the liquor business. One of the boys that ran Foodtown [grocery store, where Daddy knew the owners] told me, 'If we got short of money down there, cashing paychecks, I'd call Wayne and he'd bring me ten thousand dollars.'

"I went hunting with him one day out here west of town and he told me, 'If anything happens to me, I've got over thirty thousand dollars in my pocket. I want you to give it to my boy.' Money didn't mean a damned thing to Wayne Padgett."

Howard Donahue recalled another financial incident. "I was with him one night, we'd been fishing up to Grand Lake. Up at Langley we went into a kind of gambling and steak house. While we was waiting for them to fix us a steak, he started shooting dice. He was unlucky that particular time. He couldn't hit a lick. They had a $250 limit on the table. He lost quite a bit, so he got mad and throwed $500 out, and the man there, who knew Wayne, said, 'Wayne, you know that we have a $250 limit.' Wayne handed me a wad of money and said, 'However I'm betting, you bet $250 the same way.' In just a few minutes he lost $7,000, and said, 'Aw, hell, let's sit down and eat.' Ha ha! I couldn't no more have eaten!"

Another of Daddy's running buddies was Ricky Mitchell, who had married Bobbie Hood a year after her divorce from Homer Gafford. Ricky and Daddy would take off at the drop of a hat. They'd drive to Hot Springs or as far as Hialeah for the horse races, or they'd run up to Spavinaw or Grand Lake to fish, visit with other bootlegger friends and maybe gamble a little at the Sportsman's Bar in Spavinaw, the town Mickey Mantle was *really* from, as Daddy put it. But mainly they fished, sometimes trawling from the boat Daddy kept at Grand Lake, sometimes running trotlines, sometimes casting from the shore. Both men were good fishermen, and the catch usually included a lot of crappie (pronounced "croppy"), with bass and catfish mixed in. Daddy and Ricky would give away part of the catch and bring the rest home to the freezer. At different times, both were photographed and featured as fishermen in local publications such as the *Eastern Oklahoma Fishing Review*. One such photograph shows Daddy in khaki pants, a plaid wool shirt, and a cap, holding a stringer of crappie and smiling.

Sometimes Daddy would engage in a form of fishing that still perplexes me. Whenever the dam at Grand Lake would be closed, the portion below the dam would diminish to a trickle, exposing rocks and boulders along the bottom. As the water level sank, the fish that hadn't gone on downriver would seek refuge under the rocks. Daddy would wade out into the shallows, where he would reach down under the rocks and feel for fish, which he would catch with his bare hands. What perplexes me is that Grand Lake was known for its poisonous snakes, especially water moccasins. It wasn't that Daddy was afraid of poisonous snakes—he was afraid of *all* snakes. In fact, he had a phobia. He could hardly bear even to look at a picture of a snake. I can't understand how he had the nerve to reach under those rocks without knowing what was there. Perhaps it was his way of pushing the daredevil in him, of tempting fate.

Howard Donahue recalls an example. "I never will forget one time. Clemens had just come home from the Service. There was snow on the ground. Wayne was driving like hell—man, he drove like a crazy man, like he was *trying* to have a wreck. Clemens said, 'Wayne, if you don't slow down, I'm gonna turn the key off.' Wayne said, 'If you turn the damned key off, I'll turn this son of a bitch over.' Clemens reached over and turned the key off, and Wayne just kinked it. It went right into a tree, caved the top in—totalled the car—but it didn't hurt either one of them. Then Wayne chewed Clemens's ass out for wrecking the car!"

This may or may not have been the same accident that Bill Martin remembered: "It was sleeting and snowing in December and I just happened to see this gray car that had hit a damned tree head on, and sitting on the curb behind it was Wayne and Clemens. Ha ha ha! I said, 'What the hell happened?' and Clemens said, 'Well, he was cutting doughnuts, scared me to death, and I grabbed the steering wheel and we hit this tree.' Cutting doughnuts—Wayne was spinning the car round and round, going down the middle of the street. I said, 'Wayne, where do you want to go?' and he said, 'Oh, let's go down to the Silver Castle [diner].' So we went down there laughing and talking. I asked him, 'What do you want to do about that car?' He said, 'Aw, hell, we'll get it later.'"

One night Daddy had an episode in his Chrysler 300, a model which at that time carried the most powerful engine of any American car. It was the same car he and I had taken out to a country road where, at his urging, I had run it up to 120 miles per hour. I was seventeen. Anyway, one night coming back from a roadhouse called The Rustic Inn, he rolled it, crumpling the fenders and doors and stoving in the top. But the car had landed on its wheels, and Daddy had simply driven on home and gone to bed, unharmed.

Around the age of eleven, I had started driving his car backward and forward in the driveway, a distance of perhaps forty feet. There was no law against a minor's driving on private property, and it was good practice in using a standard-shift transmission. I had already learned to steer by driving the bumper cars at Lakeview Amusement Park. One summer evening not long after my twelfth birthday, Daddy said, "Let's run down to Morris's for a minute." Morris's sundry store was an old haunt of Daddy's and for me a source of comic books. As we approached the car, Daddy tossed me the keys and said, "You drive." I started up the car—a '49 or '50 Ford coupe—and backed out. I lurched a bit with the gear changes, but I managed the trip without stalling. Daddy seemed unconcerned about the fact that his unlicensed twelve-year-old son was driving for the first time, and in the dark!

Mother remembered another auto escapade: "He and I had been to Hot Springs. Down near Salisaw, the police got after us for speeding, and it was raining, oh it was raining! Finally he saw a road and he said, 'We're turning off right here.' When we did, we run off in a swamp. He got out of the car—mud was up to his waist—and went and got a man with a tow rope. They never did catch us."

Right after my parents were married, they had bought a '36 or '37 Chevrolet coupe, which didn't run very well. They got rid of it and bought a '38 Ford, when we were living in Baxter Springs. Back in Tulsa, Lucille remembered they bought "a '37 maroon Ford that belonged to some real nice people that lived down the block on Florence. The owner went out every morning and wiped it off and wiped the motor off. When we got it, it looked like nobody had ever stepped in it. On King Street, he bought a two-seater '36 or '37 Ford convertible. We drove that for a long time, and then he bought me a brand new Chevrolet. Then one day he told me he was going to sell it." Mother's precise recollection shows the importance of cars in the family. It also shows who was making the decisions.

Daddy's taste for fast and even dangerous driving showed poor judgment, but he was a natural and very skillful driver. He would slide into a car and be off, all in one smooth motion. If he was feeling wild, he'd drive wildly. If he was feeling impish, he'd fool the passenger next to him. One of his favorite tricks was to approach a corner and fake a lean into the turn and move his hands over the steering wheel as if he were actually starting to turn—while going straight through the intersection. The effect on the unsuspecting passenger was terrifying, but if you were in on the prank, quite hilarious. One person recalled, "Wayne could drive! And he loved to scare people. He took me on a ride one time. There was a car parked on the street, and he clipped that car so you could just barely hear it. That takes a good driver. But he'd scare you to death."

What I remember best about his driving is not his recklessness, but his easy grace, how relaxed and natural he looked as he cruised along, his right arm steering, his left bent at the elbow, with fingers lightly resting at the top rim of the window opening. He looked as comfortable as a cowboy whose body over the years had molded itself to the shape of his horse.

His car gave him the mobility that helped him become the Wayne Padgett who was known all over Tulsa. He was constantly on the move among relatives, friends, and business associates, stopping to chat, have a smoke, or drop off a handful of candy bars. And for this freedom he loved his cars, even though he was capable of willfully wrecking them. He kept them tuned up, vacuumed, washed, and waxed. If one developed a slight rattle, he would have it tightened.

Daddy had a knack for knowing if anything was wrong with a car. In addition to obvious problems, he could tell you if the shocks were worn out, if the wheels were out of alignment, if the tie rods were loose, if the valves needed adjustment, if one or two cylinders were "missing," or if the timing was off. He could tell you if the mileage indicator had been run back, and if it had, he could give a good estimate of the car's actual mileage by gauging the wear on the brake pedal. He could sight along the side of the car and, by looking for subtle ripples in the paint, tell you if the car had had body work, an indication that it had been wrecked. It's unlikely he gained much of this knowledge from school, having flunked auto mechanics twice. His expertise came from the street, from having knocked together his own jalopy, from hanging around car lots and garages, from being friends with mechanics, tire dealers, and welders, and from having pumped gas. Without his being aware of it, he had become part of a culture that had developed an intense love affair with the automobile, that big shiny machine that could lend the driver—of whatever class or economic status—immediate power (horsepower) and exhilaration (acceleration), not to mention romance.

For him, cars were also a source of income. He traded and sold them informally, and then went into business. From 1951 to 1956, he co-owned a neighborhood used-car lot with Pat Eller, the brother of his friend Lee Eller. The business was as legitimate as a used-car business can be and still turn a profit. That is, it made sense for a used-car dealer to make his products look good or even better than they are, which sometimes involved not only a cosmetic makeover, but a visit to a friend's speedometer shop to have the mileage indicator "fixed" (run back).

Was Daddy getting into the car business as a prelude to getting out of whiskey? In the 1950s in Oklahoma, there was a growing movement for legalized liquor, which would finish his business. Also trying to put bootleggers out of business was the Federal Alcohol Tax Unit, at least for a while. In April of 1951, these federal agents moved to halt liquor traffic into Oklahoma from neighboring states. In December, agents arrested four people in swashbuckling raids, and in October of the next year made a huge whiskey haul. These federal efforts were just a drop in the bucket, so to speak, but they might have set Daddy to considering another line of work. It's also possible he was simply looking for an additional source of income. He was already making a lot of money, but his expenditures were high, too.

In any case, the car lot gave him an office to hang out in and do other business. He had always been attracted to car lots, the way men in small towns were once attracted to the general store. Each lot had its office, a small frame structure furnished with an old wooden desk or two, some battered chairs and filing cabinets, a pin-up calendar, and a telephone. The rudimentary plumbing and heating fixtures gave the offices a rustic feeling. The walls were redolent with the smell of tobacco smoke. Like the gas station he had run, it was a man's world. Every once in a while he would say to me, "Let's go for a little ride," and we'd run down to one of the car lots along Lewis, where the owner would tousle my hair and say, "My, my!" and then turn away to speak with Daddy in hushed tones as I went off to wander among the shining cars. Since the age of six, I had been able to identify the make of every car on the road. Our family was deep into the car culture.

Cars were even a form of what might be called emotional currency. Bill Martin told me: "In '51 my folks had an old Ford I'd given them. It was about to fall down. Wayne come by there one day and saw that old car and said, 'It looks like they need another car, don't they, Willie?' I said, 'Ah, I don't know, Wayne. They don't go but back and forth to work anyway.' Damn, about two days later I went to work and he had this '50 model Plymouth sitting in the driveway. It was just a year old. He said, 'Hey, take this over and let your mom drive it and see how they like it. I've got to put it somewhere—I can't have it sitting around here.' He'd made up this little old excuse. So I took it over to my mom and dad and they drove it a couple of weeks. Wayne said, 'How do they like that car?' I said, 'They like it fine. When do you want me to bring it back?' And he said, 'Aw, I don't have no use for that car. Here's the title to it. Take it over and give it to them.' I said, 'Well, I ain't got enough money to pay you. We're just getting by, but I'll pay you so much a month or something.' He said, 'Just give it to them. Forget about it.' You know how he was. I said, 'You want me to bring their old Ford and see if you can sell it and get a little bit of money out of it? It might bring a couple of hundred or so.' He said, 'No, just tell them to take it down to the car lot and sell it.' He told us what car lot to take it to, to tell the guy at the car lot that he said to bring it down there. It brought around three hundred. That's the kind of guy he was. You know, if you were his friend and he liked you, you were just part of his family. He was always helping somebody."

Lee Eller recalled another example of Daddy's generosity. "I had a bad situation when I was in the banking business. The banks flew out from under us, and I was on the board and the FDIC came in and tied up everything I had. Wayne came to me and said, 'Hey, if you need money to pay bills with, I've got it.' For about three months, he made sure I had anything. And if I ever needed to borrow ten or twenty grand, he'd just hand it to me and say, 'Use it. Don't worry about it. If I need it, I'll let you know.' That's the way Wayne was. And that's the way we operated. Any cars I had, anything I had, we shared, if I knew he needed something—although it was very seldom he needed help. He didn't ask for a lot of help."

Everybody who knew Daddy has stories about his leaving groceries on a poor family's front porch in the early morning, or giving money to a widow who was having a hard time, or donating money for clothes for poor black children in what he and a great many whites called "Niggertown."*

Daddy's car lot wasn't particularly profitable, nor was the oil lease that he bought around 1953. The well was on a farm off in the woods about twenty miles north of Tulsa. I remember going there on summer nights with my parents. It would seem to get darker and darker as we turned down smaller and smaller dirt roads, until we'd stop at a wooden gate, which Daddy would swing open, and beyond which an eerie glow radiated up into the surrounding trees. And there it was, an oil derrick festooned with bare electric light bulbs, like a small Eiffel Tower, with the sound of a pump slowly chugging up the crude oil. Nearby was a holding tank and a bunkhouse, a metal chamber whose interior was heavy with the smell of oil and mud. Daddy would open and close some valves or adjust the pump or check the storage level, then scrape the mud off his cowboy boots. The work done, we'd drive to an all-night diner in nearby Collinsville and have a treat.

Later in the 1950s, Daddy bought a couple of wells from Sam Worth, part-owner of Ernie Miller's Pontiac dealership, for $25,000. Daddy's partner in this deal was Clyde Swarthout, who owned a tire company and was one of the few in Tulsa who would cheerfully hire ex-cons. These oil wells more or less broke even, like some of the other legitimate businesses Daddy went into with friends.

One that didn't break even was his loan to a family named Cottongim. According to Bobby Bluejacket, "They're real good, decent people, and he loaned them a bunch of money, to get them out of a tight spot, and they

---

* I use this corrosive word here for two reasons. First, it helps point up the paradox of my father's charity toward a race that, in general, he looked down on. (His charity was by no means an example of *la noblesse oblige*, either.) Second, I think it is important not to cosmeticize the past, which in effect is what the city of Tulsa did for some fifty years after its horrendous event, conveniently labeled "the race riot." When I was growing up in the 1940s and 1950s, my parents, other relatives, and classmates called the black part of town "Niggertown," sometimes without the least rancor, as if "Niggertown" were its actual name. Glossing over it now by substituting a euphemism would in some sense perpetuate the racism of that time, and so I use it.

had these big oil and gas leases, but they got screwed up financially." Daddy took the bath too.

But he had money to experiment with. His freedom—financial and otherwise—was made possible partly by Mother's staying home and taking whiskey orders while looking after me.

But they went out together too, leaving me at a grandparent's house. Mother recalled, "We went down to Hot Springs quite a bit, with the Hoods and Homer, and we'd rent an old cabin for three or four days or a week, during the season, for the horse races. There was a country club they turned into a casino during the racing season. One time I found a dime slot machine that was broken. You didn't have to put a dime in it. They had people walking around watching. I acted like I was putting a dime in it, and I was winning every time. Finally, I had two gunny sacks full of dimes. Then I found Wayne and Gomer Evans. They had both gone broke. Wayne asked for the $1300 I had won. We went to another place, where they shot craps. Both Wayne and Gomer won a whole lot of money, and they weren't using rigged dice, they were playing fair."

Mother and Daddy also went to local movies. Daddy liked westerns and action films with actors such as Gary Cooper, Tyrone Power, Ronald Reagan, and John Wayne, but he didn't have any favorite actresses and he didn't care for musicals or comedies.

One night leaving the theater after seeing Tyrone Power in *The Razor's Edge*, Daddy noticed that his wallet, with $450 in it, was missing. He dashed back to his seat and searched all over, but to no avail. Outside the theater, he laughed, "Well, that really *was* the razor's edge!"

They also went to Cain's Academy of Ballroom Dancing, better known simply as Cain's, where Bob Wills—and later his brother Johnny Lee Wills—played. Initially, Wayne didn't dance. Lucille danced with others while Wayne "stood around and talked and smoked and looked," according to her. Eventually she taught him "to stagger around a little." They generally went out with friends to restaurants and night clubs, where they'd drink and dance and get their picture taken, usually at a long table with glasses of ice and bottles of Coke and 7 Up—setups for the alcohol they brought themselves. Some of these clubs had big bands that played dance music and contemporary ballads while a torch singer crooned into the microphone. A photo taken at the Casa-Del, a supper club at the edge of town, shows a group of people beaming amiably: Daddy and Mother at a long table, flanked by Wesley and Gladys Pilkington (Mother's uncle and aunt), Tommie and Elda Padgett, Dolly (Wesley's sister), her son Billy Young and his wife, Norma. Billy, a drummer and bandleader, later became the secretary of Tulsa's chief of police, Jack Purdy. I list these names to show how the two sides of the law were sometimes bridged by family ties.

The Casa-Del did not inspire fisticuffs, but other clubs did. Bill Martin remembered the time "out at Roscoe Petrie's club when Lucille started a big fight. Ha ha ha! She was playing the jukebox and a guy come up there and was going to play what *he* wanted to play. She pushed him back and said, 'I'm gonna play what *I* want to play.' So Wayne come over and she said, 'This guy won't let me play,' and Wayne turned around and hit that guy and he quit sliding only after he went clear across that dance floor. And he had two or three buddies with him! There was me and Lucille and Wayne and my wife Clara and Priscilla Easley. I got two of them guys in head locks. And then we went outside, and there was this one guy—Wayne had just whipped the daylights out of him. As he was getting ready to leave, he drove by and rolled down his window and said, 'Ha ha, you can't catch me now!' There was a big rock laying there. Wayne picked that sonofabitch up and threw it right through that back glass.

"On top of that, after they left, Wayne found that guy's shoes and went back to the kitchen and got a butcher knife and cut them up into little pieces. I had my shoes off, and when Wayne came back in he looked down and saw my bare feet and said, 'Oh hell, I've cut Bill's shoes up!' Ha ha ha!"

In another fracas, one person recalled that Wayne threw only one punch, leaving his opponent unconscious for more than twenty minutes.

My parents also dropped in at Willis Newton's Music Box. Just inside the one-story yellow brick building was a bar that divided the room: to the right was a large space with booths along the walls and tables in the center, and to the left was an equal space with booths along the walls and an open dance floor. The club had live music on Thursday, Friday, Saturday, and holidays—country and western swing, with some big band stuff. At other times, a juke box provided the music. In the back was a gambling room, which Daddy frequented. According to Howard Donahue, "He knew the ones that was cheating there. He showed me how he could rattle them dice, but you really are just rattling one against the other, and you can 'kill' [control] at least one die every time, by the way you throw them.

That gives you that much advantage. It's not dishonest, it just gives you that much edge." Donahue felt that crossing the fine line between honesty and dishonesty is acceptable when it is seen as "getting an edge," a convenient moral stance that my dad shared.

From time to time Mother found herself embroiled in other situations. She recalled the night in the fifties when she took the wheel to drive home from Roscoe's because Wayne had had a little too much to drink. He sat in the middle, with Priscilla Easley on his right, and he kept laughing and reaching up Priscilla's dress. "He was wild, restless, young, high-tempered," Lucille said.

Daddy was also attractive. According to Lee Eller, "Those gals, when Wayne walked in they'd start lookin' and cookin', man! He was a sharp-looking guy, with a roll of money on him as big as his leg. He was a ladies' man, but he wasn't just crazy wild."

"He might have had a sweetie he went to see once in a while," said Bill Martin. "But as far as him sleeping with everybody in Tulsa County, that's a damned, flatass-out lie, because I knew better than that. He wouldn't take up with just everything that wanted to screw. It was just a little relaxation. He'd stay with the same one for six or seven months. Then they'd have a falling out. Then eight or nine months or a year with another one."

Daddy's girlfriends were also good-looking. As one friend put it, "He didn't go for them duds."

One of the good-lookers was Toni Rudolph, a champion swimmer. Donahue related: "She was married to Bill Rudolph, but he got killed, a train hit him, on Christmas day, between Tulsa and Arkansas. He saw one train go by, took on off, but there was more than one track, and along come another train and hit him. He had a little dog with him. Wayne started going with her after he was killed. They went together for two or three years. Maybe around '51, '52, '53.

"One time the police were really cracking down on the whiskey business, so Wayne just shut it down. He said, 'Let's go fishing.' I said, 'Hell, I can't take the time, I ain't got the money.' He kept on and kept on: 'Come on, let's go fishing, let's go up there and relax and just fish.' So I said, 'Well, all right.' Just before we left, he went to his stash and came back with a case of Canadian Club. Clemens decided to go with us. When we got there, Wayne bought a #3 washtub at a hardware store in Spavinaw—the town was about a block long—and gave me some money and said, 'Run across the street and buy a bottle of aspirin, we're gonna have a party this evening and we might need them.' We put I don't know how many cases of Cokes in this tub and iced them down, called our girlfriends"—in Wayne's case, Toni—"and went up on top of the hill to some motel cabins. Wayne knew the owners real well. None of the cabins were rented. Wayne said, 'I want to rent 'em all. We might make a little noise and I don't want to disturb nobody.' There was about eight cabins. The party lasted three days."

Everyone confirms that although Daddy would get sloshed occasionally, he was normally a moderate drinker. Howard and Clemens were the big drinkers. Donahue admitted: "I used to drink an awful lot. A lot of people liked the way whiskey made 'em feel, but I liked the taste of it. I guess that's why I drank so much for so many years. I wouldn't drink anything during the day, but I'd drink almost a quart of whiskey every night, for thirty years. In fact Wayne would preach to me about it. He'd say 'Goddamn it, Howard, you've got good health, why do you want to kill yourself?' I saw Wayne 'feeling good,' but not really drunk. He was pretty moderate."

"I saw him one time, sitting in his car on a side street. I never did find out what was bothering him. He wasn't drunk, but just holding a bottle of whiskey and a bottle of ketchup. He'd take a drink and follow it with ketchup. The way it was, if something was bothering him and he didn't tell me, he didn't tell me. If he didn't tell me, it was probably best I didn't know, ha ha! Then I could truthfully say, 'I don't know.'"

Daddy was highly sociable, but he never told anybody anything they didn't need to know. His compartmentalization of information was a safety device that he used with all his acquaintances, friends, and family, because as time went on, his information was becoming more and more dangerous.

12 *Family*

AT 2733 EAST FOURTH, THOUGH, life in the 1950s was relatively safe.

Daddy was always on the go, but he usually came home for dinner, which Mother served at six o'clock. We ate most of our meals on what we called the back porch, the small converted breezeway that connected the kitchen and garage.

This room served several purposes. In one corner was a desk and telephone, where whiskey business was transacted. Just a step away, against the garage wall, was the table where we ate. At the other end of the room, a leather easy chair was flanked on one side by an upright freezer (later replaced by a mangle iron and then a clothes dryer) and on the other by a three-shelf metal caddy with appliances and boxes of bullets and shotgun shells. Behind the chair and to one side was a professional hairdryer—a metal pole topped with what looked like a massive chromium football helmet. On the knotty pine wall above it was a gun rack with several shotguns and deer rifles. Each wall had a door: the north door led directly to the backyard patio, the south door to the driveway, the west door to the garage, and the east door—or rather, doorway—to the kitchen. Next to this doorway was a small combination cabinet-shelf that held household supplies and a radio that played country and western and popular music in the daytime and comedy shows such as "Fibber McGee and Molly" and "The Great Gildersleeve" in the evening. Attached to the wall above the radio was a manual ice shaver that resembled a large space-age pencil sharpener. The floor was of linoleum tile in a checkerboard design.

Mother served attractive, well-balanced meals. The cuisine was three-square American with a southern tinge, but occasionally she went exotic and made chow mein. Dinner consisted of fried chicken, mashed potatoes, green beans, corn on the cob, iceberg lettuce, a dessert of banana, mayonnaise, and pecans on a bed of lettuce, and iced tea. Or meatloaf, potatoes, spinach, beets, lettuce, cottage cheese and peaches, and milk. Or hamburgers, french fries, pie, and milk. Or baked ham with pineapple, sweet potatoes, peas, creamed corn, salad, jello, and iced tea. Or pinto beans with chunks of leftover ham, spinach, cornbread, iced tea, and ice cream. Sometimes she would fry the fish Daddy caught at the lake. Her breakfast repertoire included fruit juice or nectar, milk, coffee, fried or scrambled eggs, toast, french toast, pancakes, waffles, bacon, sausage, home fries, cream of wheat, oatmeal, and hot rice with butter and hot milk. The servings were always generous.

Somewhere along the line, Daddy had developed a ravenous sweet tooth. Lucille recalled: "I always had a pie or cake made, and I've seen him sit down and eat the whole pie by himself. And he *loved* rice pudding and banana pudding. I used to make a double boiler of rice pudding with raisins and nutmeg, and he would eat that whole double boiler of rice pudding, with cream on it. He loved sweet stuff." Lee Eller recalled: "My wife would fix dinner for us, and he'd bring one of those big pumpkin pies. She'd warm it for us, and he and I would sit there and eat that whole pie, steaming hot, right out of the oven. That's the way he liked it. With homemade ice cream on the side." For lunch Daddy often had candy, rather odd fare for the tough guy who was rapidly becoming what the newspapers called "The King of the Bootleggers."

According to Mother, "He finally got to where he ate better. He loved oatmeal and cream of wheat. He liked chicken and dressing, and he finally got to where he'd eat green beans and peas and corn, stuff like that." He ate the squirrel and pheasant he and Homer hunted, but he didn't care for deer meat. He did like the big, thick T-bones he got from a "friendly" butcher, usually in large, anonymously wrapped quantities passed quietly through the store's back door.

In good weather he cooked these steaks, with potatoes wrapped in metal foil, on the large portable Hastybake charcoal grill that we kept on the little sandstone patio just outside the back door. Aside from steaks, neither Mother nor I ever saw him cook anything. As Mother put it, "Making chocolate milk was about as close as he ever got to cooking."

The way he made chocolate milk had a ritualistic aura. In the late evening, he'd go to the kitchen, take the Meadow Gold milk from the refrigerator (which we still called the icebox) and a jar of Carnation chocolate malted milk powder from the cabinet. I remember his mixing the milk and powder in an oversized green mug from Frankoma Pottery—we had a complete set of Frankoma dishes, bowls, mugs, and ash trays, with their fifties Southwest look. He would stand in the kitchen, slowly drinking the chocolate milk, and he would say, "Ain't that good?" His pleasure was simple and unalloyed. For just that moment, there was nothing else in the world except that chocolate milk. Then he would rinse the mug and spoon in hot water and put them in the drainer, so as not to "mess up" the kitchen.

He was a stickler for neatness. It was all right to get dirty if you were doing dirty work—and he did plenty of that, dressed in old jeans and scuffed cowboy boots—but it was not all right to stay dirty any longer than necessary. He shaved every morning, went to the barber every two weeks, and dressed in nice clothes, usually with a slight western flair. Even his suits looked western. He always had several pairs of beautiful, custom-made cowboy boots. His few ties were of the understated variety, including string ties, but because he didn't like anything tight around his neck, he rarely even buttoned the top button of his shirt. Except when hunting or fishing in very cold weather, he didn't wear hats and I never saw him in shorts, bermuda or otherwise—the very idea makes me laugh. In those days bermuda shorts were associated with people who played golf: the leisure class. Daddy was definitely not leisure class.

Each night he carefully hung up his clean clothes and put the dirty ones in the clothes hamper. Mother did the washing, drying, and ironing. Other items went to the dry cleaners. We were such regular customers that Jake, the delivery man from Barnes-Manley Cleaners, came and went with the freedom of a family member: when picking up and delivering, he would simply knock and walk in the back door, next to which there was a clothes hook for pickups and deliveries.

As soon as an item showed a sign of wear, Daddy got rid of it. He wore only high-quality merchandise, but I don't recall ever going shopping with him, either for his clothes or mine. He wore a ring on his right hand, often a gold ring with a big diamond, though over the years the rings came and went, depending on his latest "deal." He always wore a watch, a necessity given his constant round of rendezvous. One of his flashier watches had his initials written in diamonds.

Daddy's shoes and cowboy boots were always shined, either by a bootblack or by me. I used a kit he kept in his closet. Some afternoons or evenings, he would come home and go straight into his bedroom, where, after a moment, he would call out, "Ronnie, come in here a minute." As I peered at him sitting on the edge of his bed, he'd say, "Help me get my boots off, son." He would lean back on his elbows and stick one leg out over the edge of the bed, and I'd straddle his leg, facing away from him, and take hold of the back of the boot heel. Lifting upward and forward, I'd give it a firm and steady tug, sometimes rocking it a little, and, after some initial resistance, it would slide off. I'd put the boot down next to the bed and then do the other one. He'd smile and say, "Thank you, pardner," and more often than not, pointing to a pile of change on the bed, add,

"Take this change and do something with it." Meaning keep it. Throughout the day he must have used folding money to make small purchases (often of candy), because the change frequently amounted to four or five dollars, a noticeable sum for an eight-year-old in the early 1950s. On these occasions, the pleasure of being given money was mixed with the pride of doing something right for your father and the odd satisfaction of feeling the boot resist and then give way.

Daddy bathed nearly every day, and after his bath there wasn't a spot of water left anywhere—he even wiped the steam off the bathroom mirror and left the washcloth draped so it would dry quickly.

It was the same with his Lucky Strikes. According to Mother, "There was not an ash nowhere. He was very clean in the house." Given her own high standards, such an appraisal should be seen as an understatement.

Both my parents felt that the yard around the house should be as neat and attractive as the inside of the house. They planted a hedge around the front yard and rose bushes along one side of the backyard fence, the side nearest the street. The far end of the back yard was planted with bridal wreath, bushes with small, white, fragrant blossoms. In the far, right-hand corner of the back yard was a dog pen with a chain link fence high enough to contain Daddy's enthusiastic bird dogs. Along the right- and left-hand backyard fences were flower beds.

Not too long after after my parents bought the house, they hired a gardener, who mowed and edged the lawn, trimmed the hedge, and tended the flower beds. He was a large black man named Berry, who, clad in overalls, a work shirt, and a straw hat, once a week walked the four miles from his home to our house, where he spent the entire day working, slowly but surely. Berry, who had only that name and didn't know how old he was, worked for five other clients. During the winter, he lived on the money he had saved the previous summer. He was a kind man who laughed good-naturedly the time I sprang out from behind a tree and delivered, at age seven or so, my first pun: "Berry, Berry, you're a *blackberry!*" That night Mother explained that I shouldn't say such things, that Berry was a colored man, yes, but he had feelings, too. "Colored" or not, he kept the lawn and flowerbeds in beautiful shape, as nice as any on the block.

Our neighbors knew that Daddy was a bootlegger. Mary Jane Gallup, then a little girl who lived directly across the street, remembered the oddity of seeing our garage door open, a car enter, the door close, and later, the car back out, its tail in the air. It turned out, though, that little risk was involved, because loading whiskey in your own garage was unheard of. The police figured my dad was too smart to do that.

Thousands of Tulsans knew what Daddy's laconic business card meant by "Wayne 66666." It must have taken pull to get such a memorable phone number. In any case, the neighbors didn't seem to mind having a bootlegger on the block. The ones I knew thought of him as a good, if unusual, neighbor, who would cheerfully say hello and lend them a hand. One day Daddy noticed John Gallup, Mary Jane's father, having a hard time digging up the stump of a dead tree. An hour later, Daddy drove up in a borrowed winch truck and yanked it out of the ground. Gallup's next-door neighbor, Raymond Clark, had a heart attack on a plane bound for Canada. Doctors told him that he should return to Tulsa by car. Daddy called Raymond in Canada and offered to drive up there to bring him back—a trip of more than two thousand miles. Other neighbors, such as the Blackburns and Waddingtons, were regular liquor customers.

The kids on the block liked him, too. Whenever the ice cream truck happened to come down the street at the same time Daddy was out front, they would come running: they knew he liked to buy ice cream for all of them. He was a generous, freewheeling guy who had a way of making you feel good.

He also made you feel protected. I grew up knowing that ultimately no one could hurt me, or if they did, that all I had to do was tell my father and he would "take care" of them. His name commanded respect. Even strangers automatically treated him with deference. He didn't swagger about or bully anyone, but he did have an easy way of carrying himself, which, along with his good looks and size, made his presence commanding. There was never any sense that the outside world would control us or treat us badly. Nobody treated Wayne Padgett badly, at least without suffering the consequences. The same courtesies were extended to those under his protection: his family and friends. I remember taunting a classmate in elementary school, "My daddy can whip your daddy," and experiencing the power of knowing I could say that with total conviction to anybody. My father was a tough guy, a rock-solid protector. The problem, of course, is that his extra security was necessary at all. Most families don't have fathers whose professions incur a constant, if low-level, threat to the

·

home. Daddy's protectiveness was both a welcome blessing and an unspoken curse.

Around the age of eight, I was at home in bed, enduring a childhood illness. Daddy came through the bedroom door and plunked down a stack of comic books.

"Here's something for you to read, son," he said.

My eyes grew large. There must have been fifty comic books, all of them brand new.

He smiled and left. That was the way he did things.

One day about a year later he asked me to go up to a house a block away, to pick up some money. When I knocked on the door there, a lady who looked like an ordinary housewife handed me an envelope. On the way home I took a peek: inside were twenty one hundred-dollar bills. Two thousand bucks! Previously, my parents had let me help them count money at home—sums often much larger than $2,000—but they had never trusted me with carrying it down the street by myself. It made me feel incredibly important. I knew that no other kid my age had been entrusted with that much cash.

I must have been around seven years old when, one day, Daddy offered me my first ride on his motorcycle—the first one I remember, that is. It was his big, black Harley Davidson, with saddlebags on the back and lots of chrome. He helped me up onto the seat, in front of him, and took hold of the handlebars. "Lean forward and grab hold," he said, kick-starting the engine. We rode slowly to the end of the block, where we made a left onto Columbia, and then another onto Fourth Place. Then he rotated his wrist and we roared down the street. The sudden acceleration, the throaty blast of the engine, and the wind in my ears sent a thrill though me, but then he slowed down for the stop sign—we were already at the end of the block! Two quick lefts and we were home. At the curb a small group of kids had assembled. He took them around the block, too, one at a time. They all climbed off the motorcycle with stars in their eyes. Then he took me around again. This time the exhilaration was milder, not only because it was impossible to repeat the original rush but also because I was reveling in my father's popularity and power. No one else's father had a motorcycle, and in my childish soul I knew that no one else's father would have taken the time to give all the kids a ride. Other fathers would have been "busy" or concerned about "safety" or insurance. They always backed out of their driveways carefully and drove away at a prudent speed. Daddy often laid rubber, just for the fun of it. Or, if he happened to be driving an older car that had a running board, he would let us kids hang onto the side all the way down to the corner.

He could be fun around the house, too. One of his favorite pranks was to call home and disguise his voice as that of a woman. This woman had a southern accent that was different from his southwestern twang. If my mother answered, he would deliver some alarming information: her son was in police custody, her car insurance had been cancelled, etc. If I answered, it was an anonymous girl calling to confess shyly that she thought I was really cute. Even later, after I had started recognizing this voice, if I paused in responding, he'd chuckle, "I gotcha, didn't I?"

Elda, Tommy's wife, remembered that Wayne "always liked to joke. If he'd pull something on somebody, there was the happiest man that ever was! He'd come over and tell me some big tale of some kind and then die laughing because I'd just sit there and swallow it. He always did have a sense of humor."

He was not, however, a teller of jokes. I recall only two examples of verbal wit from him, if *wit* is the right word. When I was perhaps eight years old, he pulled the old Pete and Repeat gag on me:

"Pete and Re-Pete were sitting on a fence. Pete fell off, so who was left?"

"Re-Pete."

"Pete and Re-Pete were sitting on a fence. Pete fell off . . ." and so on.

The other one involved the ice cream/I scream homonym: "I scream, you scream, we all scream for ice cream."

Though new to me, both these perennial witticisms were commonplace. Daddy's real sense of humor involved situations.

One of his pranks was rather subtle. If I wasn't in my room, he would sneak in and stand behind the door. When I returned and closed the door, I would be slowly electrified to find somebody behind it. The great thing about his technique was that he didn't shout or move, he just stood there, allowing me to go through a radiating gamut of fright.

In my teens, on warm evenings while I sat at my desk facing the open window, I would look up from my book or notebook and discover a dim face with fangs—he had let his upper dental plate drop down—quietly floating in the darkness outside. A tingling blush of terror would sweep over me, and he would break into a gleeful laugh.

He loved to play practical jokes, but there was one joke he did not enjoy having played on him. Around the age of thirteen and well aware of his phobia of snakes, I bought a life-size rubber rattlesnake, which I hid under his pillow. That evening at bedtime, he gave out a whoop, followed by an emphatic "God *damn!*" He came straight to my bedroom. I looked at him with a silly grin that froze and faded as he pointed his finger at me and shouted, in an adrenaline rage, "Don't you *ever* do that again! I'm warning you!"

Generally the threat of his punishment was enough to keep me in line. Mother and Daddy shared parental authority, but they exercised it differently. When I behaved badly, my mother would reprove me, and if I persisted to an extreme, she would give me a quick swat on the behind. She never hurt me and I never feared her. Thus she would sometimes have to resort to her ace in the hole: "Just wait till your father comes home!" Usually by the time he returned she would have forgotten the incident. Other times, though, she made good on her promise, and I would be facing the possibility of serious punishment.

Daddy was a master of intimidation. His face would take on a look of incredulity and righteous wrath, and he would grab my upper arm and shake me, demanding, "Why do you talk to your mother like that?" I did have a penchant for sassing, or, as we called it then, talking back. Also, I had a quick temper, which I got from him. That is partly why his threat of punishment was so powerful for me: it rang true viscerally.

The ultimate threat was that of being whipped with a belt. These days, such whippings are considered abusive, but back then they were sometimes considered acceptable or even necessary. If I did not show enough contrition, Daddy would reach for his belt buckle, as if to undo it, and demand, "Do you want to go into the bathroom?" (Going into the bathroom was the urban equivalent of going behind the barn.) He had taken me there for punishment once when I was little. I no longer remember the details, but I suspect that the terror he inspired at that moment was greater than the sting of the belt, and I know that he would not have inflicted any serious damage on me. In any case, I had not enjoyed this primal visit to the bathroom, so my answer to his question was invariably no.

"Then you'd better straighten up and fly right! Now go tell your mother you're sorry."

Once when I was around eight or nine, I had seriously misbehaved toward Mother and was fearing retribution. Sure enough, when Daddy got home he asked me if I wanted to go into the bathroom, and when I said no, he shocked me by saying, "Well, that's just too damn bad! I've had enough of your misbehaving." He led me stunned into the bathroom and locked the door, thus removing any hope of maternal intercession. Then he put his index finger to his lips and went "Shhhhh." Why was he smiling? He whispered, "When I start with the belt, you start screaming and crying."

As he whacked the side of the tub and I screamed and begged for mercy, my mother pounded on the door, crying, "That's enough, Wayne! Stop! Stop right now! Oh God, you're going to kill him!" When the door opened, she saw Daddy and me standing there with conspiratorial grins on our faces.

"I ought to kill *both of you!*" she shouted, tears in her eyes.

Daddy and I collapsed in laughter.

None of us had any way of knowing that this farce was a virtual reenactment of one involving Pretty Boy Floyd, his son, and his wife. Maybe it was an Oklahoma tradition.

When I was little, Daddy had spanked me a few times. For some reason, our bathroom farce was a turning point: he never laid a hand on me again. However, his power of intimidation remained undiminished until I got married, an intimidation conveyed by a sharply disapproving look that stung as much as a belt.

Although a rather wild young criminal, Daddy generally set for me an example of good manners. The words "thank you" or "much obliged" came to his lips often. He held the door open for everyone, male or female, young or old. And when he addressed an elder, he'd use "sir" or "ma'am." In conversation his voice was never loud; he was a good listener.

In restaurants, he would urge the others at the table to order more dishes, especially desserts, then he'd quietly palm the check and leave a generous tip. Dining out usually went smoothly, because the table service in Tulsa back then was provided only by women, and women found his big natural grace, sense of humor, and manly charm irresistible. Usually by the end of the meal they felt as if something personal and pleasant had transpired between the two of them—as if they knew each other. And in fact the next time he came in they did remember him. I grew up feeling that there was no shop or cafe in town where he would not be greeted with a friendly "Howdy, Wayne. How you doing?"

Actually, both my parents taught me what were then considered basic good manners. They didn't go in for the fine points, which were for the upper class, although when my mother cooked a big holiday meal, she would arrange the dishes and silverware in the patterns dictated by authorities on etiquette. Both my parents would have considered it unnecessary to use the recommended motion of the soupspoon, and we put our elbows on the table with a complete lack of self-consciousness. But my parents didn't allow me to eat messily or loudly. For ordinary meals, we used napkins, paper ones from a cafe-style dispenser, but for special dinners, crisp white linen napkins. I was not allowed to read at the table, until I convinced my parents that reading the newspaper was educational. If I finished eating first, I had to ask to be excused from the table—up to around the age of twelve.

If I behaved rudely or thoughtlessly, I was sharply reproved by both parents. For instance, tracking mud or dirt into someone's home was a serious breach of manners. And Daddy always felt that if you borrowed something, you should return it in a better condition. Likewise, a slovenly appearance was a form of rudeness, an affront to other people, as well as evidence of a lack of self-respect. If I left my shirttail half out, my mother or father would say, "Tuck that in. I don't want to have to look at you going around like that."

Both of them used friendly, informal greetings and farewells. During the 1940s and 1950s, Daddy would often greet a friend with the rhetorical question "What do you know?" or "What do you say?" To which the friend would give a rhetorical reply of "Nothin' much" or "Not a whole helluva lot." For "goodbye" it was often "Much obliged" for business associates, and "Take care of yourself" or "Be good" for friends.

Phone conversations in our house never began or ended abruptly, and it was considered very rude to slam down the receiver. This was permitted only at the end of an angry conversation. Another telephone bête noire consisted of disturbing someone's sleep. Many times my parents postponed a call, saying, "I'll call tomorow. They might already be in bed."

In addition to taking care of the home and answering the business phones, Mother also found time to be a Cub Scout den mother, to accompany me to my little league baseball games, and to host an occasional daytime party or shower for her friends (relatives and whiskey business associates).

But my parents did little entertaining at home. Neither one had grown up in a family with either the time or money to entertain. Every great once in a while a friend, perhaps accompanied by his wife or girlfriend, would drop by in the evening. For such infrequent visits, my parents kept a bottle of liquor in the house, storing it under the kitchen sink amidst the floor wax and dish soap. Growing up, I never once saw either of my parents take a drink, not even a sip of beer. As Lee Eller put it, "Wayne didn't drink much. Liquor was a business to him. He didn't come to town—as the old saying goes—on a load of sweet potatoes. He knew that in order to conduct business he had to have a clear mind." The only time I even smelled liquor was when Bill Martin or Daddy, loading or unloading whiskey in the garage, would accidentally drop a lug. Whiskey was for business or for going out. It had little place in the home.

What we did have in the home from time to time was large amounts of cash. You don't have to be a CPA to figure out that a successful wholesale bootlegger is going to have a lot of cash around—all you have to be is a thief. From 1948, when we moved to Fourth Street, until 1959, when liquor was legalized, there were several attempted burglaries of our house. The thieves got no further than bending one edge of a heavy-duty window screen before fleeing. They probably knew that Daddy carried a loaded pistol in his glove compartment. What they didn't know was that he also kept one under his pillow, a .38- or .45-caliber revolver. I remember wondering, What if you turned the wrong way in your sleep and blew your own brains out? He was more concerned with what might happen if someone broke into the house as we slept.

Robbers and Tulsa County policeman Roy Rains were the only threats to our house. Daddy was always alert to cars that slowed as they passed by, or to a car parked around the corner with a man just sitting at the wheel. It was not uncommon for Daddy to spring up from the armchair in the living room and dash into a darkened bedroom, where he could crack the venetian blinds to observe a car creeping by. He also knew if a

OKLAHOMA TOUGH

particular car had circled the block. Many were the times he said to me and Mother, "Let me know if you see a '53 two-toned Bel Aire, aqua bottom and white top, with whitewalls" or some other such car. His personal radar was extraordinary.

Riding with him around town, I'd be surprised when out of the blue he'd say, "The laws is out"—meaning that there were police nearby—and sure enough, within seconds we'd drive past a police car nestled in dark shadows, waiting for speeders. It was uncanny, and it happened time and again, both in my presence and in the presence of any number of his friends. And it wasn't just a matter of his knowing where the speed traps were on Saturday nights. It was a sixth sense he had.

As a teenager, Daddy had been wiry, but as he approached twenty, his back broadened and his arms developed. By the age of thirty he stood an even six feet and weighed two hundred pounds, all of it solid, with big shoulders and biceps (described by a friend as being "as big as a mule's hind leg"), a strong chest, a narrow waist, and slender hips. One of his favorite demonstrations was of the strength of his abdominal muscles. Sometimes when he pulled up in the driveway and I happened to be playing with my friend Dickie Gallup in the front yard, he'd saunter over and say, "C'mere, I want to show you something. Hit me in the stomach, as hard as you can. Go ahead." We would flail away until our fists hurt. He would laugh and flex his bicep and say, "Muscle." A year or so would go by, and we'd try it again, but always with the same frustrating result, until, late in our high school years, we just gave up.

Sometimes both Dickie and I would gang up and "rassle" him. We never even got close to a takedown. Sometimes he would conclude these "matches" with a demonstration of his punching power. He would hold up the palm of his left hand so that it faced him, and then from a distance of only six inches slam the right fist into it, making a tremendous thwack. Apparently this was the punch that sent so many men flying across bars and night clubs, the punch that was so short, so quick, and so hard that they never knew what hit them.

He was good with his hands in other ways, too. One day he came into the living room with a deck of cards and invited me to join him in a game of poker. Not only did he beat me, he seemed to be able to see right through the cards. It was as if he had the power of the X-ray glasses that were advertised in comic books, the specs that enabled one to see through girl's dresses. But no, it was just sleight-of-hand.

One technique was called dealing seconds, that is, dealing the card just beneath the top card. If you knew what the top card was and could withhold it until you wanted to deal it, you had a powerful advantage. So how could you know what the top card was? In shuffling and cutting the cards, you could take a quick look at, say, the card on the bottom of the deck. Then, through a series of maneuvers in shuffling and cutting, you could move it to the top. There were ways to crimp the cards so that even if another player asked to cut the deck, the top card could be restored to the desired position. He taught me how to tell when someone is dealing seconds. You do it not by watching his hands, which are quicker than the eye, but by listening to the sound each card makes as it comes from the deck. He had me shut my eyes and listen as he dealt. A "second" has a thicker sound, because it is being slipped out from between two other cards, whereas a top card, rubbing against only one other card, has a thinner sound.

Because he had large hands, he could also palm cards, which, in a game such as five-card draw, gives the palmer, who is using six cards, a heavy advantage. Palming is riskier than dealing seconds, because, if suspected, it can be easily discovered: someone grabs your hand, and you've had it.

He and I played a lot of two-hand poker, mostly five-card draw, five-card stud, and seven-card stud. To make it interesting, we played for money. Every once in a while he'd stop the play to analyze and comment on the card spread, or the odds against making a particular hand. He'd also try to cheat, and was delighted when I'd catch him.

One time he came back from a trip to Texas. He had gone down with a friend for a high-stakes poker game at a big ranch. "They thought we were rich Oklahoma ranchers." He and the friend played team poker against the unsuspecting Texans. When he wanted his friend to raise, he would make a little noise similar to a sniff, but with the air going in the outward direction. It's one of those everyday mannerisms that are so minor that no one pays any attention to them. The rich rancher who hosted the game lost $28,000 and fourteen quarterhorses to my dad and his partner.

Another time he showed me his special dice set, consisting of six dice and a dice cup. The dice were not "loaded." Anybody could detect loaded (weighted) dice by dropping them in a glass of water and seeing them float up always showing the same numbers. His dice were shaved—the minutest layer sanded off one edge so carefully that you'd need a microscope to tell the difference. By using a certain motion to shake and roll the dice out of the cup, you could get the results you wanted.

As part of these lessons, Daddy made it abundantly clear that gambling did not always involve chance. He preferred games that involved some skill, such as poker, which he played well even without the tricks, and he warned me to stay away from games such as roulette, in which the odds are stacked against you, unless you have one of those tedious systems that allows you to stand at the table all day and win fifty dollars—not his cup of tea. No, only suckers played games of chance. He spoke from experience, but never mentioned having lost the quick $7,000 shooting craps in Spavinaw.

He tried to stack the odds in his favor in many other situations. For instance, he gave himself a discount on the price of electricity. One day— I must have been in high school—he took me around to the back of our house to the electric meter.

The residential electric meters in those days looked pretty much the same as they do now. The meter was covered by what resembled a large, inverted glass jar, through which the meter reader could see the counters that registered the amount of electricity used. The jar was secured to the meter base by a lead seal that looked like a miniature padlock. It was a criminal offense for anyone other than an employee of the power company to tamper with the seal. Daddy had used a pair of fingernail clippers to make a very fine cut in the lock's inverted U-shaped top, where it attached the glass bowl to the meter. This cut enabled him to remove the seal and the bowl and to place—very carefully, since the meter was "live"—a copper penny so that the current would be shunted around the counter. In other words, with the penny in place the current would continue to flow but the meter wouldn't register it.

A week or so before the meter reader's monthly visit, Daddy would remove the penny. After all, he had to run up *some* charges. This procedure cut our electric bill at least in half, a savings that added up over the years, especially later, when he built a big house that was all-electric.

But he gave me the dire warning never to try a similar stunt. I could be electrocuted. So why did he show me? Because he took a childish delight in outwitting the power company, a delight that showed on his face as he placed the penny inside the meter and said, "Now watch the dial stop." It wasn't just the money he was saving, it was the thrill of the scam, which had to be shared.

But Daddy made "honest" money too—if the word may be applied to his used-car business. Even when he didn't have his own car lot, he bought and sold used cars. When he saw a good deal, he snapped it up, then put it on a friend's lot on consignment. Or if he heard that someone was in the market for a car, he'd keep an eye open. If that person was a friend, he'd make nothing on the deal. If that person was a stranger, he'd make as much as possible. One day he came home elated.

"I just did a deal. Boy, did I do a deal!" he announced.

"What do you mean?" asked Mother.

"I sold this old boy a car, and I crucified him. I *crucified* him!"

Daddy had picked up a car for $800 and sold it the next day for $1,800. In the mid-1950s, $1,000 for a day's work was spectacular money. During that day he had transformed the vehicle. In our driveway, he had changed the spark plugs and replaced any worn or frayed belts. He had washed it, scrubbed the tires, and waxed the body. He had polished the chrome, removing every bug from the grille, headlights, and front bumper. He had scraped and flushed out the areas encrusted with mud up around the tires. He had removed the seats and floor mats and vacuumed the interior, using special cleaners to remove stains from the upholstery. He had emptied the ash trays, washed them out, and wiped them down. He had used a toothbrush to clean every nook and cranny of the dashboard. He had dusted the light bulb inside the glove compartment. He had covered the entire engine with a cleaning fluid called Gunk, and then hosed it down and wiped it off, leaving it sparkling. He vacuumed the trunk and washed the spare tire. I have no doubt that he completed the job by taking it down to a friend's shop to have the mileage meter run back and by filling the tank with ethyl (the old name for premium gasoline). When he finished, the entire car glittered and purred, as if brand new. It even smelled fresh.

I saw him do this time and again, transforming a dirty old company car that had bounced around oil fields into one that seemed to have belonged to an elderly lady who used it only to drive a few blocks to church on Sunday. "Look for yourself: it's got only 5,000 miles on it."

OKLAHOMA TOUGH

All his nonstop wheeling and dealing did not come without a price. At one point, probably in the early 1950s, he bought an electric massager, hoping that it would provide some relief from his headaches. According to Mother, he had had "migraines" as long as she had known him, for which he took Empirin, a nonprescription compound more powerful than aspirin. The electric massager was a bulky chrome and rubber device that had to be attached to the back of the hand by elastic straps. When switched on, the motor buzzed, sending vibrations through the hand. Mother massaged his temples with it, and from time to time I would be pressed into service. I remember looking down at his head and feeling sorry for him, sorry that such a powerful man should be so reduced by pain. On the outside, he seemed so relaxed and graceful. He had a fluid, confident, manly gait, and when he wasn't feeling angry or impatient, his personal manner was rhythmical and easy. He spoke unself-consciously with an accent that might best be described as "cowboy," a soft blend of mild southern drawl and southwestern twang (I can still hear him exclaiming "Shit fire," that wonderful expression that has nothing to do with either of its components). He sat down in a chair as if it were *the* right place to be, he talked with you as if you were *the* right person to be talking with, his clothes always looked like *the* right clothes to be wearing, and all without the slightest fuss. But beneath this exterior—which I believe was not a false one—his blood pressure must have been telling a different story. It must have been hard to be Wayne Padgett, the "King of the Bootleggers"; Wayne Padgett, the guy who would fight anybody any time; Wayne Padgett, the man who felt it was his personal responsibility to help his friends even before they knew they needed help; Wayne Padgett, who had to provide for a wife and son, look after his mother and brother, and deal with crooks and cops; Wayne Padgett, whose father had met a violent end; Wayne Padgett, the Robin Hood good-guy bad-guy. Finally a doctor prescribed medication to lower his blood pressure.

He was also bothered by sinus congestion. For many years he had the habit, especially before going to bed, of coating the inside of his nostrils with mentholated petroleum jelly, to open up the breathing passages. He used Mentholatum and Vicks, both of which carried warnings on their labels: "Not for Internal Use." My mother also ignored this warning. Daddy also carried a Vicks inhaler, a plastic tube from which one could inhale menthol fumes. It too carried a warning about overuse, which of course he disregarded.

Ever since I could remember, he had a tendency to "clear his throat," probably because of mild chronic bronchitis or a minor allergy. It was one of those personal mannerisms that becomes so identified with a person that one stops noticing it. The sound of him clearing his throat was part of his vocabulary, a sound that I can hear in my memory when I visualize his face, a sound that for me has nothing to do with congestion, but only with him, a sound that is intimate and personal, friendly even, for it is a sound he made only when he was calm and relaxed.

I don't know if these conditions were related to his habit of quietly blowing little bursts of air through his nostrils, as when he was signaling a partner in a poker game. Someone once told me that this is the symptom of a rare neurological disorder, but it's possible he was just trying to keep his sinuses clear.

Our family subscribed to both Tulsa daily newspapers, the *World* and the *Tribune*. Daddy read both of them, sometimes just to check the crime beat coverage. He was especially sensitive to articles about himself. I remember his reaction to one such article, which commented on his alleged criminal activities, falsely including arrests for couterfeiting. His lips tightened and his face expressed the anger and frustration that comes from knowing that he could not simply drive down to the newspaper and punch somebody out.

"This is bullshit! I don't see how those sons-of-bitches can get away with saying crap like this. I'm going to call John Cochrane." Cochrane was his lawyer. The next day the paper printed a retraction, buried, of course, deep in its back pages, which infuriated him even more.

There were several reasons for his not wanting press coverage. The first was that it was embarrassing for his mother, even though she automatically dismissed all such articles as rubbish. The second was that it put pressure on the police to do something about the "King of the Bootleggers." They would have to raid him more often, bust his delivery boy. The third was that he was not a show-off. He even shied away from public praise. Despite all this, he seems to have gotten along well with reporters on a personal basis. He was friendly with Nolen Bulloch, the *World*'s crime beat reporter. Gene Curtis, who was assigned to the courthouse and the police station at various times, remembered that he himself "got along fine with Wayne—great." Curtis even recalled having been one of Wayne's customers.

Aside from newspapers and a few magazines, Daddy's only other reading matter was westerns. Some evenings he would sit down in the big armchair in the living room and smoke Luckies and read two or three such novels without stopping, far into the night. Zane Grey and Max Brand were two of his favorites, but I suspect that he bought anything that had an exciting cover on it: two dusty and grizzled gunfighters face to face, quivering just before the draw, or a horse rearing up as its rider blasted a man crumpling to his knees. If Daddy had a personal mythology, it was that of the Old West. Like Pretty Boy Floyd, he admired colorful outlaws such as Billy the Kid and the Dalton gang. According to author Michael Wallis, late nineteenth-century dime novels had described Billy the Kid "as a bloodthirsty killer," but by the publication in 1926 of Walter Noble Burns's *Saga of Billy the Kid*, the tide had turned, and in the 1930 movie *Billy the Kid*, Johnny Mack Brown portrayed him as a "frontier superhero."[1] Likewise, Emmett Dalton, who had once been taken on a booster trip by Tulsa businessmen, published his memoirs in 1931 under the title of *When the Daltons Rode*. Dalton's description of the typical outlaw sounds as if he were describing Daddy: "An outlaw's got to be cagey as a coyote to live even a short time in the land of his father. The alert outlaw acts a good deal by intuition. His wits and sense become acute as a wild animal's. The ordinary pitch of faculties is not sufficient. His life constantly depends upon the accuracy with which he judges men."[2] Dalton upheld the code of the West, which called for intense loyalty to one's buddies. You never ratted on your friends. As Wallis put it, "The unspoken silence in a lawless clan was a social bond."[3] Similar to the Mafia's *omertà* (vow of silence), this solidarity was a personal bond that filled in the yawning gap left by the fraternal and professional groups that Daddy felt to be unreliable. But honor was not only among thieves. Daddy also admired the straight-shootin' western hero as portrayed by Ronald Reagan, Randolph Scott, and Joel McCrea. When my parents and I went to the movies together, it was usually to see a western, and usually at a drive-in theater.

The first drive-in movie theater in Tulsa was the Hi-Way 66, named for the famous highway it was near, way out in what was then a rural area.

The theater's name was spelled out in pink neon lights in lariat shapes, next to a blue and pink cowboy on a horse that continually reared up. Beside the horse stood an immobile green neon cactus. As soon as the 66 opened, in the late 1940s, my parents joined the others who flocked to it and soon learned the rituals of the drive-in.

Because the drive-ins usually charged by the head, children would often duck down on the back floorboards, sometimes covering themselves with a blanket. A more elaborate ruse involved cramming as many people as possible into the trunk. Those who used the drive-in as a Lovers' Lane would park in the back rows; families used the middle and front rows. Before the film started, the screen would dance with the beams from spotlights that many people outfitted their cars with in those days, in imitation of police cars. The concession stand, a drab cinderblock building next to the projection booth, would be thronged with people buying popcorn, peanuts, soda pop, hot dogs, chili dogs, corn dogs, and the entire spectrum of popular candies, usually toting them back to their cars in flimsy little cardboard carriers while pre-feature footage played on the screen, urging patrons to stuff themselves and warning that they had only ten minutes, then nine, then eight, etc., until show time. The voice-over could be heard through the individual speakers that hung on poles next to each car, and which, thanks to a coiled speaker cord, could be brought into the car, adjusted for volume, and hung inside the window. Some people brought Windex and rags for cleaning their windshields—not a single bug must come between them and the huge screen.

Each Tulsa drive-in had its special flavor. The Airview was graced with the deafening sounds of airplanes arriving and departing from the nearby airport. The trashy Skyline, on the far north side of town, was where tough kids went to fight. (It was at the Skyline that I later saw the notorious film, *The Moon Is Blue*, notorious because one of its characters dared to utter the word *pregnant*.) On the south side near the Arkansas River, the Riverside was home to voracious mosquitoes. The respectable Capri, located out on the Sand Springs Road, catered to a blue-collar crowd, including us. The Admiral was the only duplex drive-in in Tulsa: at the last moment you could change your mind and see a different movie. The Bel-Aire had a bland, menthol overtone, like the cigarette of the same name. The new Sheridan presaged the shopping malls in its lack of character. The best drive-in was the Apache, best because Daddy knew the owners (when they were at the ticket booth we always got in free) and he could vouch for the spotlessness of their kitchen and the quality of their food—their chili dogs would never growl in your stomach.

In the late forties and early fifties, the three of us went to the drive-in fairly often. In fact, it was the thing the three of us did most together outside the home.

One night the Admiral was showing a first-run western with Joel McCrea. We were about fifteen minutes into the film—Joel was riding higher and higher into the mountains—when Daddy said, "Hell, I've seen this movie."

"How could you have?" asked Mother. "It just opened."

"I don't know, but I've seen it. You wait, this other cowboy will come along in a minute, an old boy Joel McCrea used to know."

And sure enough, the old friend did appear.

This prophecy and fulfilment went on for some time. My mother and I were fascinated and my father was baffled by his sudden onset of clairvoyance. Then finally he said, "Shit, I know what it is! I read this *book*."

I remember another drive-in incident. We arrived a little late for the last show. The entry gate was shut. I can't be sure that our late arrival was unintentional, since it provided us with an opportunity to enter through the exit—without paying. We cruised in quietly with lights off. In fact we had snuck in successfully any number of times—another drive-in ritual. But this time a man with a flashlight fell in behind us on foot, huffing and puffing.

"Wayne, there's an usher behind us," my mother said.

"I know," Daddy said, but he continued to cruise, as if in search of a good parking spot. Every time the usher would catch up to the back of the car, Daddy would gently accelerate, forcing the panting usher to redouble his efforts.

Finally Mother asked, "Wayne, why don't you stop?"

Daddy grinned. "Oh, I just want to run him a little." And the three of us burst out laughing.

Another sweet memory I have of him is seeing him watch the rain, which seemed to fill him with a hypnotic pleasure. If a good rain came up, he'd go out onto the small front porch of our house and stand there, sometimes even in his underwear, to watch it come down on summer nights. What was it that made this man, ordinarily so active and uncontemplative, stand there for twenty minutes, as if transfixed? Sometimes I would join him, partly because I liked the rain too, and partly because I hoped to see what was so calming and fascinating for him. Once I asked him point blank why he went out on the porch like that. His reply was "I love the rain," said softer than usual and with an inflection that told me that he himself understood this fascination no better than I did. Sometimes lightning would streak its way across the sky, highlighting the two elms, their leaves now audible and spattering, and the sweet, clean smell of fresh rain making the world feel, for a moment, so simple and innocent.

Until I was perhaps eight or nine, Daddy, Mother, and I went to the annual rodeo at the fairgrounds, inside a huge yellow building called the Pavilion. The rodeo consisted of stunt riding and lariat tricks, clowns, fanfares, calf roping, bronco busting, and bull riding, along with a cavalcade led by a cowboy star such as Roy Rogers, Gene Autry, or Hopalong Cassidy waving majestically from atop a prancing stallion. My parents indulged my every whim, buying me helium balloons, cotton candy, Cracker Jacks, cap pistols, autographed pictures of Roy or Gene or Hoppy, commemorative programs, live chameleons, tin sheriffs' badges—you name it. The rich, loamy, reddish-brown dirt on the floor of the Pavilion looked gorgeous.

My parents liked the rodeo as much as I did. My mother always enjoyed a spectacle, and Daddy had grown up with the cowboy mystique. The romantic image of the cowboy—free, brave, and straight-shootin'—was irresistible to him. Hadn't his father grown up on a ranch, busting horses? Hadn't he himself attended a high school named after one of America's most beloved cowboys, Will Rogers? Hadn't Rogers grown up just outside of Claremore, where Verna and Grover had met and married? Wasn't northeastern Oklahoma where the likes of Jesse James and Cole Younger had roamed? Wasn't this where great cattle drives from Texas made their way to the stockyards of Kansas? Wasn't Tulsa where Bob Wills got his start? Wasn't this, after all, a part of the country that was called Indian Territory until only fifteen years before Daddy's birth? The poet Ted Berrigan once said that Daddy reminded him of John Wayne and the "code of the West" that the actor embodied by being rugged, decent, fearless, and faithful to one's friends.

And then there were Daddy's cowboy boots, some of which were cus-tom-made and elaborately tooled, in alligator or snakeskin, boots he prized and kept immaculate, and whose hard, pointed toes, incidentally, could come in handy if some smart-aleck picked a fight. But there were no fights at the rodeo, where a lot of good old boys and their families enjoyed the show and took home a little of the Old West. Daddy was no exception, though for him the fast car had replaced the fast pony.

Every once in a while, when the summer evenings would start to cool off, my parents and I would go out for a ride, sometimes rather late in the evening. We might just cruise around town, though we'd often end up passing through what was called downtown (the center of town), whose streets, so busy during the day, were eerily empty at night.

All three of us loved the smell of bread being baked, so every once in a while we would drive to one of the big commercial bakeries, such as Rainbow. Daddy would send me in a side door—left open because of the heat—with a quarter to buy a loaf of warm bread. The baker, invariably a skinny old guy dressed in white with a white cap, would chat with me or briefly explain how the bread was made. When I got back in the car, the smell of the bread would cause us to tear open the wrapper and eat half the loaf—white bread with nothing on it—as we cruised around. For me, it was one of the pinnacles of human experience.

Another pinnacle involved our night drives out into the country—which in those days was only fifteen minutes away from our house and which today has been overrun by housing developments and shopping centers. Daddy is said to have known every country backroad and cow-path, knowledge he had picked up while hunting and while evading police and potential hijackers. I recall long night drives out to the east and north of town, down dirt roads where the only living things were the big Oklahoma crickets that made their amazingly loud music in the dark. When I'd get sleepy, I'd lay my head on my mother's lap and stretch my feet over to my father's lap, and suffused by the creamy light from the dashboard with its gauges and radio band, I'd drift off among the gentle vibrations from the road.

It was Mother who had the radio on. She liked popular and country and western music, which she would sing along with. Daddy seemed fas-cinated by her ability to sing. According to her, "He liked music, but he couldn't get his tune together. He couldn't whistle, either. But he always used to have me sing to him, whatever was popular. Just sitting there at home. And if somebody came over, he'd have me sing. Wayne thought I was the best singer that ever was. 'Jeannie with the Light-Brown Hair' was his favorite song, that and 'Peg of My Heart.'"

Driving along one day, he asked me about the new school year. I had just started ninth grade. After I rattled off the names of my courses, he said, "Latin? Say something in Latin."

"Like what? I can't speak much Latin yet."

"Say anything."

"America est patria mea."

He laughed. "What's that mean?"

"America is my native land."

"I'll be damned! Say some more."

"America est patria mea. America est patria tua. America est patria nostra."

"What's that mean?"

I told him.

"Damn! That's really something!"

Years later, when I returned from living in France, he had me speak French to him, and became as dazzled as before. To him, it seemed sort of miraculous that his wife could sing and his son could speak a foreign language.

Daddy was far more interested in these things than in big events, such as holidays, either national or religious. For the most part, he let Mother handle them. He maintained his adult record of never attending church, even on Easter. At Christmas he did go out and buy the tree and fit it in its stand, but that was about all. Mother was in charge of buying the presents, including most of those from him to us. He did give her at least one special gift, usually jewelry. Decorating the tree and wrapping gifts was not man's work; Mother and I did that. The three of us spent Christmas Eve together unwrapping the gifts, which were piled up high around the tree, evidence of my mother's generosity, her willingness to spend, and her desire to please us. To me, the gifts—except the shirts and socks—were magical, but Daddy took it all in stride. He would thank us and smile, but it was hard for him to get excited about receiving a new bathrobe or belt. Besides, he was not effusive. He was a man. His role was to make the money that made all this possible.

Easter, Thanksgiving, and Halloween made even less of an impression on him. He was no longer religious, he cared little for American history, and he didn't believe in the supernatural. For some years my mother fixed traditional holiday dinners for the three of us, which we took in the dining room—the only time that room was used—but eventually she stopped.

She did so partly because we had our holiday meals elsewhere. The three of us would convene at Grandma Verna's, where other Padgetts and Tuckers would join us for dinner. Or just Mother and I would go to her parents' house, which by the 1950s was only six blocks away.

Early on in my parents' marriage, my father and my maternal grandmother, Daisy, had begun to feud. The matter was never discussed in my presence, but Daddy let it be known that he thought she was a meddling, bossy old bag—the archetypal mother-in-law. In fact, Daisy was a domineering, critical person, but she did have her reasons for disliking Daddy, with whom she struggled for control of my mother. The struggle became so bitter that he refused to speak to Daisy or to set foot in her house, and he refused to allow her in our house when he was in town. It was clear that I was not to mention my grandmother's name in his presence. And so, on Easter after church, on Thanksgiving and Christmas Day, my mother and I would drive the six blocks to Noah and Daisy's house for dinner with them and other relatives on their side of the family. Neither my father nor Daisy, both of whom were incredibly headstrong, would budge an inch. They maintained a rift that went straight through the center of our family.

Relations with other relatives were better. Verna and my mother always got along extremely well. And my father's first cousin Alma, Roy Padgett's daughter, was in some ways more like a sister to him. In fact, from around 1951 to 1959 Alma Montgomery was at our house five days a week, working for us.

When the media reported that Bill Cook, a fugitive killer who slept with one eye open and therefore could hold his terrified captives at gunpoint indefinitely, had hid out one night on Tulsa's Reservoir Hill, Alma and Tom Montgomery decided to move from there. They moved into the first house Daddy had bought on Fourth Street, and Tom got a regular job as a night watchman out at the Douglas aircraft plant. Tom let his daughter Sharon and me ride on the electric gate he guarded and walk around the aircraft parked nearby—violations of security, of course. But nobody was going to see us from the Douglas plant: it had the distinction of being the largest building in the world without a window.

Daddy liked both Alma and Tom, and he knew that she was honest and loyal. Hadn't it been her father, Roy, who had stepped in and helped the family when Grover died? It was only natural that Alma, now living across the street, should go to work for Daddy. His entire whiskey business was made up of family and old friends, people he could trust.

Alma remembered a raid on our house. As the county police knocked on the back door, she removed the speaker pieces from the phones and walked out the front door and to her house across the street. With the pieces removed, the police couldn't talk to the caller, although the caller, a customer, could be heard. The squad, led by Roy Rains, searched every nook and cranny of the house. By the time they left, the place was a total mess, with the beds crooked and unmade, the drawers of clothing a jumble, the couch moved out from the wall and its cushions piled up. Years later, when I first heard a couple say that coming home to a burgled apartment made them feel violated, I immediately knew what they meant, even though the circumstances were considerably different.

There weren't more than perhaps four or five county raids in all, and we had advance warning for all of them. Daddy had a friend in the police department who called him whenever the county raiding squad obtained a search warrant for our house. I remember two such raids. In the first, Daddy told me to hide "the books"—two standard office ledgers. I took them out to the doghouse in the backyard and crawled through the small doorway. The doghouse, with its floor covered with a thick layer of hay, was a perfect place for a child: it was cozy, dark, and, because of its small doorway, inaccessible to grownups. Inside, I hid the books up in a secret slot next to the roof, invisible to the naked eye. Needless to say, the raiders didn't find the books.

On another occasion, I was playing catch in the backyard with friends, when some gentlemen in suits and hats came to the gate. "Which one of you lives here?" one of them asked. I knew right away that they were foes. "I do." "Where's your momma and daddy?" he asked. I said, "I don't know." In fact, I didn't—wasn't she at home? When they knocked again,

OKLAHOMA TOUGH

Mother answered the back door. She had just returned from Tommie's house next door, where she had secreted the books in a custom-built plant. With the phone "fixed" and the books gone and no liquor in the house, the county was stymied once again. I was delighted by their grim expressions.

"You didn't want to get caught by them," said Alma. "The city didn't do anything but make you pay a fine, but the county's laws were a lot stiffer. You could get time."

During the 1950s, Alma was not only a part of the family, she became a part of our household, taking liquor orders, helping clean, and picking me up at school. She also became a good friend and companion for my mother, as was Alma's daughter Sharon for me. The four of us often drove out to Pennington's drive-in cafe for hamburgers, black-bottom pie, and Cokes, followed by a movie. She or Mother took Sharon and me bowling once a week.

One time, the police stopped Alma and Mother a few blocks from our house. Sharon and I were riding on the front fenders. Given the very slow speed, it was safe, but of course against the law. The policeman told them he was going to take them "downtown." Mother replied, "Oh no you're not. Not dressed like this!" She and Alma were wearing shorts. "We'll go home and change first." He then learned that Mother was Wayne Padgett's wife. "I'm gonna tell Wayne about this," he warned, and then let them go. As he drove off, my mother snorted, "The old fool!" and we all laughed. Resistance to authority was endemic in our family.

In the summer of 1954, the four of us, accompanied by Alma's husband, Tom, took a trip to Colorado to see the sights. Daddy did not go.

By this time, a pattern had developed: Daddy was going one way and Mother and I another. He was a good provider and a steady disciplinarian. He cared about how I did in school; he even attended the Open School nights and took part in the brief parent-teacher conversations. He was extremely proud of my academic success. Like a big brother, he enjoyed joking and horsing around with me. But the fact is that usually he didn't spend any extended length of time alone with me, other than the brief runs down to a car lot or to the sundry store. Most of our interests didn't intersect. For example, I loved baseball, but I can recall his playing catch with me only once, when he came home one day and found me alone in the yard, throwing a ball high in the air to simulate a fly ball. We played catch for a few minutes—he was well coordinated and he had a good arm—but he quickly lost interest. He never watched me play little league. It was Mother who cheered from the sidelines. The necessity of selling pop and peanuts at sports events as a kid had made sports unpalatable to him, but his absence at my games was also due to his reluctance to be locked into any regularly scheduled activity.

He was, however, more than willing to help me sell magazines. When I was in junior high school, the Curtis Publishing Company, publisher of the *Saturday Evening Post* and other popular magazines, organized a subscription sales contest at our school. Seeing that I was gung ho to win the top prize (a bicycle), Daddy spent his evenings driving me around to visit many of his friends and customers, who would take a quick look at the Curtis brochure and say, "Give me that one, that one, that one, that one. . . ." I won the contest hands down. It was a rare chance for him to help me with my "schoolwork."

Daddy took me swimming only once, at the newly opened McClure Pool. I had never even seen him swim, so I was amazed when he immediately climbed to the top of the high dive, took a few steps out onto the board, sprang into the air, and executed a perfect dive into the glittering blue water.

Another rare moment I remember was when he took me to Oiler Park to see an exhibition baseball game, around 1952. Players from various major league teams had been selected to tour and play local teams, in our case the Tulsa Oilers. The real reason for our going was to see my idol Mickey Mantle, the Oklahoma boy who had become a major star with the New York Yankees. The press called him "The Commerce Comet," after the little northeastern Oklahoma town where he had grown up, but Daddy insisted that Mantle had really grown up in Spavinaw, where he had been very close to an uncle. The uncle, it turned out, was a good friend of Daddy's, and so, after the game, in which I saw Mantle throw a perfect strike to the catcher on the fly all the way from the right-field fence, Daddy and I, along with the uncle, were admitted to the locker room. There, amidst the hubbub and steam, stood Mickey Mantle, clad only in a white towel, as radiant as a young god. I shook his hand and we talked briefly about playing shortstop, which was my position and had been his as a kid. But Daddy was far less interested in Mantle than in his uncle, whom he had pulled aside for a private conversation. He had a deal to discuss, and he just wasn't interested in baseball.

And I wasn't interested in hunting. When I was little, he had taken me rabbit hunting, but the sight and smell of limp and bloody rabbits had caused me to vomit. Seeing Daddy and Homer Gafford gut and skin squirrels also made my stomach lurch. At the age of around eight I had fired my BB rifle at a bird in our front yard and, to my utter horror, hit and killed it. Hunting was not for me. I never liked fishing, either: the fish stank, their eyes were ghastly, they finned you when you tried to take them off the hook, and their guts were disgusting.

In general, my father didn't know how to spend time with me. I ascribe this partly to his family history. His father and his father's father had grown up on farms, where the father-son relation didn't need "cultivating." It was based on working together in the fields and in the barn. Living in the city, Grover had no way of relating to his boys, because they didn't work together. His inexperience carried over to the way his three sons raised their boys. That is, aside from disciplining, they left child-rearing mostly to their wives. By the time I was eight or nine, I was pretty much a "momma's boy."

Fortunately, Daddy and I did share an interest in cars. When he asked me what I wanted for my sixteenth birthday—driving age—I told him I wanted an MG, preferably an old TC, TD, or TF model. The MG was a modest British sports car, not flashy but rare in Tulsa. Without my knowledge, Daddy bought an oil field company car, spruced it up, drove it to Kansas, where it wouldn't be recognized, and traded it in. On a sunny afternoon in the spring of 1958, three months before my birthday, I was out in the front yard when he pulled into the driveway in a bright red, shining, streamlined-for-racing MG-A, the latest model, and for just a moment I had the strange feeling that this was going to be my car, and when he got out and looked my way, the realization flooded me that yes, this *was* going to be my car, all mine! It was an unbelievably great surprise, the kind of feeling he liked to create in people he loved. I might add that it is easily the best birthday present I have ever received.

"Go ahead, drive it around the block," he said. That I didn't have a driver's license made no difference to him.

All in all, life looked pretty good. We all awoke every morning in a nice house in a nice neighborhood. We had nice clothes and cars. Alma came across the street to help. The customers usually didn't call in their orders until the afternoon. I'd come home from school and play outside (or, after 1950, watch television). In the late afternoon Bill Martin would come by to shoot a few baskets with me, chat with my parents, pick up the day's orders, and head off to the plant. Except for Daddy's headaches and an occasional pain in his knee, we were all in good health and we always had plenty of money, with a nightly gross of anywhere from $800 to $2,000 in the early 1950s and $1,200 to $3,500 later in the decade. Bible thumpers aside, people liked and admired Daddy. Everywhere we went, they would smile and say, "Hi, Wayne. What you been up to?"

First and foremost in Daddy's devotion was his mother, and although she had enough love for all three of her sons, Wayne was the one she counted on. Robert had made a new life in California. Tommie had stayed in Tulsa, but he was still the baby of the family.

At the start of World War II, Verna had gone to work at Spartan Aircraft as a rivet inspector. Now that she was earning more and the boys were no longer dependent on her, she was ready to divorce Nick, whose drinking had gotten much heavier.

Spartan Aircraft was owned by John Paul Getty, who at that time was living in Tulsa. One day at the factory, Getty, then in his early fifties, noticed Verna, in her early forties but looking much younger, and invited her to an art exhibit. A few days later she found herself looking at paintings in the company of the man who, a decade or so later, would be described by *Fortune* magazine as the richest man in America, worth $700 million. The magnate conducted himself like a gentleman with her, but on the subsequent date, Getty's chauffeur took her aside and said, "Verna, if you play your cards right, the sky's the limit." Restraining her anger, she replied evenly, "I don't know how to play my cards right." Getty relinquished his pursuit.

At Spartan she had met Ralph Combs. They dated and she found that she liked him. The disintegration of the marriage was too much for Nick, who hit the bottle even harder, and finally Verna divorced him.

After the war, she worked part-time for Daddy, answering phones and taking orders. Then, with the boys moved out and Nick gone, she sold her house and bought a little duplex at 308 (now 312) South Xanthus and became a real-estate agent. She lived in one side of her duplex with Ralph Combs, whom she had married, and rented out the other.

Tommie had always followed in his big brother's footsteps, but with less panache and success. Bill Martin recalled that "Tommie bought his whiskey off Wayne on credit. He'd come over and make a payment maybe once a week. When the bill would get so big—maybe around ten thousand dollars—you know what Wayne would do? He'd say, 'Aw, his bill's getting too big. Let's just scratch that off and start him a new bill.' He did that lots and lots and lots of times. He always looked after Tommie as if he were his son, instead of his brother. He always took care of him."

Both brothers were quick to fight, but Tommie, a skinny six foot six, was not built for street-fighting, especially against an opponent such as Charley Wood. There are several possibile causes of the fight, including sexual jealousy, but the upshot was that Charley pistol-whipped Tommie, cracking several neck vertebrae. A May 18, 1961, photograph in the *Tulsa Tribune* showed Tommie, on crutches and in a neck brace, being helped by Daddy out of a courtroom after testifying. Charlie was found guilty of assault and battery with a dangerous weapon and sent to the county jail. Tommie also filed a civil suit.

As Bill Martin told it: "Tommie sued Charley and got all that money. It was all right as far as money went, but Wayne still wasn't satisfied with the outcome, so he told Charley he was going to whip his ass and told him where and when. Charley was a big guy, and he had big shoulders, big arms, and everything. He had hands like a goddamned grizzly bear. A big, tough son of a bitch." Another person told me that over the years Charley had gotten "a little wacky." Wacky or not, Wood was shrewd enough to use his six months' jail sentence to weight-train for the fight. When word got around about his preparation, friends urged Wayne to train too, but he dismissed the idea, the way he had once sloughed off a boxing manager's suggestion that he take up "the sweet science." Howard Donahue remembered that "when Wayne and Charley were younger, they had had a hell of a fight, and Wayne whipped him." That was then. Charley was ready this time.

As Donahue told it, "Charley had gotten out of jail the day before. I was working at Gene Downing's car lot over in West Tulsa. Charley drove up and got out of his car with a pistol in his hand. He walked past me, stopped, and said, 'You son of a bitch, I ought to just kill you.' See, I testified when he beat up Tom—I just testified as to what happened. Which wasn't good for Charley. I guess Charley figured I shouldn't have told the truth. But here Tom was a good friend of mine, Charley was a good friend of mine—what are you going to do? Just tell the truth and let it take its course, right?

"The next day he had cooled off. He came by and said, 'Hey, let's go get a cup of coffee.' On the way, he told me, 'That goddamned Wayne's a cowardly son of a bitch. He won't fight me.' Charley was a big boy: he lifted those weights and all that bullshit. I said, 'I ain't taking sides, but you can rest assured that Wayne'll goddamned sure fight you.'

"The very next day, Gene and Wayne pulled up at the lot and Charley was already there. Wayne was driving. Charley came right up to the car door: he figured he'd hit him as he was getting out of the car. 'Come on, get out of there, you goddamned cowardly son of a bitch!' Wayne kept motioning to Gene to get out, and Wayne got out Gene's side. Wayne and Charley met right in front of the car. They clashed. They swung at each other a few times. Big as they were, you'd hear it go swish when they'd swing, but they wasn't connecting too much. They hit each other a couple of times. Wayne put his leg behind Charley's leg and throwed him. Wayne got hold of his leg and pulled him around and then stumbled. The traffic started stopping out in the street. Charley picked up a rock—they were both on the ground—and Gene stopped him and said, 'Hey, the law's going to be here and I can't afford that. Break it up.' The fight didn't last that long. It was a kind of a toss-up. Wayne got in his car and drove off. Charley said, 'Well, I was wrong, wasn't I?'"

I happened to be home on vacation from college when Daddy returned from the fight. He looked ragged. "I just had a fight with Charley Wood," he explained, pulling down his lower lip to show where it had been torn away from the gums and was still bleeding. He was now over forty and still getting into fights for his "little" brother.

Both Wayne and Tommie were highly protective of their mother. One time her new husband Ralph got rough with her, and the hot-headed Tommie drove over with a pistol and offered to blow his brains out. Lucille recalled: "Wayne was a little more subtle. He'd kind of talk Ralph out of it. He might slap him around, jerk him around a bit, make him behave."

Robert was blissfully free of all this family drama. After serving in the Army Air Force in World War II and getting married, he attended the University of Southern California, becoming the student body president and graduating with a degree in education. He then went to work for Pitney Bowes, the postage meter company, the youngest sales representative the firm had ever hired. In no time his sales territory expanded beyond Los Angeles. He had a family, a job with a future, and a new life. As his wife, Mary Margaret, put it, "There was no way in hell he was ever gonna go back to Tulsa."

According to her, "Bob was very fond of Wayne," and I know Daddy respected Robert. And although the two of them had gone different ways, they were both Padgetts to the core, and they knew it. You could tell by the way they looked at each other and stood and talked together, at the edge of family gatherings on the rare visits Robert made to Tulsa in later years.

Like his brothers, "Bob could charm the socks off anybody," Mary Margaret recalled. But all three brothers were extremely jealous husbands, and they were marked by the trauma of their father's death. Tommie never spoke of his father—Elda, his third wife, didn't even know where Grover was buried. Robert, who spoke of his father very rarely, finally told Mary Margaret, after forty-two years of marriage, that Grover had killed himself. She noticed that "tears were running down his cheeks, the only time I ever saw him cry." But then he abruptly said he didn't want to talk about it, and the subject was closed forever.

Daddy's sense of family went beyond blood relatives. Whenever Nick, now his ex-stepfather, hit the skids, Daddy stepped in. According to Lucille, "Nick just drifted drunk from place to place. They'd throw him in jail and call Wayne, and Wayne would go down there and bail him out, buy him some new clothes, and get him a place to live and give him a little money. But it wouldn't last. Soon as his money was gone he'd be back out on the street."

One relative for whom Daddy continued to have no sympathy was Daisy, his mother-in-law. Their mutual enmity had not abated. But Daddy found it hard to dislike his father-in-law, for Noah was kind, gentle, and salt-of-the-earth, "the sweetest little old thing," as one person fondly put it. Standing at perhaps five nine and weighing 135, the wiry Noah had gone from farming to working in a shipyard to running a small downtown cafe with Daisy (Daisy's Waffle House) to working as a pipefitter in a machine shop. In the 1950s, he would drive home from work in his old blue Plymouth, return his standard-issue black lunch pail to the kitchen, and go in to scrub the heavy grit and grime from his hands and face.

Although Noah was docile and henpecked, there was a point beyond which he would not be pushed, no matter what. When Wayne and Daisy had their initial falling out, my dad told the Hueys to stay out of his house forever. The Hueys left, but soon Noah returned and said to Wayne, "You big son of a bitch, my daughter and my grandson live here, and as long as they're living I'll come back any damned time I please." Wayne replied, "Mr. Huey, you're welcome here any time."

Lucille said, "Daddy loved him. And Wayne loved Daddy. But Momma was bullheaded and Wayne was bullheaded." Daisy had been against Wayne from early on. She had warned Lucille, "Someday you'll hate him as much as you love him."

As far back as I can remember, both my parents, when tucking me in, would give me a light kiss on the lips and say, "Goodnight. I love you." This ritual lasted late into my elementary school years, though the tucking-in and kissing gradually were abandoned. The verbal part continued until I went to college, even though my parents grew further and further apart and my adolescence made such avowals of love more and more awkward. The ritual helped maintain our pretense of family unity, a pretense that was fading fast.

13   *Things Fall Apart . . .*

MY PARENTS' MARRIAGE HAD evaporated, but in many ways they continued to behave as if everything were fine. Alma recalled that they "always kept up a pretty good front, but they definitely had a problem. I never saw a family that could keep it all together but not together. When you walked into that house, you thought it was a family."

Mother helped maintain this façade. "I just shrugged it all off, ignored it, thinking it would pass. Actually I wouldn't let myself think about it." The word nowadays is *denial*.

By the age of fourteen, I had begun my own compartmentalization. I was showing signs of being like my uncle Robert. I made good grades and spent more and more time alone in my room, reading and writing. I too had branched off the mainstream of the family by going inside myself. Now when I went into my room, I shut the door. Daddy could no longer walk past, look in, and say hello. If he opened the door without knocking, I would give him a stare to let him know that he was intruding. Since I couldn't compete with him, I was cutting him off.

Of course, there was nothing unusual in this burgeoning father-son conflict. With puberty, my sense of self was wobbling and coalescing around a new center, one located inside me, not out in the family. And this new self, a male self, was reenacting the ritual of discomfiting the father, so it could grow on its own. Like most fathers, Daddy chafed against my growing resistance to his authority, and the struggle between us was on.

Gradually over the next four years—after which I left home for college in New York—I could be sullen with him, if not arrogant, and I found him increasingly bossy, if not dictatorial. I wanted to let my hair grow long (free and natural); he insisted on keeping it short (neat and presentable). I wanted to read books and listen to music, he wanted me to mow, edge, and rake the lawn. If dinner was ready, I saw no reason to hurry to the table, because I was reading about, say, the origins of the universe, but he would insist hotly that I come to the table immediately. Neither he nor I understood the father-son conflict, I because of my callowness, and he because it was a conflict he had never had the chance to experience with his own father (and stepfather). Deep down he was proud of me, but the situation didn't allow him to enjoy my company very much. There were times during that period (1957–60) that I disliked him intensely.

What I tend to forget is that we got along well enough. Recently rereading the letters I wrote in my senior year of high school to my friend Dick Gallup, then a freshman at Tulane, I found six references to my father, only one of them negative. I also tend to forget the immense gratitude I felt the day he drove up in my new MG, and the little moments of fun we had together.

Part of my antagonism toward him came from the growing social pressure I felt as the son of the King of the Bootleggers. In the third or fourth grade, I started to realize that society considered bootlegging shameful, but only rarely did his profession cause me any embarrassment, such as the time at school when some classmates huddled and whispered in the back of the room, then giggled and peeked in my direction, passing among them my father's business card. For a moment I felt as if I had been stabbed in the chest. I didn't know that my father was unintentionally making me feel about him the way he had felt about *his* father: the father was someone you didn't talk about, a source of shame. Of course, my father was alive and a source of power and pleasure too, and the truth is that, like all my father's family and friends, in my heart I didn't think there was anything morally wrong with selling whiskey. Nonetheless, by the time I got to the eighth grade, it pained me to have to list his occupation on school records as "car dealer" and to lie to my schoolmates, not knowing if they knew I was lying. Equally awful was knowing that few of the girls I liked would be willing or permitted to date the son of a well-known criminal.

But he was an outlaw I loved, just as I loved the romance of his being one. This romance even had its own liturgy. How many times I sat at the table in our den and listened to my mother repeating brand names over the telephone as she wrote them down: Ancient Age, Four Roses, Seagram's Seven Crown, Seagram's VO, Old Grandad, Old Crow, Johnny Walker Black, Johnny Walker Red, Ballantine, Kentucky Tavern, Haig & Haig, Old Forester, Canadian Club, Gilbey's, Belmont, Glenmore. . . . These names had a magical ring for me: the unpredictable Johnny Walker (was he red or was he black?), the Canadians and their Club (a country club?), the comical and harmless Old Grandad, the dinner-date suavity of Four Roses, and the regal dominance of Seagram's Seven Crown (wow, seven of them!). Each brand name had a special ring that reverberated with its own vignette, which took on a different nuance when Daddy pronounced these same names: things were serious now at the Canadian Club—there were clouds over the golf course.

At the age of thirteen or fourteen I read the *Iliad* and the *Odyssey*, in which the Greeks offer numerous libations and taste the fermented grape with great delight. Wine sounded so good—even better than my beloved Grapette pop—that I told my mother I wanted to see what it tasted like. A few days later she announced that the bottle was in the refrigerator. I poured some into a glass, marvelling at this liquid that had so enchanted the ancient Greeks—even the great Odysseus himself—and slowly brought it to my lips. I drank deeply and ughk! It was sweet and sticky, with some terrible acid attacking the back of my tongue. I emptied the glass into the sink and washed the disappointing red liquid down the drain.

This experience was in line with our family's agreement about drinking. My parents made it abundantly clear to me that if I ever wanted to drink, I could—but only at home. Under no circumstances was I to drink outside the home. Their great fear was that I would suffer the fate of so many other young Tulsans: in a drunken blur I would smash my car into a culvert at 110 miles per hour ("Four Youths Killed in High-Speed Crash"). So for me, without its aura of forbidden fruit, booze lost its allure. As a high school senior I did get plastered at a party one night, but only because I didn't know that the drink being served—a clear moonshine poured from a gallon jug and called White Lightning—had the kick of a giant mule. Both my parents would have been upset by this incident, my father less than my mother. He knew that young men have to be a little wild. By then it was one of the few things he and I agreed on. However, my idea of wild rang with the magic of names such as Kerouac, Ginsberg, Burroughs, Camus, Sartre, Hesse, Rimbaud, Miles Davis, Jackson Pollock, and Franz Kline, names a universe away from that of Max Brand.

In my junior year I got a part-time job in a bookstore and started a literary magazine. I invited my friends Dick Gallup and Michael Marsh to be co-editors, and my friend Joe Brainard to be the art editor. Dick and I wrote to writers we admired, asking them for material, and in the spring of 1959 the first issue of *The White Dove Review* appeared, a collection of poetry, prose, and art in a simple 5½-by-8½ format. The contributors to that first issue included Jack Kerouac, Paul Blackburn, and Clarence Major. Over the next year or so, four more issues appeared, with work by Allen Ginsberg, Robert Creeley, LeRoi Jones (Amiri Baraka), Ron Loewinsohn, Peter Orlovsky, Gilbert Sorrentino, and David Meltzer, as well as local writers Ted Berrigan, David Bearden, Martin Cochran, Dick, and me. My mother contributed twenty dollars toward the production cost of each issue (around ninety dollars) and bought me the saddle stapler we used for binding each issue, but my father seemed to take no notice of the venture. That is, until one day he stopped by my bedroom door and said, "You could be put in jail for publishing this." He was serious.

"What do you mean?"

"Sending obscene material through the mail."

He was referring to the use of the word *fuck* in one poem, the first time that word had appeared in *The White Dove*. Only a year before, the publisher of *Lady Chatterly's Lover* had been prosecuted for using the word *fuck*. To my knowledge, no one had ever published anything in Tulsa with *fuck* in it.

Daddy wasn't giving me legal advice, he was expressing his moral disapproval. I had heard him utter the f-word only once, the year before, to a buddy at a car lot. He used other swear words at home, with great flair, but not the f-word, not in my presence, anyway. I remember thinking, Here's a guy who breaks the law every day of his life, and he's all hot and bothered about *fuck*!

But the oddity of the larger situation dawned on me only years later: at one end of our house was the office of one of the biggest whiskey businesses in town, while at the other was the "office" of an avant-garde literary magazine. Really, though, I was simply imitating my dad: I had my office desk, I operated a cottage industry, and I pursued a project that most people would have considered bizarre. But what was truly bizarre was that Daddy was reading Beat and Black Mountain poetry.

One *White Dove* contributor, Ted Berrigan, at that time a graduate student at the University of Tulsa, thought of my father as a legendary figure, the last cowboy. A few years after *The White Dove*, when Ted and his young wife were on the lam, eluding her outraged parents, they holed up at my parents' house for a few days. Some months afterward, a man knocked on the door and asked my father if he knew a Mr. Ted Berrigan.

"Who are you?" my father asked.

"I'm a private investigator hired to locate Mr. Berrigan."

"Then get the hell off my goddamned porch."

Then, one day near the end of my senior year in high school, as I was going out the front door and Daddy was coming in, he announced grimly, "One of these days, you'll come back home and I'll be gone," meaning that he was going to leave Mother. I gave him a perplexed look and he went on past. And then I felt angry for his having transferred this emotional load onto me. Why didn't he sit me down and really talk about it? For one thing, that wasn't his style. For another, I doubt that he wanted to talk or even think about the whys and wherefores. But also, somewhere inside him, it is possible that his announced departure resonated with the fact that one day *his* father had been suddenly gone. At least Daddy was giving me some advance notice.

But it was a notice that I didn't need, for I would have been a moron not to see that the marriage was hopeless. In fact, throughout my high school years I kept asking myself why they just didn't get it over with, and start new lives free of the awful pressure of pretending that everything was okay. When it came time for me to go far away to college, I jumped at the chance to escape the emotional tension in our house. Later, when it became clear that I was never going to move back "home" (to Tulsa), I felt guilty because it meant that I was implicitly rejecting my parents—which I was, without really wanting to. But for me the only other option was to return and be torn to shreds emotionally. I didn't have the strength to contend with their feelings.

Over the years, my parents had had fights. Around the age of eight, I was awakened one night by their voices, hers tearful and his angry, as she kept badgering him—about infidelity, it turned out—and he kept warning her to shut up. As the level of intensity rose, I began to pray to God (whom I didn't believe in) to stop their arguing. Then Daddy slapped her and she burst into loud sobs. I ran into the living room crying "Stop it! Stop it!" and grabbed his leg in a feeble attempt to pull him away. He shoved me aside brusquely and ordered me back to bed. Mother took me to my bedroom, calming herself down and telling me it was all right, as Daddy slammed the front door, got into his car, and squealed away, presumably back to his girlfriend, leaving us shattered.

In such cases, his tendency was to blame—and even provoke—the victim, for he needed an excuse to become angry enough to hit Mother. She recalled one incident that took place when I was about fourteen. "One night I was getting supper ready and he set in—he always set in so he'd have an excuse to get up and leave and go meet his girlfriend—and I jumped up and he knocked me half way across the room." I slammed my hand down on the table and shouted, "I *hate* this violence!" This surprised Daddy so much that, after a moment's pause, he took a few steps and was out the door and gone. Fight or flight. When he was prevented from fighting, he fled. There was no in-between, such as discussion.

It took me many years to see the relation between my father's lying in bed as a child hearing his mother weep and my doing the same thing when my mother cried, although his childhood circumstances were far more severe than mine. His childish helplessness engendered in him a rage to fight, whereas mine led to a desire to flee from it all.

Things Fall Apart . . .   137

These scenes, and others in which I saw the flash of my father's anger, instilled in me a gut-level aversion to violent aggression. Only twice in my life have I been involved in fisticuffs, and in both instances the fracas was started by the other party, and both times I reacted by grabbing my adversary and hurling both of us to the floor and holding him there until we were separated by onlookers. At the very moment when I saw that I could inflict some serious damage on the immobilized attacker, my burst of energy switched to something akin to passive nonviolence. Seeing my attacker so vulnerable made it impossible for me to hurt him. That I have never struck a woman (typically seen by men of my generation as physically weaker) probably comes as much from this aversion as it does from my thinking that such an act is morally repugnant.

Surely there were men like me in Daddy's generation, but I saw scant evidence of them. Daddy was very much a man of his time, when the ultimate authority of the husband was the norm, and when bullying one's wife or girlfriend did not have the social stigma it has today. Our now widespread concept of "abusive relationships" didn't exist. Most of Daddy's friends slapped their wives around from time to time, just as guys did in the movies and crime novels, believing that that was what a husband had to do when the little woman got out of line. Otherwise, their wives would walk all over them, wear the pants in the family, subject them to public humiliation. No, you had to remind them who was boss.

Being boss meant having the freedom to do what you wanted and keeping the wife in line, for in the Padgett family—and in the entire society—one of the worst things that could happen to a man was to have his wife "run around on him." You couldn't let that happen. It was better to keep your wife at home with the children, and if some man made even the suggestion of a "forward" remark, to punch him out, the way Grover had knocked the flirting salesman off the front porch. Lucille said, "Wayne was jealous of everybody that looked at me. I didn't look at nobody." She knew better. Also, most men were afraid to "look at" Wayne Padgett's wife, given his knockout punch.

All three Padgett brothers were extremely jealous, partly on account of their own "running around." Bill Martin mimimizes Daddy's philandering, describing it as insignificant by the day's standards, but apparently one relationship did become rather sticky. You will recall that Daddy and Homer Gafford had been taking the Easley clan to the cleaners in poker games. Daddy was playing with fire in other ways: he was having an affair with Priscilla Easley, whose gun-toting father and husband were both whiskey customers as well.

Priscilla and her husband Griff had children roughly my age, close enough for us to play together. Our parents went out periodically for dinner and dancing. According to Mother, "Griff was a *good* dancer, and he and I could really dance together. He was a handsome man, muscular but not tall." Apparently, Griff was attractive enough to make Daddy jealous. "One night I had on a pretty red velvet dress and the prettiest high heel shoes to match it. This dress was just gorgeous, long sleeved and cut down to the waist and then kind of full. We were sitting at the table and everything was going just fine, and Griff said, 'Let's dance.' I said, 'OK.' Wayne reached over and pushed me down again and said, 'You're not gonna dance.' I said, 'I'll dance any time I want to.' He pushed me back down and took a glass of whiskey and poured it down that dress. I just got up and went on and we danced anyhow."

We children were unaware that things were beginning to boil. We went to movies and the amusement park together or played in the yard. On the Fourth of July, the two families would convene for a cookout and fireworks at Griff and Priscilla's house, which was located just outside the city limits and therefore exempt from fireworks laws. Because our fathers spent large sums on a variety of fireworks, we had quite an extravaganza.

Despite appearances in the Griffing family, all was not well there either. In fact, the handwriting was on the wall, in capital letters. And it was in my father's hand. It's hard to know when Daddy and Priscilla began their liaison, but it was well before 1959. It was perhaps after Priscilla divorced Griff that she took up with Daddy, because after the divorce she hung around our house a lot. Lucille recalled: "Every Saturday night, a bunch of us would all go dancing. Wayne just kept on fiddling around with Priscilla. He said, 'I'll dance with you and then I'll dance with Priscilla, so she won't have to just sit there.' But he wasn't fooling me none. But that's the way we'd do. She'd come home and stay all night with us."

At that point, my parents were still sharing the same bed.

One morning, when Mother returned from taking me to school, she "caught Daddy and Priscilla all loved up. They forgot to lock the back door. They were in the kitchen, and didn't hear me come in. So I run her off."

Such a life was hard for her, but, as she said, "I didn't want to give up, I wouldn't turn loose." She could not envision a future without Wayne.

In February of 1957 the whiskey business and its payoffs to policemen were rocked by a grand jury investigation. Bootlegger and payoff conspirator Bill Edwards had ratted. The grand jury handed down seventy-eight indictments for liquor, gambling, and prostitution conspiracy, reaching as high as Police and Fire Commissioner Jay Jones and Chief of Police Paul Livingston. Jones, according to a February 22, 1957, article in the *Tulsa World* was "a church-goer and announced 'dry'" who had "led successful campaigns on platforms of honesty and integrity in office" and had "maintained a strong public stand against liquor and vice." Total payoffs in Tulsa were estimated at $25,000 per month.

In January 1958, fifteen defendants were found guilty of liquor conspiracy, including Jones and Livingston, who were fined and sentenced to one year in a federal penitentiary. Mother says that both Jones and Livingston were on the take from Daddy, who somehow was not even indicted. He was leading a charmed life.

That same month, a federal grand jury probe opened in neighboring Creek County to investigate the connection between bootleggers and law enforcement officers in that county. Meanwhile, Tulsa police turned up the heat on bootleggers, grabbing 2,120 fifths of booze in the month of April alone. It was not a good time to renew the payoff system.

In the late 1950s, Daddy had made yet another move toward financial diversification. In 1956 he had sold his interest in his car lot, telling Mother he had lost money on the deal. It's equally possible that he had made a profit, but had some private use for the money—it wouldn't have been the first time he had spent money without Mother's knowledge—money he felt was his, after all. His new venture was the Sheridan Club, in partnership with two friends, Gene Downing and Bob Amos.

Tulsa's tremendous expansion to the south and east was still in the future; in the late 1950s, the club at Fifty-first Street and Sheridan was located outside the city limits, conveniently exempt from city ordinances. Coincidentally, at some point between 1935 and the late 1940s, the club

OKLAHOMA TOUGH

had been owned by none other than the ubiquitous Ned VanDeventer, the man who had run the poker game the night of Grover's death.

The club was, as one patron described it, "just an old ratty-looking gray and white building, one story. Sitting to the left of it was a garage apartment. There was a sign outside that said SHERIDAN CLUB. As you approached the building, the door was on the far right. Inside was a little foyer and then, on the right, the cash register, where Bob Amos stayed, day in and day out. That's where they kept the Cokes and ice, right there by the register, a little piece of a U-shaped bar, because all they sold there was set-ups. There were tables and chairs to the left, with a partition, with a wide opening, beyond which was a big dance floor and a jukebox. The liquor was hidden in a back room." There was also a small bedroom and a kitchen. The jukebox played a variety of country and western and pop music. While Bob handled the cash register, Daddy and Gene made sure that no customers got rowdy, and if they did, bounced them out.

One patron remembered Gene Downing well: "Wayne was good with his dukes, but that Gene, he fought Golden Gloves, kept a punching bag in the garage, worked out all the time. Indian, too. Those TU [Tulsa University] football players would get drunk—those 250-pound football players—and start throwing their weight around. Gene and Wayne would knock their heads together and throw them out of there: bang-bang-bang!"

On April 7, 1959, Daddy himself got thrown out—or, rather, voted out—of his steady profession.

That day Raymond Clark, our neighbor across the street, was sitting in his living room, when he heard the front door open. A voice asked, "Would you like to buy some tomatoes?" Door-to-door tomato vendors were common in those days.

"No," said Raymond.

"Would you like to buy some bananas?"

"Hell, no."

"Well, now that you've voted me out of business, I guess I may as well give you my last bottle."

Raymond turned and looked at the man. It was Daddy, holding out a bottle of scotch and smiling.

THINGS FALL APART . . .

Although Daddy had contributed money to the "dry" cause, he had seen the change coming. The citizens of the state of Oklahoma had finally decided to end the charade of prohibition and to legalize the sale of alcoholic beverages. As the *Tulsa World*'s lead article put it the next morning, "The people's decision also marked the end for prohibition's delivery man, the bootlegger. And finally, it appears likely to put at rest once and for all Will Rogers' remarks about Oklahoma remaining dry as long as the voters can stagger to the polls." Prohibition would continue for a few months, until the state legislature worked out the details of the new law.

But Daddy had already made up his mind. He would not descend to becoming a pint pitcher selling by the bottle after-hours, so small that federal officials would ignore him; nor would he, as some bootleggers did, turn to selling drugs, which were anathema to him. And he most certainly would not stand behind a counter all day long in a state-regulated liquor store, like a grocer. Nor would he stroll around in an automobile showroom, wearing a suit and tie and trying to convince some guy that the new Buick was the way to go. It was all too boring, too tame. No, he would have to find a more interesting way to make money. In the meantime, he would slowly wind down his whiskey business—over the course of one year, it turned out. Little did he or anyone around him realize at the time that his getting out of bootlegging was to have serious consequences for him.

But, as his little surprise for Raymond Clark shows, he himself had a sense of humor about it all. And when he cleared out his secret stash beneath Tommie's garage floor for the last time, he left one item behind on a little table: his card that read "Wayne / MA 66666." Then he cemented the floor shut. At thirty-seven, he had lost his job.

The Sheridan Club turned out to be transitional. It gave him not only an "office" and an occasionally exciting fight but also the perfect excuse to stay away from home: he was working. Well, yes and no. He was also making deals on the side, such as handling hot merchandise.

In late 1959 Daddy was seeing a girl named Pam, a friend of Gene Downing's girlfriend. The four of them spent time at Grand Lake, water-skiing behind Daddy's cabin cruiser, drinking, and partying. One person told me, "That little Pam was out there skiing topless, and in '59 that was unheard of. Wayne got her to put her top back on. They went to a bar in downtown Langley. Pam had a bathing suit on and had it unzipped in the back and you could see her butt, and the bar lady said, 'Wayne, this is not like you at all. You're gonna have to ask her to zip up her bathing suit, or get her out of here.'" Pam was wild and fun, but he was looking for something else. Like love.

By the spring of 1960, Daddy was out of the whiskey business. Most of his customers had settled their bills, except for a couple of bootleggers. I recall his telling me about one of them. Daddy had asked to be paid several times, then lost his patience. He drove to the guy's house, knocked on the door, brought out a revolver, and said, "I want my goddamned money, now!" The guy paid up.

Daddy complained so bitterly about the few welchers that he gave the impression that he had been stiffed out of huge sums, just as he had complained about losing money in the oil business and the car lot. But he lost very little at the end. Except, of course, his job.

The fact is, it had been a perfect job for him. It had been exciting, lucrative, and bold. Its success had thrived on his social and professional contacts, which he cultivated with verve and charm. It had enabled him to support his family, help the needy, loan and give money to friends, and have girlfriends on the side. And with no boss or time clock to punch, it had given him tremendous freedom: at the drop of a hat he could take off with his hunting buddies, run up to the lake with his girlfriend, join in a poker game, or drive to Joplin to socialize. His success at bootlegging had enabled him to become not only the "king" of his profession, but also, with his easy sociability, manly good looks, fearlessness, personal integrity, and generosity, an admired and, on a local level, a legendary public figure, somewhat like Pretty Boy Floyd and John Wesley Harding.

Years later, longtime *Tulsa Tribune* journalist Roger Devlin related the following anecdote in his daily column, "The Rambler":

Ah, nostalgia! Several days ago we informed you that the Little Theater was having a problem with some of its costuming for a forthcoming show, and we invited anyone who could help to phone the theater's box office—WE [*sic*] 6-6666.
    Then came a call from a Tulsa businessman.
    "Did you recognize that number when you printed it?" he asked.
    "No," we admitted. "Why?"

"Once upon a time," the businessman chuckled, "I dialed that particular phone number a lot. It practically was tattooed on the minds of countless Tulsans, and if they wanted to help a friend they'd reach into a wallet and pull out a business card with that WEbster 6-6666 printed big right in the middle.

"That was the phone number," he chuckled, "of one of Tulsa's finest, most prominent, well-publicized bootleggers."[1]

Had prohibition stayed in place, Daddy could have continued his life as a combination John Wayne-Robin Hood. But when it didn't, he turned to peripheral businesses, such as the Sheridan Club. The money wasn't nearly as good, but the place did have fringe benefits.

One of them walked into his life on October 9, 1959. She was a tall, curvaceous, dark-haired beauty, and across her face flickered the naughty-innocent look of Natalie Wood. Her name was Louise, but everybody called her Kam. She was seventeen.

14   *. . . And Get Reconfigured*

"I WALKED INTO THE SHERIDAN Club and I saw Wayne, and I thought, 'Oh my god, that's the most beautiful human being I have ever seen in my life!' I was just in awe," Kam remembered.

"As the night went on, I told my sister and my girlfriend to just go on and I'd be along later. After they left I walked up to the front to where he was bouncing and said, 'I don't have a way home, my friends ran off and left me.' He said, 'Oh, that's OK, I'll take you home when we close.' That was the beginning. He did take me home, you know, just dropped me off. And he said, 'You girls come back,' because we were definitely good for business. That's kind of what started me going out there. Then later we'd always stop and have breakfast on the way home, and then later he'd stop and pick me up on his way *to* the club. I'd go out there and stay all night with him, until four or five in the morning." Like Pam, Kam was uninhibited and fun, but unlike her, Kam was head over heels in love with Daddy.

He had already stopped sleeping with Mother. Around 1955 he had accused her of infidelity and moved into the guest bedroom. In their relationship, he made the sexual decisions. Lucille: "When he wanted to have sex, he'd just take hold of me and lead me off to the bed. He'd never say anything . . . oh, only maybe when we were having sex he might whisper little sweet nothings in my ear." She was not sexually aggressive toward him, "because you'd never know how he'd respond to it. One time I went in and started to get in bed with him, and he flipped out of it like a tornado. I had to wait until he was in the mood. He wasn't oversexed, but he wasn't undersexed. He was very normal."

In light of his experience and aggressiveness in general, he was sexually modest. "He wouldn't come out and say anything about sex. No, no, no. And you'd never see him without his clothes on. Even after a bath, he never came out naked," said Lucille.

Kam confirms his modesty: "When we first started going together, he was real bashful. He used to get pretty well loaded so he wouldn't be so bashful, sexually bashful." He even told Kam that he could count on one hand the number of women he'd slept with—an exaggeration, but by comparison with the sexual tallies of many of his friends, emotionally accurate. According to Kam, "He could be gentle, sweet, and giving, a *very* passionate person, the opposite of what friends thought (Mr. Cool)."

Life around the Sheridan Club had its comic moments, too. Kam recalls that one night during a raid, she was lying on the bed watching TV with Gene Downing's girlfriend, Sandy. The police told the two girls that they were under arrest for prostitution. Kam said, "I didn't know it at the time, but Wayne knew one of these raiding guys, and he had him go back and say that to us. As a joke! Ribbing, ribbing, all the time. Disguising his voice, calling people and teasing, the biggest tease in the world. He ribbed me from the day I met him."

He enjoyed a good time away from what had become for him the joylessness of family life. Weekends when Mother had gone fishing with her parents, he and Kam would run up to Joplin. "We had a great time in Joplin. A little after we started going up there together, his friends Bud and Treva opened up a bar, the Bar Seven Club, a beautiful bar! Before that we went to the Black Orchid, Little Bo Peep's, and Mickey Mantle's Dugout."

One night Daddy and Kam were having dinner in Wilder's Buffet, an established and AAA-approved Joplin bar-restaurant, when he revealed something shocking. He had already told her about his father's death, that is, the version that he in fact no longer believed: that Grover's "poker-playing buddies put a hose down his throat and poured acid into his stomach, then took him home and poked him in the garage window." Why had they supposedly done this? "Wayne said he was a gambler, a fighter, a scraper, a scuffler, and he beat them a lot in poker and the firemen that he worked with were just mad at him. And Wayne swore to himself that when he grew up he was gonna take revenge on these men." At dinner that night in Wilder's, he added to this tale. The following dialogue is from her memory.

"Up above us here blew off one time," he said.

"What?"

"Yeah, it used to be a gambling casino, upstairs here."

"How'd it blow off?"

"Dynamite," he said

"Is that right?"

"Yeah."

"How do you know?"

"Because I blew it off."

"Why'd you do that?"

"Because the last one of the men that was still alive that helped kill my father was up there."

"What are you saying?"

"They're all dead."

Kam stopped breathing.

Daddy bore down: "Some of them died on their own, the rest of them are *all dead*." The implication was that he had killed them.

Kam couldn't believe it, but she did. Which was exactly what he wanted. He wanted to cast himself both as the little boy who avenges his father's murder and as somebody not to be messed with. Using his childhood fantasy of revenge, he was creating his own legend, and like all good fabricators, he was using just enough truth to make it cohere emotionally.

In fact, there had been a gambling club on the floor above Wilder's. And, in fact, an explosion had rocked the club, on September 3, 1959, only a month before he and Kam had met. Approximately five sticks of dynamite had been detonated on the roof, tearing a four-foot hole in it, blowing a large section of the cornice onto the street below, shattering windows along the block, and injuring six people inside the building. But several aspects of his story don't ring true, aspects the young and dazzled Kam would not have known about. In the first place, Grover tended to lose money at cards, not win; second, it is quite unlikely that an entire group of firemen would suddenly conspire to murder one of their own, especially a loser, over a card game; third, it is hard to believe that Daddy could have found out the names of all the conspirators, tracked the living ones down, and killed them; and fourth, Daddy was not the kind of person who would endanger the lives of innocent people—the explosion occurred at 8 P.M. on a Thursday night, with the restaurant and bar below filled with customers and the street outside frequented by pedestrians. But the weakest part of his story lies in the fact that the dynamite was placed on the roof in a spot directly above the office desk of the club's owner, who was downstairs in the restaurant at the time of the blast and hence unharmed. The only fatality was that of an employee named Charles Greenwood. Let's say, despite all the reservations above, that Daddy *was* responsible for the blast. Let's say, as he did, that he killed the last of his father's murderers, Greenwood. This "murderer," then, would have been only fourteen or fifteen at the time of Grover's death, for Charles Greenwood was born in 1918. In 1933 the Tulsa fire department did not have a fifteen-year-old poker-playing boy murderer in its employ.

It is quite possible, though, that Daddy knew who *was* behind the blast, and knew that the culprit or culprits would never be discovered. A grand jury investigation two months after the incident had turned up nothing. Hence, Kam would never know the truth. Claiming to have been responsible for an unsolved crime was a ploy he would use more than once: it was an easy way to build up an intimidating reputation without any real risk of prosecution, since he hadn't committed the crime.

Later Kam asked him, "Did you do that because you loved your father so much?" and he replied, "He wasn't a father to us. He had a nice car and took us places once in a while, but that's about all." Daddy told her he just didn't care about him. He was still unwilling to think about the ramifications of his father's suicide. Instead, he "just didn't care about him."

Had Grover been alive at this point, he might have been able to steer Wayne in a new direction, as Daddy began casting about for new sources of income.

His first move was to sell his one-third interest in the Sheridan Club, around the end of 1960. It's possible that he put the proceeds into Padgett and Stone Investment Company, which he formed in early 1961 with his friend Fred Stone. As far as I know, Fred was a legitimate businessman who bought, sold, and developed real estate, which was the goal of Padgett and Stone.

It was perhaps Padgett and Stone that owned a piece of property on East Eleventh Street, part of which was serving as his brother Tommie's used-car lot. It was there that Daddy had sold my MG when I went to college in September of 1960. During the following summer he had me mow the high grass and weeds on the rest of the property, to make it presentable for the future buyer, the Midas Muffler chain. Within the next few years, Daddy acquired, both alone and in partnership with Fred Stone, property all around town, as well as up at Grand Lake. In most of these acquisitions, of course, the money was going out, not coming in.

A more immediate source of income was the increasing amounts of stolen property he fenced for some of his shadier associates, many of whom he had known through the whiskey business. When prohibition in Oklahoma was repealed, some bootleggers switched to burglary, robbery, and insurance arson. The crime rate in Tulsa soared: from 1959 to 1960 the property loss doubled. It was similar to what had happened when national Prohibition was repealed in 1933. Organized crime's two main sources of income had been booze and gambling, but when the former dried up, the Mob moved into drug dealing, prostitution, loan-sharking, hijacking, etc. Daddy's shift followed a similar pattern.

One summer in the very early 1960s, I came back to Tulsa from college and found the hedge around our front yard gone. My parents had planted it when we first moved into the house, and over the years had kept it neatly trimmed. What had happened? "Your daddy pulled it up," Mother explained, many years later. He was trying to find some jewelry that his friend Pete Bishop and accomplices had burgled from Oertle's, a Tulsa discount store. Daddy, who was the jewelry fence for the job, remembered burying the loot under the hedge, but he forgot exactly where. Using a winch truck, he pulled up half the hedge before he found it, so he went ahead and pulled up the rest.

Somehow Daddy got the idea to go into yet another line of work. For many years he had associated with criminals, policemen, lawyers, and

OKLAHOMA TOUGH

judges, and he had loaned money (at no interest for friends, at shark rates for others). Why not combine his involvement with the legal system and his willingness to loan money? Thus, on May 21, 1961, he went into the bail bonds business.

Making bond seemed like an easy way to make money. It mimicked the way Daddy thought that slick businessmen operate: by having money, you make money. He expected to do very little actual work, because with his reputation few of his clients were going to risk jumping bail. But, as I described in a rather jolly letter (October 31, 1961) to a friend, one client did:

> A fellow who had my father post bond for him skipped out of town. My father, with his usual adroitness, pursued in green Chevrolet up to Collinsville, where the culprit had taken refuge. Ha ha! Vain man, to think he could escape the wrath of Wayne. Wayne, after locating the fiend, demanded that he open the door, to which the demon replied, 'Not by the hair of my chinnychinchin.' So Wayne proceeded to kick the door in, manacle the quivering escapee, and stuff the poor man in the trunk of the car for the whole trip back to Tulsa.

Knowing the Tulsa underworld inside and out helped his business, but making bond was not always clean. Some of his cash-poor clients paid him in "merchandise." According to Kam, "he started befriending the real crooks, running around with extremely tough people. He was a real closed-mouth person and they all trusted him with their lives." As we shall see later, going into bail bonds turned out to be a very bad move.

Throughout everything, Daddy continued to be a dutiful son, dropping by to see his mother almost every day. He helped keep her home and car in good repair. Behind her old garage he built a larger one, in which he stored tires, furniture, and other large objects. When not in town, he phoned to check on her.

He also continued to help his many friends and relatives. If one of them needed something, he supplied it.

In the spring of 1962, I wrote my parents to say that I was thinking of dropping out of Columbia. On April 26, Daddy wrote me one of his rare letters:

Dear Son,

Received your letter this evening. Weather here couldn't be better. Everyone here is fine.

Stick the school out if you figure it best—if not call me and I will come after you anytime you say. If you need anything—let me know.

After you grow older—you will get really tired. If you don't look it outside you will sure feel it inside.

When you come home—I'll send you to Mexico. Until then—take care of yourself.

Love,
WP

Fortunately, I managed to complete my sophomore year. Daddy bragged to his friends that not only was his son in college, he was at Columbia, an Ivy League school. Over the years, many of them have told me: "Your daddy was really proud of you."

Now he was even driving to New York to get me. I don't know why he didn't just send a plane ticket. At the end of school the previous year, Mother had driven to New York to pick me up. Maybe now it was his turn. Maybe he felt guilty about not contributing to my weekly allowance (my mother had gotten a job as a cafeteria cook and was sending me an allowance). Maybe he was concerned about my morale or my health (my lung had spontaneously collapsed that spring). Or maybe he was curious about New York, a city I don't think he had ever visited.

He arrived with my cousin Jimmy Pilkington. Two years older than I, Jimmy was the son of Wes and Gladys (Happy) Pilkington, my mother's uncle and aunt. I had played with Jimmy and his little brother Johnny all during my childhood. Jimmy, now a student at the University of Tulsa, was free for the summer. Because of a strained lower back, Daddy enlisted Jimmy's aid, and the two of them drove nonstop from Tulsa to New York, 1,350 miles.

I don't recall where Jimmy slept that night, but I do remember offering Daddy my room, on 115th Street near Broadway. It had a single bed, so I told him I would make myself a pallet. Daddy adamantly refused. I offered to find him a hotel room nearby, but he refused it as well.

"But where will you sleep?" I asked.

"In the car."

"You mean all night? What if someone tries to break into your car? There are some weird people in New York."

"Let 'em try," he said, taking a small knife from his pocket.

"How could you hurt anybody with *that*?" I asked, referring to the two-inch blade.

"You don't have to hurt 'em. All you have to do is drag it once across their forehead. It cuts some big veins, and the blood pours down in their eyes and blinds them. Then I wouldn't have any trouble at all."

I was taken aback by this violent image. Wouldn't it have been easier just to get a room? And sleeping in the back seat of the car? No wonder his back hurt! But I knew it was pointless trying to persuade him to do otherwise.

Besides, he was quite congenial about giving two friends, Pat Mitchell and Joe Brainard, a lift back to Tulsa. He had known both there. Pat had become my girlfriend, and Joe and I had left Tulsa together on the train to go east to art school and college, respectively. Daddy, Jimmy, Pat, and I drove down to the Lower East Side to pick up Joe, then we stopped at a gas station on Bowery. A drunken bum staggered up, stopped, extended his arms and hands, and slowly rotated his body from the waist, shouting, "Da-da-da-da-da-da-da-da! I'm John Dillinger! Da-da-da-da-da-da-da!" Daddy found this very amusing. Years later he would smile at me out of the blue and make that machine-gun noise, "Da-da-da-da, I'm John Dillinger!"

The five of us headed for Tulsa, nonstop as usual. My driving scared both Jimmy and Daddy—unusual in light of the latter's driving record—so only ten miles into New Jersey I was demoted to the back seat with Pat and Joe. Throughout the trip, Jimmy was unusually animated, drumming out syncopated rhythms on the dashboard and steering wheel as we zoomed along. Later I learned that he had taken "pep pills" to stay alert, pills that my father had gotten for him. Apparently at that time Daddy didn't consider benzedrine to be a drug. For him it was what truck drivers took to stay awake, a stronger version of No-Doze. The real amphetamine wave hadn't quite yet broken over Tulsa. In any event, Daddy didn't take any of those pills. Years later, he told me that he had in fact never taken a pep pill or any other kind of illicit drug, a claim that everyone who knew him has confirmed.

Joe, using a style that is a cross between Dostoyevski and Gertrude Stein, wrote a semifictionalized account of that trip. Here is an excerpt:

Back in Tulsa again, by way of free ride from Ron's father: Ron being a Columbia University student, also poet, and Ron's father being a John Wayne with $80 cowboy boots. I wear desert boots. Pat usually wears very basic black flats, tho she looks better in high heels. They complement her legs. Very nice. Yes, Pat too made the big move back to Tulsa. The three stooges make the big move back to Tulsa. The three fuckado's make the big move back to Tulsa. The big move back to Tulsa was made by Pat, Ron, and myself.

The trip back was as normal as possible considering John Wayne drove (in $80 cowboy boots) and we, the three "Tulsans in New York" were his passengers.

"Lunch," Ron said again to his father with $80 cowboy boots driving like a madman directly aiming at Tulsa with serious conviction of direction. Yes, Ron's father was anxious to get home, home to Tulsa. Home to space and lightness, white square gas stations and shining car lots. Ron's father is obviously from Oklahoma. We Marx Brothers minus one are obviously only flounderers. Floundering because we are neither New Yorkers nor Oklahomans.

It was my turn to be by the window: goody. It was open, with my arm and head stuck out, and the wind stinging my face making it even harder to breathe. I sang louder, but no one could hear me: the wind blew the volume back down vibratingly into my throat. I sang the worst songs in the world not knowing why; not knowing why I sang the worstest songs in the world: "The Tennessee Waltz," "Tell Me Why," "Dancing Matilda," and "The Thing," Others too, yes, many others. And more others. Many many etc.'s.

We slept. Ron's father drove. We smelled the dry grass: bad at first then heaven. We entered Tulsa. Ugh!

"Ugh! Ugh!!" we sang, "Ugh! Ugh!" as we entered Tulsa. Ugh! John Wayne smiled and we three sang "Ugh! Ugh!"

An indescribable farce began, simply indescribable, quite simply unbelievable. A farce which could only possibly occur between a woman and two men, a girl and two boys, in a car driven by John Wayne wearing $80 cowboy boots driving from New York to Tulsa, Tulsa, Oklahoma.

We sang "Oklahoma."

I stayed in Tulsa for several weeks, until two classmates from Columbia arrived. One of them had shoulder-length hair and wore an overcoat day and night. He seemed fascinated by our lawnmower, going so far as to mow the lawn, wearing his overcoat, in summer! I was relieved that Daddy didn't witness this event. In any case, after a couple of weeks in Mexico with my classmates, I returned to Tulsa, where I spent a lot of time out driving around or seeing old friends. I didn't see much of Daddy. He was still living at home, though in fact he spent little time there. It had become a place for him to sleep, if even that. He preferred the company of his girlfriend.

Kam's real name was Louise May Thompson. She was born on February 22, 1942 (four months before me), in the little town of Okemah, Oklahoma, about fifty miles south of Tulsa. She grew up on a farm outside Okemah, with her father, mother, three sisters, and two brothers. Her father kept cows and horses, but he also worked as an oilfield pumper and an operator of heavy-duty construction equipment, mainly around Okemah. Having entered first grade at the age of five, Kam was able to graduate from high school in 1959. Shortly thereafter, she accepted her sister Gen's invitation to move to Tulsa.

Kam moved in with Gen and got a clerical job. It was only five months later that she walked into the Sheridan Club one night and saw Daddy, "the most beautiful human being I had ever seen." After they started going together, he set her up: "Wayne gave me the money to get an apartment. He went to a friend of his that had a warehouse and he bought, all in one trip, everything a living human needed for a house. I'm talking sheets, towels, shower curtains, pots and pans, coffee pot, silverware, set of dishes, everything. I was eighteen then, his 'sweetie.' He didn't want me to work, so I could run around with him."

By 1962 she had moved again, this time to a mobile home he bought for her.

Kam recalled: "We had so many blissful times. Mmm. He just amazed you. At times, you know, an absolutely magnificent human being. When you're desperately and hopelessly in love with someone, it's almost like a fairy tale. You just idolize each other.

"Wayne bought a cabin and 410 acres up at the Lake. He and I used to build a big fire in the fireplace and pull the bed over by it, because that was the only heat the cabin had, and we'd be up there in the winter. We'd go hunting in the woods back behind it. It was like a dream. Beautiful. Of course he was still married, ha ha! Which made it better! Added spice.

"He took me around his friends up at Grand Lake, and they had been friends with Wayne *and* Lucille, but they all kept their mouths shut. People just didn't tell anybody anything about Wayne's business."

His jealousy surfaced early in the relationship. Kam confirmed: "When we'd go out, if someone would walk by and look at me—and they looked at me day in and day out—he'd say, 'Have you been with that son of a bitch?' So I watched the carpet when we went out to clubs, then I looked at the ashtrays, but I dared not raise my eyes up and look at another human being."

Weekends, they ran up to Joplin to go to clubs, over to Hot Springs for the horse races, and even out to Las Vegas, where an old friend of Daddy's was working as a casino pit boss. Kam was a fun-loving, tall, and attractive young girl, and he was a big, tough, handsome guy with a bankroll. And, as Kam put it, "He had charisma. Some people have it, and some people couldn't buy it. He had it." The two of them must have turned heads every time they walked into a room.

Both liked going to clubs, but whose idea was it for her to move to such a club mecca as Las Vegas?

According to Kam, both of them liked the idea. "He was still married. I was going to move out to Vegas and get a job serving cocktails, and later he was going to get a divorce and move out there."

He felt he couldn't get a divorce until I was on my own, and he made that clear to Kam from early on. Kam told me: "Wayne and I had been going together for three months. He told me he had a son, in his last year of high school. He said, 'I don't really have a marriage. It's been over for a long time. It's nothing that you're breaking up. But I was raised without a father and I'm going to stay [married] until my boy's out of school.'" Unaware of all this, I blithely went off to college for four years, thereby postponing the date of my father's projected break until 1964. If Kam wanted to marry him, she would have to wait.

In the meantime, there was Las Vegas. But why Vegas? Because, Kam said, "He knew some people out there and it was away from Tulsa and he loved it where the money was."

OKLAHOMA TOUGH

The "away from Tulsa" is significant here, for it is in the early 1960s that Daddy began to think about moving away for good. He wanted a fresh start. He later told me that he was tired of Tulsa.

Kam continued: "So I moved out to Las Vegas. I lived two doors down from Harvey Pugh and his wife Beulah Lee. I knew them real well. Wayne sent me to them."

Harvey was a short, baggy man with a world-weary face and a limp, the result of smashing his car into a culvert at high speed one night.

"In Tulsa I had been working for a dentist. His brother told me to look up Mitch DeWood, the musical director at the Flamingo," Kam said. "So the day after I got to Vegas I went to the Flamingo and looked up Mitch DeWood. I thought he might help me get a job as a cocktail waitress—I'd just turned 21. He asked me, 'Do you dance?' I said, 'Of course.' He said, 'I'm having auditions this afternoon. Stick around.' Before it was all over, I had a job in the revue. I called Wayne in Tulsa and told him all about it. He said, 'Go ahead, nobody there knows you.' I went ahead and was having the time of my life.

"Wayne came out to see me. Our show was in the lounge. He came in and sat down. The music started. I was the center girl because I was the tallest, and I came spinning out and took the position. He looked up there, and the next girl came out, and pretty soon he turned his barstool completely around, with his back to me, for about thirty seconds, then got up and walked out and went into the casino. That night, after we got back to the apartment, it was 'I don't want you doing that. I want you to come back.' I said, 'No, I'm not going to. You're married, you go home.' He got mad, jumped in his car and drove back [to Tulsa], but he called me every night from the Cheyenne Club. Every night. That's when they had the string on the phone."

Using a piece of string, Daddy was able to rig pay phones so that he could call anywhere for only a nickel.

Finally Kam did move back, probably in the summer or fall of 1963.

In June 1963, having finished my junior year of college, I came back to Tulsa with my girlfriend, Pat Mitchell. We had tried to get married in New York a few weeks earlier, but the waiting period conflicted with our planned return to Tulsa for the summer. Finally my mother said to us, "Why don't you just take the car and drive up to Miami and get married." Miami, Oklahoma, is a small town with no waiting period. Pat and I were married there on June 21 by a justice of the peace, with no family in attendance. In that sense it was like my parents' wedding. I don't remember where my father was at the time, but I do remember that afterward his attitude toward me changed. He became more relaxed, less critical and controlling. I in turn relaxed around him, and we began to get along better than we had in years. My marriage was one more step toward my independence from the family, and hence a step toward his freedom from obligation to me and the marriage that had been prompted by my conception.

Kam moved to a one-bedroom house at Ninth and Sheridan, a property of Padgett and Stone Investment Company. For all practical purposes, Daddy was living there too.

At the same time, he bought Mother a new 1964 Chevrolet. Their daily lives had grown further apart, and she still knew nothing about Kam.

About a year later, Mother got a call from her aunt Pearl, who told her that she had seen Wayne in a car with a beautiful young girl. Mother explained it away. He was just giving someone a ride. Over the years she had suspected infidelity and she knew things weren't right at home, but she had been holding on, hoping things would get better. But what if they didn't? Finally there was an opening in the denial she had surrounded herself with. She gave in and called Henry Noble.

Henry was one of Daddy's old friends, the middle-aged, mild-mannered owner of The Rustic Inn, where Daddy regularly cleaned out suckers in a poker game. Henry's ability to remain calm and to wield a small utility chain enabled him to fend off even his most violent patrons, but when Mother asked him pointblank about Daddy and this girl, Henry was unable to lie to her, partly because he liked her and saw her as an innocent victim. He told her who the girl was and where she lived. Mother got in the car and drove to Ninth and Sheridan.

Kam remembered it well. "The funny thing about it—and I know that she knew it—Wayne was there with me, and when he saw Lucille coming up to the door, he scooted back to the bathroom. She knocked on the door. I opened it and she said, 'Are you Kam?' I said yes. She said, 'I'm Lucille, Wayne's wife.' I said, 'Do you want to come in?' She said yes. I made us a cup of coffee and we went in the living room and sat down. He evidently bumped something or made some noise, and she asked me if Wayne was there and I said no. His boots were sitting right there on the floor. She started to cry and said, 'That's a very familiar sight to me.' I felt so sorry for her, I really did.

"We sat there and drank a whole pot of coffee. We made him stay in that closet a long time." Tough guy Wayne Padgett, the guy who was willing to go up against any man in town, wasn't brave enough to be in the same room with his wife and mistress.

Kam continued: "Lucille said, 'I see how beautiful you are, and I see now I'll never get him back.' I was twenty years younger than she was, and it made me feel even worse. I felt like a homewrecker. So I told her, 'I'll get in my car and leave, and if you can get him back, I promise you I'll back off out of the picture.'" Mother left. Kam packed her clothes and drove away.

Mother returned that evening and confronted Daddy straightway, demanding a divorce, which in fact was the last thing she wanted. In an extremely rare and perhaps unique display of guilt, he began to weep. He offered to come back to her. Perhaps Mother finally admitted to herself that Kam wasn't really the problem and that their marriage had been finished for a long time. After all, they hadn't slept together for years. They hadn't even been able to talk about their relationship, only to argue. Now the whole situation was finally out in the open. In a fit of pride, disorientation, and pain, she refused his offer.

Kam related: "I called in a few months, and he answered the phone, at my place. He said, 'Where are you?' 'Right now I'm in Buffalo, New York,' and he said, 'Why don't you come home? Nothing's changed. I'm right here. Come home.' I came back, and that was the end of that."

Well, not quite. Lucille recalled: "I went back and told him I was ready to go get a divorce. That was on a Monday, February 17, 1965. I told him, 'Pick me up in the morning, we'll go to John's [John Cochrane, their lawyer].'" At that time, Cochrane was a friend who handled our family's legal affairs, civil and criminal.

Daddy objected to infidelity as the grounds for their divorce, so Mother agreed to "incompatability." But because her church—she had started attending her parents' church, the Church of Christ—doesn't recognize incompatability, and thus wouldn't recognize any future marriage of hers, Daddy said that if it came up in the future, he would testify to them that the grounds really had been infidelity. Mother generously agreed to this arrangement.

Two days later, on February 19, 1965, the divorce decree was made. Lucille said, "I went home sick, about as low as anybody can ever get. Depressed. Wouldn't open the curtains, wouldn't eat, wouldn't sleep. I stopped working." Since late 1962 she had been employed as a cook in the DX-Sun Oil Company cafeteria in downtown Tulsa, where her mother was chief pastry cook. Now she was having a nervous breakdown.

The divorce settlement awarded Mother four pieces of property: our house on East Fourth Street, a piece of rental property on North Peoria, two lots on Admiral near Peoria with a garage and body shop, and two lots out near Mingo. There was no provision for alimony.

Daddy received the one-half interest in the two parcels of land at Ninth and Sheridan that he co-owned with Fred Stone.

Daddy later told me he gave her two-thirds of everything. When Mother sold her property a few years after the divorce, the total yield was $47,000. According to Kam, Daddy had squirreled away $30,000 in cash, which, with his interest in the two other properties, represents noticeably more than one-third of the total assets. There was also his cabin and lake property, which he quietly liquidated, probably the very month of the divorce. Had Daddy been confronted with the truth of these numbers, he doubtless would have rationalized his action by asserting that our family assets were almost exclusively the result of his ingenuity and risky work. When caught in a deceitful act, he always had a justification that made him more comfortable with himself. In fact, he would become hotly self-righteous.

In any event, Mother made an obvious mistake in allowing Daddy's lawyer to represent both her and Daddy—John Cochrane knew which side of *his* bread was buttered—but she was too numb to feel aggressive or vindictive.

The divorce was granted on March 29.

I was in New York, practicing my own denial of their situation, preferring that neither of them discuss it with me. I kept telling myself that the divorce was a good idea, which, given the ciurcumstances, it was. But I used that facile thought to forestall any deeper probing of the subject, and I was totally insensitive to my mother's feelings.

Years later, she told me, "It boils down to one thing. Wayne was wild and he was just too young to be tied down. That was where the whole problem started." He had been more or less coerced into marriage, albeit with a girl he was sweet on. On the other hand, he had been married to her for more than twenty-three years, and they had been through a lot together, including some very good times. He had come of age as her husband and the father of her child. And whether or not it was his responsibility to be "around" until I got out of school, as he told Kam, he had never asked for a divorce. On some level, he felt guilty about his betrayal and virtual abandonment of Mother, but it was a guilt he could not face. Instead, it made him angry, and he blamed *her* for alienating *him*. He claimed that she spent all her free time with her relatives and that she lavished *his* money on them, buying them expensive furniture and clothes: a textbook case of projection, since it was a perfect description of his own behavior toward his mistress. But even with all his confused anger, recrimination, and bitterness, he still had, as we shall see, a soft spot for Lucille.

15 *New Wife, New Life*

With the divorce, Daddy was finally free, right? Not quite, for his ties to Lucille ran deeper than he had thought. According to her, "He was living out there with Kam, but he'd come over every morning, even after we were divorced, and I'd cook him breakfast."

This raises a number of questions. Why, after the way he had treated her, did she allow such visits? Was he compelled by his abhorrence of abandonment? Did he need to maintain his macho view of himself as a man with two women? Was he having second thoughts about the divorce or about Kam? Did he find being divorced somewhat disorienting? Did he unconsciously fear that he was losing an important part of his past? Was he trying to apologize to Mother or to appease his guilt? Did he think he still owed her something? Did he feel sorry for her? Did he have a hidden sentimental streak? Whatever the cause, it certainly wasn't sexual.

Or *was* it, partly, in some strange way? Lucille recalled: "One night, he knocked on the back door, came in, and wanted to go to bed with me. I wouldn't. He said, 'I've just got to go to bed with you one more time. You're the best woman I was ever in bed with in my life.' I said, 'That's just too bad, you waited too long.'" He had shown no sexual attraction for her for years, but this final proposition shows that this connection to her had not been entirely severed by the divorce.

For years Daddy had been postponing his marriage to Kam, saying that he had to wait until I was out of school. I don't know what excuse he used after I graduated from college, but when I was awarded a fellowship for study in France, to begin in September of 1965, he recycled his old line. Kam pointed out that I was as old as she was, that I was married and perfectly able to take care of myself. Besides, her parents were wondering why she and Wayne had been dating for six years if they weren't "serious." She put her foot down, and on September 16, 1965, five days before my wife and I sailed for France, they finally got married, in a small civil ceremony, in Lawndale, California, not far from the Los Angeles International Airport.

When Kam's father died that year, Daddy bought a house and asked her mother to live there free of rent, as long as she wanted. He quickly became the father figure among Kam's relatives.

At some point Daddy had made the acquaintance of Jack McBride, a thief and, it was rumored, an occasional hit man. Based in Tulsa, where his wife owned a bar, he moved around the West and Midwest, carrying out robberies set up by associates in their various locales.

It was Jack who introduced Daddy to Pete James, around 1964. Jack brought Daddy into Pete's restaurant, The Royal Peso, in Inglewood, California, and the two of them, roughly the same age, hit it off right away. Pete's people were from Missouri. His dad had come down to work on a farm in northeastern Oklahoma, where Pete then went to school, through the eighth grade. Over the years, Pete's business ventures—Peter James Enterprises, with corporate offices in Compton, California—had proved successful in real estate, land development, oil leases, and restaurants. It is said that Pete also liked to play high-stakes poker, and that he brought Daddy into some games around L.A. In general, Pete was a shrewd and determined fellow.

According to Pete, he and Daddy never had any formal business dealings together. Hearing early on of Daddy's falling out with friends, Pete decided not to mix friendship and business.

But Pete thought Wayne was wonderful to be around. According to him, Wayne, with a heart "as big as a bucket," would come to people's rescue time and again. The two of them were like brothers. Pete even rented the little duplex apartment at Verna's for about three years, during which time he was going back and forth between Tulsa and L.A. He trusted Daddy, but he was careful not to get on Daddy's "bad side." Daddy could be quite intimidating when he wanted to, especially when it was useful. The way people speak about this power of his reminds me of the way he looked at me when I had misbehaved as a child. You felt as if you were facing Doom. Pete was later to be on the receiving end of this look.

For the next couple of years, Daddy and Kam spent a lot of time out west. The geographical change marked a change in the tone of his criminality. He had begun a new life as a full-time crook on a more extensive scale.

One major venture was a phone scam. Beginning in 1965, he and Jack McBride traveled up and down the West Coast and across New Mexico and Arizona. McBride had gotten hold of special keys that enabled them to empty the coin boxes of pay phones. But you not only had to open the box, you also had to manipulate something inside to release the coins. The two of them emptied many, many phones, laundering the change in Las Vegas and converting it to greenbacks.

Back in early 1963, the FBI had opened a file on one Wayne Padgett as part of an anti-racketeering investigation. Their information was minimal: initially they didn't even know his correct address. But over the next twelve years, the FBI amassed 1,300 pages of files on him, with information provided mostly by informants and law enforcement officials conducting surveillance. On July 14, 1964, the agency approached Daddy directly, getting nowhere, of course. The first three years of files mention investigations of burglary, bank burglary, fencing, and a hotel robbery. The files also mention that Padgett openly speeds through Tulsa and that he supposedly owns a brothel in Georgia, and go on to discuss his financial and marital status. A July 29, 1965, file states that "the Sheriff's Office at Tulsa, Oklahoma, has been working with a view of developing any type of prosecutable case against Padgett." From informants, Tulsa police know that Daddy has been fencing and probably masterminding a local burglary ring, but they have no evidence. These local violations were of minor interest to the FBI.

In the spring of 1965, Daddy gave me a call in New York.

"I need your help," he said.

"What is it?"

"I've got some stamps and I need to find out what they're worth."

"Why don't you get them appraised?"

"Well, I don't want to. I'll just send them to you."

"What kind of stamps are they?"

"They're from foreign countries."

"Daddy, let me ask you something. What are you doing with foreign stamps?"

"Oh, a guy owed me some money." This was his standard non-answer.

A few days later a large parcel arrived, with mint sheets of stamps from various Southeast Asian countries and the United Arab Republic. I remember one group that reproduced the head of an Asian king in row after row, in different denominations and colors. These were definitely not of the "One Hundred Stamps for 99 Cents" grab-bag variety you used to see advertised in comic books.

My wife and I took a selection to a stamp dealer, who looked at them carefully, then raised his eyes to mine.

"Where did you get these stamps?" he asked evenly.

"From my grandfather. He died not long ago and left them to me. I have no idea of what they're worth."

"Uh huh," said the dealer, lowering his gaze to the stamps. "I'll tell you what. My strong suggestion is that you not offer these to any other dealers."

He handed them back to me.

"Why not? They're in perfect shape," I said, controlling my voice.

"I'd just suggest that you not try to sell them to a dealer."

I had no choice but to continue to play innocent.

"Oh, you mean I won't get much for them. I see. OK, maybe I'll just keep them. Thanks for your advice."

My wife and I retreated as decorously as possible. We never did find out why the dealer suspected they were hot. Perhaps, like art dealers, stamp dealers subscribed to a theft-and-counterfeit bulletin that alerted them to philatelic thefts and scams.

Anyway, we sent the rest back to Daddy, withholding a few sheets for our artist friend Joe Brainard, who incorporated them into his collages that were sold a few years later in a show of his work in New York.

In early January of 1966, the Oklahoma City FBI field officers did hear something that must have caused them to prick up their ears. An informant told them that Wayne and a colleague had been burglarizing telephone coin boxes in California. On January 4, the San Diego Police Department had phoned the Sapulpa, Oklahoma, Police Department to discuss Wayne Padgett, "kingpin of telephone coin box thefts." Apparently, he had returned from the West Coast to Tulsa in November 1965, then gone back to the Coast in January, then returned to Tulsa sometime after February 15.

On April 5, two of "Padgett's associates" were arrested in San Jose, California, and charged with burglarizing telephone coin boxes. The two suspects, employees of West Coast Shows, a carnival outfit, had $18,000 in coins on them.

A May 11 file says that Padgett and a colleague spend a lot of time at Jake's on the Shore, a restaurant near Marina del Rey, in Los Angeles County. According to Kam, they did go there, for one reason: the abalone. They also liked a restaurant in Gardena, not because of the nearby gambling, as the FBI might have surmised, but simply because of the custard, which Daddy had a weakness for.

But the FBI wasn't interested in Daddy's culinary preferences. A June 6 file notes that on May 31 a California license plate was issued to Wayne Padgett, who gave his address as 2533 Lakewood Boulevard, Long Beach. That location turned out to be the Ray Johnson Used Car Lot. Meanwhile, agents were trying to learn where Daddy and Kam had been married. One report gives Miami, Oklahoma, and another gives Las Vegas. A September 20 file estimates that $50,000 to $100,000 had been stolen from coin boxes in Los Angeles and San Diego. In October, Padgett's accomplice, who had been driving back and forth between Tulsa, southern California, and Nevada, was seen exchanging $7,000 in coins at various casinos in Reno, but Padgett himself was not there. The San Diego FBI office at first claimed to have a witness who could finger Daddy and his accomplice, but apparently the witness did not prove reliable. In the end, the FBI did not have one iota of evidence.

My wife and I had returned to Tulsa from Paris via New York in late September of 1966, living in the now vacant house on East Fourth Street. Mother had met and married C. E. Shaver, a fellow who traveled around the country setting up temporary promotions between car washes and large department and discount stores. She was on the road with him. On November 29, my son was born. We named him Wayne.

I noticed an immediate change in Daddy's attitude toward me, just as I had when I had gotten married. Daddy completely relaxed. Kam agreed: "I saw it myself. Because he said to me a thousand times, 'I don't ever worry about that boy. He's smart and he's good and he'll always take care of himself.'" From the day my son was born until the day my father died, we felt thoroughly at ease around each other.

We did argue about the American involvement in Vietnam. Daddy thought that America had every right to be there, to fight the Communists. I thought that our military presence in Vietnam was misguided and immoral. Daddy said that if he were younger he'd be proud to serve his country. I replied that I would go to prison before I served as anyone's cannon fodder. Our rather heated discussions, with no place to go, inevitably petered out. Our lack of common ground was typical of the time, even commonplace. But our political disagreements had no personal sting.

In retrospect, I wonder about Daddy's patriotism. What had formed it? His guilt over not serving in World War II must have played a part, a war that had made a deep impression on him. Late in his life, he and an East Side buddy would slowly drive up and down the streets of their old neighborhood, remembering house by house who had gone to war and not come back. He felt he owed these fellows something. At other times, his patriotism sounded like thinly veiled xenophobia, and I wonder whether or not his desire to see America shielded from outside threats wasn't an unconscious enlargement of his desire to protect his mother and brothers from menace. Of course, it is likely that he absorbed something of his civics lessons in school, as well as the patriotic surge that ran through the country during World War II. I never heard him or his friends say anything unpatriotic, and in reading about other American criminals, I've noticed that many of them were highly patriotic. What is it that prevents such people from realizing that they themselves are menaces to their own country? When Daddy argued that young men should not burn their draft cards because it was illegal, I scoffed and said, *"You're* one to talk about legality!"

"That's different."

And there it stood.

I remember the first time I talked with Daddy about Kam. He, my wife, and I were sitting in a cafe in Tulsa having coffee. I broached the delicate subject.

"What's your girlfriend's name?"

"Louise," he said quietly, "but everybody calls her Kam."

"Do you get along well with her?"

"I get along real well with her."

The first time I saw her was on November 5, 1966. She had called to ask me to come over to their house to pick up some frozen meat. I didn't know what to expect, but when I saw her I was bowled over. She was young, friendly, vivacious, and curvaceous. I think it was on a second visit, this time accompanied by my wife, that Kam put on one of her old Vegas costumes and demonstrated a belly dance, complete with Middle-Eastern music, without the slightest embarrassment. In any case, I came away from the first visit feeling elated that I did not have to dislike her, and, frankly, I was charmed.

It may have been around this time that Daddy brought up the possibility of our working together in Vegas. He gave me the lowdown on beating the house at blackjack by counting cards. If you are able to keep track of which cards have already been used from the deck, you can make a good guess as to which cards will be left when the deck gets down to the final eight or ten cards, especially if the unused ones happen to be either aces, high cards, or very low ones. Armed with this knowledge, you have an edge. Fine, but why did he need me?

"I can't play *and* keep track of all the discards at the same time. I need somebody to watch the game and keep track for me, and then give me a signal."

We ran through the deck a few times, trying sample hands. I told him that, although I didn't have a photographic memory, I could handle the general idea.

"This is legal?" I asked.

"Oh yes, but if the the casinos suspect you're doing it, they'll throw you out. So you have to go real easy."

Some months passed while he was away. I brought up the blackjack idea again. It sounded like fun, like riding atop a load of whiskey when I was a child.

"Ronnie, the casinos have gotten wise. Now they're using more than one deck and they're shuffling all the time. It's no go."

Thus ended what would have been our first caper.

But real crime was serious. The very day my son had been born, there was a knock on my father's door. The FBI report reads as follows:

> Wayne Padgett, 3819 South Jamestown, Tulsa, Oklahoma, was contacted at his residence on November 29, 1966. He appeared at the door to that residence in response to a knock, when asked if he was Wayne Padgett, he replied his name was Sam Brown. Immediately thereafter he admitted his identity.

When asked if he knew Cleo Epps, he hesitated briefly and then stated that he had "signed her bond" in September 1966, as a result of her arrest on an indictment by the federal grand jury at Tulsa, Oklahoma.

Asked about a conversation he had had with Cleo Epps, Daddy replied that he "would have to talk to Cleo before discussing that." The FBI agents then served him a subpoena to appear before the United States grand jury on December 6, 1966, to answer questions about obstruction of justice and conspiracy to commit bribery.

For many years around our house I had heard talk of Cleo Epps. (Who could forget such a name?) Daddy always spoke of her with a respect bordering on reverence. And what was that stuff about obstruction and bribery?

The *Tulsa Tribune* devoted a long article to Cleo.[1] Born on a farm between Blue Mountain and Magazine, Arkansas, she and her two brothers moved to Oklahoma in the mid-1920s. The article described her as "an intelligent woman with an innate love of children, [who] finished a college education during a time when most men and women dropped out of school without finishing the eighth grade." She became a teacher in a one-room school, got married, and then divorced her alcoholic husband.

OKLAHOMA TOUGH

"One of her former students had this to say: 'She was the most warm, helpful lady that I ever knew. She'd work with all the kids and give them all the help and love she could. She was more like a mother than a teacher . . . she really cared.'"

Cleo remarried, this time a bootlegger.

"She was always strictly against whiskey," said one of her friends. "But when her husband started selling it, she decided, To hell with it, and got in it all the way. That's the way Cleo was—she was either in or out." But she herself never drank.

For years afterward, she had a running battle with law enforcement officers, sometimes driving her own truckloads of whiskey in from Missouri. Strangely enough, one of the men who considered her a friend was Jack MacKenzie, Creek County investigator and former highway patrolman who many times arrested her.

"I never lied to her, I never mistreated her," says MacKenzie. "She respected me for that, and I respected her because even though she did wrong, she was always straight with me."

Cleo Epps was not a soft, feminine-type of woman. Big and strong, she dressed in workman's clothing—usually tattered and smeared with paint from one of her many construction projects around her home or a neighbor's house. Even in later years, she could "swing a sledge hammer better than any man," recalls a niece. "She could sit on a plough from sunup to sundown and never even look tired," says MacKenzie. "And she was always helping someone—especially if they had kids. If somebody's house would burn down, she'd load up a bunch of furniture and groceries and carry it to them."

MacKenzie went on to describe her as "a kindhearted ol' gal." She opened her doors to anyone in need, including the criminal element, who knew they could count on her for a handout, a meal, or a safe night's rest. As the *Tribune* put it, "She was a soft touch for panhandlers or persons down on their luck, easily giving without expecting anything in return."

Bobby Bluejacket, the one who as a youth had blown an adversary's head off, remembered Cleo: "The story's never been told of the hundreds of people that would come through town and who Cleo would help. Cleo was a terrific gal. I always had a great deal of respect for her."

The parallels between Cleo and Daddy are many. Nolen Bulloch, the Tulsa reporter who gave Daddy the title of King of the Bootleggers, had earlier bestowed the title of Queen on Cleo. Some years older than Daddy, she was something of a role model for him.

Cleo's only serious arrest had been for conspiracy to violate liquor laws, for which she had been sentenced, on June 14, 1966, to eighteen months imprisonment plus a $2,000 fine, followed by two years probation. Her conviction was being appealed, but now she was being investigated for obstruction of justice and conspiracy to commit bribery in that same case. Daddy was also implicated.

Between Cleo's conviction and sentencing, she had been approached by an individual from the Avalon Club, a nearby nightspot, who claimed he knew someone at the Montmartre Club who, for $5,000, could get her sentence "fixed" by going through a Tulsa attorney who was a close friend of Judge Allen E. Barrow, the magistrate in the case. Whether the judge could have been fixed or whether it was merely a shakedown to get money from Cleo has never been clear.

Cleo supplied the following information to the FBI. The initial offer of a fix was made a few days after her May 26 conviction. A man had come to see her at the Western Capri Motel, which she owned. She took him to a secluded dining room, leaving Daddy to cover the front desk. Cleo heard the proposition and declined it. The man left. Then Cleo discussed it with Daddy, who advised her that "if there was anything to the offer, she would be stupid not to go for it and that an appeal of her conviction would cost her more."

Cleo's attorney could not advise her to accept the offer, but he did confirm that an appeal would cost her more than $5,000. Having then decided to accept the offer, Cleo asked friends to loan her money, but she didn't tell them the purpose of the loan.

The man came back to the motel the next day to meet with Cleo. Daddy walked in and threw an envelope on the desk, saying that it was all he could raise on short notice and that he would have the rest before the sentencing date. Cleo argued that the money should be put in escrow, but the man pocketed the envelope, without examining the contents, and left. Daddy told Cleo it contained $2,000.

Two or three days later, another friend lent her an additional $2,000, but she refused to give it to the fixer, this time insisting on an escrow arrangement. Meanwhile, she had Daddy do some investigating to find out if the judge and others really were friends. It turned out they were. They belonged to a number of the same clubs.

Cleo saw no more of the man until after her sentencing. Having gotten nothing for her money, she repaid Daddy, using the second $2,000. The man made numerous promises to return her first $2,000. At the time of her disclosure to the FBI, the sum was still unpaid.

Cleo concluded her remarks by adding that "she and Padgett had been close friends for a number of years and had helped each other by lending one another money over the years. In this regard she advised that prior to borrowing the $2,000 from Padgett she had earlier borrowed about $23,000 from him to complete the new motel which she is now building. She advised she has been repaying Padgett $500 or $1,000 at a time and only owes him $4,000 or $5,000 at the present time."

The FBI agents who tried to interview Daddy at his home had been given the power to serve the subpoena, since, as a November 25 teletype from the Oklahoma City field office to Washington headquarters said, "Past experience disclosed that it is necessary to conduct fugitive type investigation to locate witness Padgett for interview. Padgett uncooperative with law enforcement agencies and goes into hiding after every interview."

The Tulsa Police Department's description of Daddy at this time gave his hair and eyes as gray, his height as six feet, weight as two hundred pounds, and his build as heavy. Among his marks and scars were the initials *W.P.* tattooed on his left forearm. His occupation was listed as car and real-estate dealer.

For some mysterious reason, the Tulsa County Sheriff's Office advised the FBI that it could "locate no record identifiable with Wayne Merriott Padgett in their files." Both that office and the Tulsa Police Department said the same thing about Cleo Epps. How could the King and Queen of the Bootleggers have no files in these offices? Perhaps there was no love lost between local law agencies and the FBI.

The grand jury reconvened on December 6, 1966. On that same day, an article in the *Tribune* stated that Russell Cobb, Jr., a successful oilman and son of a Tulsa police commissioner, had in fact called a probation officer to put in a good word for Cleo. He had done so because Bill Curlee, owner of Tulsa's Montmartre Club, had given him $1,000 to do so. An unnamed party had asked Curlee to help. The probation officer had notified the judge, who in turn notified the FBI and U.S. Attorney John M. Imel, and the whole thing blew open. Daddy told the *Tribune* that he had no idea why he had been subpoened, but that he resented a previous *Tribune* article that incorrectly described him as having been charged with counterfeiting and hijacking.

I was so obsessed with my one-month-old son that I paid scant attention to the investigation, which Daddy dismissed, along with the *Tribune*'s reportage, as "bullshit."

On December 8 the grand jury recessed until the following month. On January 30, U.S. Attorney Imel, who was handling the investigation, told the FBI and the Department of Justice that in his opinion a violation of the law had occurred, but that the matter was on hold pending an opinion from the Department of Justice.

On March 1, Daddy, Kam, Pat, and I drove over to Hot Springs, Arkansas, to take in the races at Oaklawn Park. Back in the 1880s, there had been seven gambling houses on Main Street alone, protected by a corrupt police force. Although illegal gambling had been closed down in 1946, it slowly crept back. Under Orval Faubus—the governor who in 1957 defied a Supreme Court order to desegregate the schools—Hot Springs was wide-open with prostitution and illegal gambling. When Winthrop Rockefeller defeated Faubus, though, the town straightened itself out, and by the late 1960s off-track betting and casino gambling were kaput.

We spent four nights there. In a letter to a friend, I wrote, in a rather jocular mood, "We're back in Tulsa again after five warm, fun days at Hot Springs, where we stayed in a great motel, called room service every five minutes, flicked ashes on the carpet, stole the towels and soap, and had a ball." Pat recalls that "we got motel rooms, and that first evening went out to dinner at a tourist showplace. I wore a fur that belonged to Kam: we had to get dolled up." Getting dressed up and going out to dinner was contrary to our spartan, artistic lifestyle, but doing it with a handsome crook and his foxy moll turned out to be fun.

The morning after our arrival, Daddy took me along to a trainer he knew, at the racing stables. The two of them chatted for a while, then got down to the nitty-gritty. "Anything going today?"

"Well, Wayne, I can tell you one thing for sure. Our horse was sick, and when we got him back on the track for a few races it was just to work him back into shape. So the odds on him have gone up. But if he's feeling good today, he'll run away with the third race."

"How'll you know if he's feeling good?"

"The jockey will know. When he first comes onto the track, if the horse is ready, the jockey will stand up in his saddle."

At the track that afternoon, Daddy and I placed a few bets just for fun, losing in the first and second races. Afterward, we moved to a spot where we could get a good view of the horses entering the track and then get to the betting windows quickly. We craned our necks. The horse in question came out onto the track, and the jockey. . . . What did he do?

"Was he standing up or what?" I asked.

"He was kind of standing up. I think."

We couldn't tell if he was standing or squatting or what, but we edged toward the windows, I toward a two-dollar window, Daddy toward a higher echelon.

I bet four dollars. I didn't like that semi-standing ambiguity. Daddy put down fifty.

The horse went off at something like twelve to one and he breezed home a winner by two lengths. Daddy and I looked at each other. Damn! The guy *had* been standing. We should have bet more. Oh well, we had won enough to place a few more bets.

Daddy also got useful tips from his contacts in Las Vegas. Al Benningfield, later Daddy's lawyer, recalled going out to Vegas with him and Johnny Eller: "When we went out there, Wayne knew everybody. Johnny and I'd shoot some craps, talk to the hookers in the lounge, this that and the other, but Wayne would disappear for an hour or two at a time. He was always: 'There's a guy I gotta talk to.' He came back once and said, 'You want to make some money? There's a horse running, Santa Anita, third race'—something like that—'and it's going to win.' Johnny put $500 on the horse and won.

"If there's that much money at stake, there's something crooked somewhere. Somebody's figured a way to pay somebody off, because there's hundreds of millions of dollars bet every weekend. People can be bought off, especially in horse racing. Let me tell you one thing Wayne told me.

He knew somebody with a quarterhorse at Ruidoso, in the All-American Futurity, who had given the guy who pushes the button to start the horses $30,000. Well, how's this guy going to control anything? He was paid $30,000 to *not* push that button unless this man's horse was facing forward in the gate. If the horse was looking around this way or that way and not ready to go, the button would not be pushed. Wayne knew the man who owned the horse."

Actually, Daddy was part owner of a horse in Hot Springs, but it didn't run while we were there. It had come down with a cough.

We rounded out our stay by taking in a few night clubs and a gambling joint, but we seemed to enjoy going to the track. The night before we left, we had a private birthday party for Daddy—his forty-fifth—in one of our rooms. Needless to say, Daddy footed the bill for the entire trip.

Near the end of March my wife, baby son, and I rented a car and drove to New York, and a month after that the U.S. attorney closed the file on Daddy in the Epps obstruction of justice case.

About a week later, Lucille's father was released from the hospital after recovering from a heart attack. But he lived less than another month. On May 21, Kam wrote me, "Your dad said that Noah's funeral was the best he has ever been to, and when he came home he sat down and wrote this poem about him:

> **To Noah**
> He was great in my eyes
> yes, although small in size
> his dry humor and wit
> always did fit
> when his face creased with a grin
> you knew he was a friend
> he loved his family right to the last
> we are all sure he had a good past
> if there's a heaven I'm sure he'll be there
> and his words will be, I'll declare
> The fishing will miss him and so will I
> time will go on til bye and bye
> goodbye my friend for this is the end
> but I know for you it will only begin.

As far as I know, this is the only poem my father ever wrote, and no matter how inept it is, the very fact that he wrote it suggests the depth of his feeling for Noah. Mother confirmed this in a letter written to me a few days later: "Your father was at the funeral and it hurt him so. He stayed at the hospital with me a lot. He really liked Noah."

Maybe it was time for a vacation.

In May of 1967 Daddy flew to Alaska in a friend's private jet for a hunting trip. It was his first visit to Alaska, which he later described to me as "the most beautiful place on earth." A newspaper photo shows the hunters and guides standing around their trophy, a two hundred-pound bear skin. Among the hunters was Jerrold Wilson, the punter for the Kansas City Chiefs. Daddy sent me a postcard, dated May 29 with an Anchorage postmark: "18,000 feet high in plane, ears popping but beautiful scenery. Why don't you ever write—like I do. Wayne P." A little witticism about his infrequent correspondence.

In Alaska he took the opportunity to visit one of Kam's brothers. On a postcard to Kam, he wrote: "Up in the clouds, honey. Love you very much. Rough air now, can't write well. Take care of everything. Don't forget the other dog. YAAIH [You are all I have.] With your brother. He says hello. Love you, Wayne."

He brought back an assortment of matchbook covers for her, from the Kansas City, Missouri, airport; the Sky Room at Boeing Field in Seattle; the Juneau Municipal Airport, from Gil's Cocktail Lounge in Seward; the Hotel Captain Hook in Anchorage; and the Glacier Park Lounge in Valdez.

On June 30, when the friend with the private jet flew to New York on a quick business trip, Daddy and Kam hitched a ride. They took a taxi from Teterboro Airport to the Manhattan apartment that my wife, son, and I had moved into, three months before. Because I had next to no money, I had rented an unfurnished, rather wrecked tenement apartment on East Thirteenth Street. I think Daddy was taken aback by my bohemian digs, but he said nothing, other than to ask where I had gotten the gigantic wooden spool that, turned on its side and painted white, was serving as a makeshift table. I had found it up the block, outside the telephone company. A photograph taken that day in our living room shows Daddy holding up his grandson and beaming.

He and Kam took Pat and me out to dinner. We walked to John's, an Italian restaurant around the block. In the back room was a very long table, in the center of which was a small mountain of candles, more or less melted together. We were seated at the only available space, at the near end of the table. At the far end I noticed two attractive young women and the actor E. G. Marshall. Daddy was suitably impressed not only that we were "having dinner with E. G. Marshall," but also that E. G. Marshall seemed to have not one, but two girls in tow. Years later when we talked on the phone, Daddy would sometimes say, "Hey, I saw your old friend E. G. Marshall on TV the other night."

We had only one bed in the apartment, so Pat and I made a pallet for ourselves in the living room. The next day Daddy and Kam went out for breakfast and took a walk over to Washington Square Park, pausing to get their pictures taken in a photo booth. Later they had lunch. It was a lovely spring day. But his friend was flying back out that night.

Before Daddy left he took me aside and told me that he had "fixed" the phone in the little bodega a few doors away. He had drilled a tiny hole in the box, and if I inserted a hatpin, did this and that in a particular sequence, I could make long distance calls for the cost of a local call. I never had a chance to avail myself of this opportunity, because shortly thereafter the phone, like all the others in the neighborhood, was replaced by a new model, as part of a general upgrading.

When Daddy and Kam got back to Tulsa, she wrote that the visit had allayed some of Daddy's worries about my living conditions. (My wife felt that they had done a creditable job of concealing their dismay at our apartment.) Kam also mentioned that Daddy, true to style, had just visited the ailing father of a friend.

My mother's marriage to C. E. Shaver had taken some bad turns. After one argument, probably in the middle of 1968, he had punched her in the face and ordered her from the car, leaving her on the highway at night outside of Fort Collins, Colorado. She told Daddy about it, and about the $10,000 of hers that C. E. had kept, probably in their mobile home.

OKLAHOMA TOUGH

One afternoon, Daddy called Mother to tell her that he and Jack McBride had tracked down C. E. They had seen him coming out of a supermarket with a woman and a child. Did she want them to kill him? Mother said most definitely not, but that she *would* like to have her money back. That night, when C. E. was out, Daddy and McBride broke into his mobile home and tore it to pieces looking for the money. They even stripped off the wall paneling. But they found nothing—or at least said so—and the wily Shaver never reappeared. By September, Mother was working at the cigar stand in a Tulsa supermarket and renting a room from her Aunt Gladys and Uncle Wesley. She had filed for divorce. I told her that if I ever saw C. E. again, I would take a baseball bat to his head.

Would Daddy have killed Shaver? "No," said Mother, "but McBride would have."

In New York, I was writing poetry and screening poetry submissions for the *Paris Review*. Back in Tulsa, Daddy was telling his friends, "Imagine. I have a son who lives in New York and is a poet!"

16   *Arizona Highways*

WHEN DADDY AND KAM HAD COME back to Tulsa from California as man and wife, they rented an apartment and then bought two houses, one on South Jamestown (the one where the FBI came knocking) and the other near the Tulsa International Airport, which they rented out. But they continued to spend a lot of time out west, so Kam's sister Joan occupied the Jamestown house.

From 1966 to 1968, Daddy was moving back and forth between Tulsa and Arizona, mainly Phoenix, Tucson, and Scottsdale, handling stolen property for Donald Sparks and Jerry James, two guys he had known back in Tulsa. He shifted some of the merchandise in Tucson through a local bondsman, the rest in Tulsa or in Kansas City's "Italian" neighborhood. He was probably fencing for Tulsa associates, as well.

According to Kam, Don Sparks was "a cowboy who rode rodeo, a tobacco-chewing, quiet guy, a country boy all the way, a little guy, but muscular. Jerry James was a great big guy, overweight and hyper, a high-rolling go-getter. They were completely the opposite. To us they were real friendly and fun to be around."

To the FBI, Sparks and James were less amusing. In fact, they were two of the Ten Most Wanted men in America. In 1967, Daddy and Kam had lived a few doors down from them in a Scottsdale apartment complex, where you could rent by the day, week, or month. Sparks and James needed to keep moving around. As a precaution, Daddy rented his apartment under the name of Wayne Johnston. It was there that Kam had become pregnant, in August of 1967. The conception was accidental, as mine had been.

Sparks and James, along with wife, Nell, and girlfriend, Joan, respectively, moved on to Tucson. Daddy and Kam returned to Tulsa, then went back out to see the two couples. Kam and Wayne were staying at the James's, a ranch-style stucco house with a front yard, cactus, and sliding glass doors leading to a backyard patio—a typical southwestern house, located at the end of a dead-end street, with desert beyond. Under the alias of Mr. and Mrs. J. W. Jones, Jerry and Joan had been living there for three months. It was January 23, 1968.

Daddy had stashed his Cadillac at a shopping mall, but had forgotten to unload his clean shirts from the trunk. Jerry drove him back to the mall to retrieve them. The women set about cleaning house.

Kam was shaking a rug outside the patio door when a swarm of men crashed in from every direction and one of them, holding a shotgun, shouted, "Freeze!" She froze for a moment, then took a step.

"I said *freeze!*" the man growled.

"Well, I'm putting a robe on," Kam insisted. With her silk pyjamas outlining her pregnancy, she felt vulnerable before a stranger.

The agent lifted the cushion out of an armchair, making sure it concealed no weapons, and told her to sit down. He himself turned a dining room chair around and sat on it, facing her, never taking his eyes off her. No one had said anything about a search warrant, but she could hear the tank covers rattling on the toilets.

The agent said, "What's your name?"

"I have nothing to say to you without an attorney."

"Not even your name? You've been well schooled," he said.

She fell silent as the searching continued. Finally the agent said, "Well, Mrs. Padgett, I thought I'd let you know they have your husband locked up downtown, if you want to call a bondsman."

According to FBI records, as Bureau agents had moved in to surround Jerry James's house, other agents saw a big white Cadillac Eldorado with two occupants leaving the area:

> Occupants of vehicle observed Bureau cars and immediately took off at a high rate of speed. Pursuit immediately instituted by Bureau Agents covering escape routes, while other Agents went to the house and arrested [blacked out, but probably Joan Taylor] who identified herself as [blacked out] when Agents entered the house. Pursuit at high rates of speed ensued in areas of highway construction, congested school areas, and heavy traffic toward outskirts of the city. Bureau cars gave chase at speeds of up to 95 miles per hour, but were outdistanced by the Cadillac and Cadillac observed by Bureau cars traveling in opposite direction on a different road. Agents' effort to stop this vehicle by signaling unsuccessful, so vehicle was rammed by Bureau car to prevent escape and further high speed chase through town.
>
> Driver of the vehicle identified as Wayne Merriott Padgett, who refused to furnish any information other than his name. Padgett refused to identify other occupant of vehicle or whereabouts at moment, and denied knowing [blacked out, but probably Sparks or James]. Since Padgett was driving vehicle purchased by [blacked out, but probably James] and had just left the [blacked out, but probably James] residence, he was arrested for harboring.

The January 24 *Arizona Daily Star* front-page photo of Daddy, as well as his subsequent mug shots, show him wearing a windbreaker with no shirt beneath. He had never gotten to the clean shirts in the trunk of his car. The look on his face is the same as one sees in the mug shots of veteran criminals, not that of the cocky kid in the mug shot taken twenty-seven years before in Houston. Or is it simply the face of a forty-seven-year-old man who had left the house without a comb, who had removed his upper plate, and who had been through a massive and draining adrenalin surge?

When Daddy and Jerry James had left the house, James was driving. Momentarily losing the feds outside of town, the two switched seats without stopping the car—quite a feat, considering the size of both men—and, as Daddy later told Kam, he slowed the car down but didn't stop as James bailed out and hit the ground rolling.

The FBI, the Border Patrol, State Liquor Control officers, Pima County sheriffs' deputies, Tucson city police officers, and the Arizona Highway

Patrol unleashed a massive manhunt, even calling in a helicopter from Davis-Monthan Air Force Base, scouring a large area five miles east of the city. But James, hiding all night in the desert, eluded them. The next morning he made his way to Don Sparks's rented house, where agents then moved in and arrested both of them. The two put up no resistance, though there was a virtual arsenal in the house. Back at James's house, agents had found a large supply of burglary tools and weapons, as well as a roomful of fur coats and silver services.

Coincidentally, their arrests came exactly thirty-four years after John Dillinger had been arrested, also in Tucson, the last time he ever would be arrested, before being gunned down in Chicago.

Jerry Ray James, twenty-eight, originally of Oklahoma City, was wanted on charges of attempted burglary, carrying a concealed weapon, and assault with a dangerous weapon, in Mays County, Oklahoma; burglarizing a bank at Mobeetie, Texas; and escaping from a Mississippi jail. Donald Eugene Sparks, thirty-eight, whose previous home was in Electra, Texas, was wanted on a federal indictment for residential holdups in Gadsden, Alabama. Now both fugitives were held in lieu of $100,000 bonds. It turned out that Jerry's girlfriend, Joan Taylor, was wanted in El Paso for bank burglary, conspiracy, interstate transportation of stolen property, and transportation in aid of racketeering. Her bond was set at $10,000. Neither Kam nor Nell Sparks was charged. Eventually, Sparks and James were extradited, then tried and sent to prison. Joan Taylor was released on bail in Oklahoma City and married the bondsman, who, two years later, shot and killed her.

Late in the afternoon of the first raid, Kam had been followed to the airport by FBI agents, who told her she would not be welcome in Arizona anymore. She took a 6 P.M. flight to Tulsa on a one-way ticket.

Meanwhile, Tulsa bondsman Pete King was flying from Tulsa to Tucson to post Daddy's $1,000 bail. King was a friend, and besides, he favored making bonds for professional crooks. He also owned Tulsa's Reeder Hotel, where a lot of small-time hoods lived. It was on Boston just two blocks north of the Orpheum Cigar Store, a walk-in bookie joint operated by none other than Ned VanDeventer.

I remember wandering into the Orpheum one afternoon when I was about fourteen, because I was curious about it. Inside the door was a glass display case with cigars and a cash register. An old smell of dust and tobacco smoke hung in the air. At the far end of the long room were some large blackboards high up on the wall, with lines, words, and numbers in white chalk. Off to the right, someone rose from a chair, so I turned and walked quickly out the door. It never occured to me that Wayne Padgett's son would have been welcome there, or that the business operated under the protection of the police department, whose headquarters were only three blocks away.

At the January 31 preliminary hearing in Tucson, the commissioner ruled that there was no evidence that Daddy had any knowledge of the warrant against Jerry James. Besides, the fugitive had been harboring *him*, not the other way around. Daddy's charge was dropped. The legal decision was sound but, according to Kam, the $1,800 that Daddy had paid the local "fix" man might not have hurt, either.

By July 12, Assistant U.S. Attorney Dianos, noting that no new information had turned up to implicate Daddy, closed the case against him.

Years later, Kam said that she and Daddy had gone out to liven up the Christmas holidays of Sparks and James, but given the date of the FBI raid, January 23, one wonders about the extended length of this Christmas visit. Obviously, they were up to something more than holiday cheer. Daddy later told one of his Tulsa buddies about taking part in residential robberies in Arizona. In one, he and his accomplices dressed up in police uniforms to gain easy access to a wealthy home, robbing the occupants at gunpoint. His direct involvement in these armed robberies—a quantum leap in crime that makes my heart sink every time I think of it—would have taken place in the two years before the FBI raid. Kam confirmed that Daddy took part in these stickups, though she didn't remember the police disguises. She recalled spraying his silver hair brown for one job, and his wearing a ski mask for another. Generally the trio wore business suits, white shirts, and ties. They wanted to look nice.

17 *The Dixie Mafia*

ON MAY 7, 1968, A FEW MONTHS AFTER the FBI raid in Tucson, Kam gave birth to a boy, Wayne Merriott Padgett, Jr., in Tulsa. It was her idea that he be named after his father.

Kam recalled: "We were living in an apartment in Arizona. We had our home and were married, but we were out there running with the wild bunch. That's where I got pregnant. And I just decided that it was a nice thing to do. I was twenty-six years old and I was ready. Wayne didn't say much about it, other than 'Oh you don't want to have this baby,' and I said 'Yes, I do.' He said, 'I can't stand to be around pregnant women,' and I said, 'Why not?' He said, 'Well, when Lucille was pregnant she never had a sick day and I was sick at my stomach the whole time.'"

According to Mother, *she* was the one who felt ill. I believe he transposed the sickness idea to justify his reluctance, while using the opportunity to badmouth his ex-wife. Sometimes he would describe the past in ways that had enough truth to make his account credible, while shaping it to his own purposes, as he had in telling Kam that he had dynamited the gambling club in Joplin.

About this same time I sent Daddy a copy of *The Poet Assassinated*, a fantastical novella by the modernist poet Guillaume Apollinaire that I had translated from the French. The volume was illustrated with wacky and delightful photographs by Jim Dine. I don't know what I thought my father would see in such an outré book; I probably sent it to him as tangible proof of what seemed to be my early success as a writer. I also wanted him to continue to be proud of me, and apparently he was: a few years later I noticed the book on the shelf in the headboard of his bed, a position it maintained thereafter. I doubt, though, that he ever read more than a few pages of it. Cubist literature was, to put it mildly, alien to him. In subsequent years, I simply told him whenever I published a new book of poems, thereby relieving him of any obligation to try to understand my work, and relieving myself of the disquieting feeling of how different we were. Instead, I preferred knowing that at any time, day or night, I could ask him for anything and that he would deliver, no questions asked—his way of showing affection for me, an affection I, although far away in many respects, still needed.

A June 26, 1968, FBI file, relying on a neighborhood informant, notes that a FOR SALE sign has appeared in the front yard of Daddy's house on Jamestown. Daddy's plan was to use the proceeds from the sale of this house to help finance the construction of a big new house, and when the sale went through, in August of 1968, he, Kam, and baby Wayne moved into the North Memorial rental house, where, according to Kam, a couple of bank robbers on the lam holed up in the garage apartment. Kam cooked for them, but Daddy delivered the meals—if she never saw them, she couldn't be implicated in harboring. Daddy also harbored an Alaska bank robber.

Daddy's 1968 FBI files make a passing reference to a burglary of Newcomb's Clothing Store in Woodward, Oklahoma. A July 30 entry mentions Cleo Epps and her Western Capri Motel, Daddy, and fencing. It notes that because Daddy doesn't fence "hot" money, it is doubtful he was involved in the robbery of Tulsa's Home Federal and Loan Association. But there's a rumor that he was fencing men's suits. In a September entry he is described as a "very good Ace lock picker." In October he and a friend have bought $5,000 worth of tires, but apparently it's a legitimate transaction. By April of 1969 he is one of ten prosecutable targets for interstate gambling, but the following month he is removed from the list. The FBI was grasping for straws. They didn't even seem to know that he was handling "slugs," plain metal disks the size and shape of a quarter, for use in vending machines.

Daddy, Kam, and Wayne Jr. were still living on North Memorial when Neil Armstrong set foot on the moon, on July 20, 1969. A few days later Pat and I, on our way to California, stopped in Tulsa to borrow a car from Daddy, who told us the route to take, where to eat, and where to stay the night, describing the trip like a crooner singing "Route 66": Oklahoma City, Elk City, Shamrock, Amarillo, Tucumcari, Albuquerque, Gallup, Winslow, Flagstaff, Kingman, Needles, Barstow, San Bernardino, and on into L.A. I wasn't surprised by his knowledge, but I had no idea that for the past few years he had been burning up this route, driving the 1,461 miles from Tulsa to L.A. nonstop. When I asked him what he had been doing in California, he grew typically vague: "I went to see a guy about something." Meaning: it's private.

When Pat and I returned to Tulsa a few weeks later to leave off the car and retrieve our son, we were stunned to hear that Daddy had given the two little Waynes—ages two and one—a Clorox bath.

"You gave them a *what*?" we asked.

"A Clorox bath. They had been out playing in the backyard, where there's all them chiggers, so I gave 'em a Clorox bath. It kills the chiggers. Don't worry, I take a Clorox bath after every time I go hunting."

Neither boy seemed to have suffered any ill effects from being soaked in bleach water.

Daddy and Kam lived on North Memorial for two years while building a large ranch-style house on their new property just west of Tulsa in Creek County. On December 8, 1969, Kam wrote me, "We are all great. Papa has been quail hunting a lot and as usual he's doing real good. I've fixed three dinners of them already. The contractor has started on our new house. It sure is going to be big and nice." She also mentioned maybe getting a few cows and horses, planting a garden, and relearning country life. At that time, the countryside there was still rural, with pasture and rolling hills dotted with stands of trees. It was a quiet and pretty spot, sparsely populated.

The gray stone house was built with money from the telephone coin boxes. The cost wasn't all that high, since, according to Kam, "eighty percent of the stuff was stolen. Every light fixture in it was stolen, every inch of carpet, every piece of tile that went in the three bathrooms was stolen. We stole all that stuff, piece by piece—Don Goodson, Wayne, and me." Don was the boyfriend of Kam's sister Joan. "They'd go out every night and get a truckload of light fixtures or a truckload of tiles or whatever they wanted. The windows came from a house under construction. As for the carpet, I was the driver and they got the carpet. It took about three trips to get enough carpet to cover the house. That's why it didn't quite match: it took several homes. Isn't that awful? They watched 'em lay it that day, then went and got it that night. Brand spanking new. 'Give us thirty minutes.' 'Give us an hour. If anything happens, flash the lights.'" Another source told me that some of the two-by-fours, cement mix, and roofing were also stolen from construction sites.

Midway through, Daddy dismissed the contractor and finished the job himself. His friend Pete James called to say that because he was getting divorced he had a lot of extra furniture. Would Daddy like to have it? Daddy drove a truck out to L.A. and brought it back, fancy contemporary design.

During one of my visits to this new home, Daddy took me to dinner at a nearby roadhouse, the Avalon, an unassuming place off the beaten path west of Tulsa, near the Sapulpa Road. The Avalon had been built and was run by a woman named Billie Popovich, but Cleo Epps also had money in it.

We each had a T-bone steak, a baked potato, and a bottle of beer, followed by coffee. Daddy, of course, had somehow already paid the check.

Then he said, "Let's go around back. I want to see some people."

Behind the Avalon was a small house where Billie and her husband lived. They welcomed us into their modest but tidy living room. When Daddy introduced me as his son, they became extra cordial, saying, "Oh, we've heard so much about you. You live in New York, don't you?"

"Yes," I said, "right there," pointing to the television screen, where police were pursuing crooks on a New York City street in an episode of *Kojak*. Suddenly everyone began watching *Kojak*. Then Billie's husband guffawed, "Look at them damned fools," and provided a real-life critique of the portrayal of a gun battle. Daddy and Billie agreed that neither the police nor the crooks would behave that way. It had looked credible enough to me. Then my eyes wandered to the things on top of the TV. I expected to see something like a ceramic palomino or a copy of *TV Guide*. One object looked like a gun.

"Is that a gun you have there?" I asked.

"Yes, it's a .45," Billie replied.

"I hope you don't mind my asking, but why do you keep a .45 on top of your TV?"

Looking like a farm woman talking about the unpredictability of weather, Billie said, "Why, honey, you never know who might come through that door."

The conversation turned to the use of handguns in the commission of crimes and the controversy over the death penalty. As a social liberal, I believed that the death penalty was not only immoral, but also ineffective as a deterrent. That night I kept my mouth shut.

"Now, there's some people who are gonna kill you, law or no law, it don't make no difference," Billie's husband said. "But there's a bunch of others, and I'm one of 'em, who would think twice about doing armed robbery. Because if you go in with a gun, you'd better be ready to use it. Facing the chair would make me think twice, I tell you."

Both Billie and Daddy knew a lot of criminals who were scared by the thought of the gas chamber or electric chair.

Billie got up and lowered the volume on *Kojak*. I sat back and listened as the conversation turned to gossip. The three of them exchanged a lot of information in a short period of time; then they started reminiscing about the good old days in Nevada. Billie's husband had known a way to beat the slot machines. You held the handle down while you stuck your fingers up the payoff chute and fiddled with the internal mechanism to make the machine pay off. However, it wasn't quite that simple. There were two conditions. First, you needed a lookout—Billie, in this case—to make sure that no one noticed this suspicious activity. And second, you had to have your fingers broken and reset in a configuration that matched the machine's. When I expressed interest in this last procedure, Billie's husband held up his left hand: the fingers were oddly misshapened, and, as it turned out, now unfit for the task: Vegas had redesigned the payoff chute.

On another of my visits to Eighty-first Street, Daddy asked me if I needed a jacket.

"Not really."

"Come out here a minute," he said, heading toward the two-car garage.

When he switched on the garage light, I saw row after row of clothes racks filled with sports clothes.

"Jesus Christ!" I said.

"Take what you want."

"Where'd all this stuff come from?" This was the normal question to ask, allowing him to provide his stock answer.

"Aw, I'm just storing it for a friend. But he owes me some money, so take anything you want."

I knew what he was saying, and when I repeated that I didn't really need anything, he insisted. To make him happy, I selected two windbreakers, neither of which was my style.

The next day a uniformed policeman drove up to the house, followed the driveway around to the back, and parked, right in front of the garage doors, which were wide open. He then walked around to the front door,

       OKLAHOMA TOUGH

rang the bell, and asked to speak to Wayne Padgett. When he learned that Daddy wasn't home, he left. The next day I was surprised to find the hot merchandise still in the garage, but I knew there was no point in asking Daddy about it. I never saw the policeman again, and Daddy distributed the merchandise as he wished.

Pat and I stayed a few nights at Daddy's, then moved on to her parents' house and then to the new house my mother and Daisy had bought.

FBI informants described Daddy alternately as the fence or the kingpin for any number of burglaries. As far back as July of 1964, sources identified three burglary and robbery rings—somewhat interchangeable—in and around Tulsa, one of which was called "the Wayne Padgett gang." A December file includes him in "some of the better fences in the Tulsa area" (an interesting choice of adjectives). An April 5, 1965, file states that "any large burglary or robbery in the Tulsa area is masterminded by Wayne Padgett." In May some drill bits were stolen from the Hughes Tool Company in Perry, Oklahoma, but all the FBI could do was to put the information in Daddy's file and drop the investigation for lack of evidence. In June they tried to link him to the robbery of the Sterling Hotel in Miami, Florida. From July to September the agency investigated, without success, the phone calls made from Virgil Edgar's Conoco service station, where Daddy not only was hanging out but was thought to be part owner. By October he is said to have recently returned from "the coast." Then there is mention of his burglarizing telephone coin boxes. In March, Automotive, Inc. in Fort Smith, Arkansas, was burglarized by a ring that included Wayne Padgett, according to an informant. A spring 1967 file quotes an informant as saying that it would be extremely difficult to "come up with a specific robbery or incident that would directly implicate either Padgett or [name blacked out] in view of the fact that they were normally the 'brains' behind various criminal activities and were not directly involved in the participation of the crimes." In April a Wayne "Shorty" Miller was shot to death in a Sapulpa bar, the same Shorty Miller whom the FBI suspected of fencing stolen goods to Daddy.

The August 1967 information that "Wayne Padgett has ceased all activities at the present time" was accurate: he had been occupied with the Cleo Epps grand jury, Noah's death, and his trips to New York and Alaska.

For a few years, the files meander along. In August 1972, though, Daddy is again "targeted for intensive attention" under the FBI's Anti-Racketeering Program. The agency had his Eighty-first Street address, suspected him of continuing to fence, and knew that he had real-estate investments and part ownership of the Cheyenne Club. The report also notes that goods stolen from Treadway's Western Store down in Musko-gee had been recovered from Mack's Bait Shop in Ketchum. In May 1973 the Sun 'n Fun Shop in Ada was burglarized. A June 1973 file reports that Wayne Padgett is actually participating in burglaries. The agency has asked field offices in Jefferson City, Missouri; Kansas City, Kansas; Wichita, Kansas; Topeka, Kansas; Little Rock, Arkansas; Springfield, Missouri, etc., to provide any information, but apparently they have none. Perhaps their lack had something to do with the area where many of the burglaries were taking place. According to Lee Eller, "Up around Grove, Oklahoma, is a hotbed of the escape-hatch boys out of Springfield and St. Louis and so forth. There's a lot of Mafia dealings around Springfield and St. Louis that funnelled into Grove. You know, you can stand out there around [Grand Lake] and get lost. A highly protected area—from the law. If you moved in there and kept your mouth shut, no one would know who you were."

The agency did a lot of legwork, investigating phone, car registration, bank, and real estate records, but the remainder of their information came from informants, whose veracity fluctuated. For example, in one ludicrous moment the agency goes off the deep end by noting that Daddy is said to be organizing a thieves' union, which robbers can belong to by paying dues of ten dollars a month! Another tidbit describes me as a graduate of Annapolis who translates from English into several other languages, whereas I had graduated from Columbia and I translated from French. Initial reports had Daddy and Kam marrying in Las Vegas, then in Miami, Oklahoma, whereas in fact they had been married in California. Daddy's larger-than-life image and penchant for secrecy generated a lot of rumors. If a big burglary occurred, then Wayne Padgett must have been behind it, right?

The fact is that over the years he *had* gone from doing occasional fenc-ing for small-time thieves to handling larger jobs for much rougher cus-tomers. Many of his earlier associates had been childhood buddies who were not dangerous, but later, especially after he became a bail bondsman, he began to work with truly malevolent characters.

Tom Lester Pugh and Albert McDonald were two such men.

A chunky 175 pounds at five foot seven, Lester Pugh was an armed robber, burglar, and murderer, among other things. He was, according to one acquaintance, "short, fat, and crazy," a man who "got off on the use of power."

Albert McDonald was a big fellow with curly hair. In the mid-1960s, he and Cleo Epps planned on getting married, but, working as a bouncer, he was arrested for carrying a gun—a violation for a former felon—and sent back to prison. After his release, he started running around with Lester Pugh.

In 1970, Pugh was charged with placing a bomb in the car of Tulsa district judge Fred Nelson, injuring him critically. During the investigation, Cleo Epps appeared before a grand jury. A few years later the *Tulsa Tribune* presented the following scenario. Cleo kept dynamite on her farm, for removing tree stumps. When McDonald and Pugh asked for some, she complied. But it worried her, so she told her police friend Jack MacKenzie. Then Judge Nelson's car blew up, with the judge inside. (It so happened that Nelson was running for office against Albert McDonald's lawyer.) Cleo was very upset about the bombing. According to MacKenzie, she wept: "I never dreamed they'd do something like that . . . what if that little [Nelson] girl had gotten into that car with her daddy?"[1]

Cleo had agreed to appear before the grand jury, on the condition that her testimony remain secret. In the closed courtroom, she wore a facial disguise and a red wig. But word leaked out. On November 12, 1970, Pugh and McDonald called Cleo and told her they needed to talk about storing some whiskey. She met them in a parking lot in West Tulsa.

Riding in their car, she received two bullets in the back of the head. A little over three months later, her body was found at the bottom of a cistern. Pugh and McDonald were charged with her murder. She had told the district attorney that the two of them would do her in.

Cleo's brother, Tom Gilbert, had found her body. But how? Gilbert said it was simply the result of legwork, "correcting" a remark of his son (for a while himself a deputy sheriff) that it was on an anonymous tip. Many people believe that the tip came from Daddy. According to this scenario, Daddy, knowing that Pugh and McDonald were involved—apparently he had asked them not to kill her—went to them and said, "Look, Cleo may have ratted, but she's dead now, and there's no reason for her body to be left like that. I'd like to see her buried properly." The culprits felt that enough time had gone by for the lime they used to decompose the body, so they told Daddy the location and he relayed the information to Gilbert, either anonymously or on the condition of absolute secrecy.

Lester Pugh was a busy man. Another of his colleagues, Arles Delbert Self, who had testified against him, was found shot to death. In October of 1972, Pugh was convicted of that murder.

Bad ends came to other associates of Daddy's. On July 15, 1971, Tulsa crime figure Martin Edwards was missing. His police record went back to 1937, when, at the age of sixteen, he was charged with burglary. But from then until the state went wet, most of his police record consisted of traffic and liquor infractions. In fact, he was arrested so many times for driving without a license, liquor possession, and drunkenness that one police officer said, "We lost count." He also carried a pistol, which he used in shooting his older brother Cordon in the leg during an altercation. Martin had two other brothers, Bill and Jack, the latter sometimes known as "Cadillac" Jack. All four brothers were bootleggers.

Martin was one of those indicted by the 1957 grand jury that had sent bootleggers and major police officials to jail. He was fined and given a year in McAlester State Penitentiary, his bootlegging business was put on hold, and just about the time he got out of prison, the state went wet. As with many other bootleggers, it was at this point that his criminal activities branched out: he was charged with armed robbery, bank robbery, and burglarizing parking meters, and later suspected of having bombed a club right across the street from the Tulsa County Court House. One of his two partners in the 1964 parking meter burglaries, which took place in the middle of downtown Tulsa, had been none other than Don Sparks, Daddy's Ten-Most-Wanted friend. Martin Edwards was running with the rough crowd that included Pugh and McDonald.

On September 28, an anonymous phone tip led reporters to a shallow grave in a desolate area north of Sand Springs. The reporters notified authorities, who began digging. About a foot down, they hit pockets of lime, and when they unearthed a hand, they called the medical examiner. The body was quickly identified by its tattoos. It was Martin Edwards. He had received five bullets in the head, three from the back, two from the top. Lime will usually destroy a dead body, but unusually heavy rains had caused a chemical reaction that turned the fat in Edwards's body into soap. In effect, Martin Edwards had become a life-sized soap carving of himself.

My mother told me that Daddy told her how Edwards was killed. For some reason, Edwards had put out a contract on Daddy. He hired two men to do the job, even paid them in advance, but he insisted on seeing the grave where Wayne Padgett would be laid, out in the middle of nowhere. The two assassins liked Daddy and they were beginning to think that Edwards might tell what he knew about the Epps slaying, so after showing him the gravesite, they shot and buried *him* instead.

Another version has it that Raymond Cates, a Tulsa car dealer, had hired Edwards to kill Howard Donahue, Daddy's old race-car-driver friend. Edwards subcontracted the job to Pugh and McDonald. When Daddy heard about it, he interceded, asking the dual assassins to lay off Donahue. Instead of shooting Donahue, they killed Edwards.

Both versions jibe with a Tulsa newspaper account of a "doublecross-power play in the underworld" and the reports indicating that originally the grave had been dug for a different victim.[2]

In late 1973, yet another grand jury investigation was called, this time to investigate the Epps slaying. Daddy was subpoenaed, but took the Fifth in response to the four questions he was asked. He was recalled the next week and asked the same questions. When he again refused to answer, the judge ordered him to jail without bond. On the way, Daddy took a swing at a TV cameraman and mistakenly slugged a deputy sheriff, who promptly filed assault and battery charges against him.

I called Daddy from New York.

"What's this whole thing about?" I asked.

"A bunch of bullshit." (His usual answer.) "They're just out to nail me."

There was no way he was going to "cooperate." But in addition to that, there really was no way he could answer the four questions posed to him: (1) Did you talk to Tom Gilbert about the recovery of Cleo's body? (2) Did you talk to Lester Pugh about the $2,500 reward for the recovery of the body? (3) Did you know where the body was before it was found? (4) Did you get any money for the recovery of the body? As the *Tulsa Tribune* put it, "Several courthouse observers term the queries 'suicide questions' because of possible underworld reprisal if Padgett answered. Additionally, a 'yes' answer might have subjected Padgett to charges of being an accessory after the fact of murder and income tax evasion if he had failed to report the reward."

After a month of testimony, the grand jury was dissolved and Daddy was released. Later Albert McDonald was convicted of the murder of Cleo Epps and sent to prison, where he was killed by an inmate. Pugh survived an attempt on *his* life, also in prison. The level of violence among Daddy's associates had dramatically escalated. Now they even had a name: The Dixie Mafia.

Unlike the Italian or Jewish Mafia, the Dixie Mafia was an unstructured group of hoodlums across the South and Southwest who got to know each other through personal recommendations. Larger cities had clusters or gangs, but often their members were interchangeable. Of course there were the specialists, such as safecrackers, who would work first with this gang, then with that one, and the "steer artists," who would set up a job but not take a direct part. Because Daddy had access to so much information, he was an ideal steer artist.

As Al Benningfield, a lawyer and friend of Daddy's, put it, "Wayne told me that there wasn't any Mafia around Tulsa, though a bunch of guys might get together to do something. If people had a deal working, they knew they could trust Wayne, whether or not he went in on the deal. I'm sure he had the connections to put deals together, or to tell them who to go see. A lot of things went down, and because Wayne was on the edges or made some suggestions, they'd come back and give him some money. It was a sort of reward or token of thanks. A finder's fee type of thing."

Daddy's information could be valuable. Benningfield recalled: "I had a client, a real good rich client, who played poker at a country club here in Tulsa. There was $30–40,000 on the table. I guess just as a favor to me, Wayne told me, 'You tell that guy that the next couple of weeks, watch it, because there's somebody new in the game and he's gonna cheat 'em.' And sure enough the next two weeks a stranger walked away with a lot of money. Wayne was well connected enough to know when somebody was about to be run in on a game."

One well-known Tulsa-area member of the Dixie Mafia was John Dillon, who in his day eluded the FBI longer than anyone else on their Ten-Most-Wanted list. Dillon's criminal career began in 1931 at age sixteen. Subsequently, he was convicted of grand theft auto, interstate transportation of stolen vehicles, violations of wartime regulations for tire rationing, bootlegging, burglary, forging stolen traveler's checks, and finally, in 1961, drug dealing and bail jumping.

When he was not serving time, he worked as a farmer, used-car salesman, carpenter, sawmill operator, and mechanic. In fact, a sheriff called him "one of the best mechanics in Oklahoma." At his garage, he did specialty work for bootleggers, souping up their cars and fitting them with "plants." It was Dillon who installed the plants in my uncle Tommie's delivery cars, as well as the plants at Bobbie Hood's house. A farmer he worked for described him as "a good tractor driver who was nice to kids." His wife Lorine, the sister of Tulsa bootlegger Sam Bryson and one-time bootlegger herself, told me that he was a wonderful husband, kind, gentle, and courteous to her at all times. She also said that he never smoked, drank, or womanized, a statement confirmed by others. Dillon's mother described him as "a good boy that I loved with all my heart." On the other side, an FBI press release warned that his "deceptively mild appearance masks [his] demonstrated vicious nature," but the only evidence of his viciousness was their charge of his being part of a gang that tried to run down a police officer who found them changing their license plates on a country road. All of his convictions were for nonviolent offenses.

Dillon's final conviction, in 1961, was for dealing drugs, most of which were burglarized from pharmacies. A few days before sentencing, he went on the lam. Over the next several years, apparently he borrowed large sums from crime figures in St. Louis, who, when he did not repay them, had him beaten and threatened him with murder. On March 2, 1964, police found his body, weighted with oil rig equipment, at the bottom of a cistern in Rogers County, Oklahoma. His skull was cracked, his lungs were filled with water, and his fingers had been cut off—not necessarily in that order.

While on the run, he had returned to his farm outside of Tulsa to see his wife. Late at night, two men came to the door. He told her he'd be back in a few minutes. She never saw him again.

Exactly what happened next is uncertain. A Tulsa-area crook named Burns Trusty, Jr., later testified that his colleague Bob Jenkins had driven the car while Martin Edwards, in the back seat, hit Dillon with a hammer. One source told me that according to very reliable information, Dillon had been hit in the head from behind by a pistol wielded by Jenkins. In 1974, Lester Pugh testified that Jenkins had killed both Dillon and Epps.

Ruby Charles "Bob" Jenkins is a particularly interesting character. There is no doubt about his criminal life: it was heavy and sometimes violent. Bootlegging, cattle rustling, whiskey hijacking, pistol whipping, armed robbery, prison escape, and murder were his stock-in-trade. But he was more than a northeastern Oklahoma country boy gone bad. One source who knew him described him as very intelligent. Former Tulsa D.A. "Buddy" Fallis told me that Jenkins was "physically rough, but a cut above the others when it came to mental discipline. He testified for us, and I've never seen a stronger witness on the stand. I'd say the defense lawyer had met his equal, if not his superior. Bob had a lot of native intelligence about him. He was not an impulsive person." Kam described him as "a kind of a deep-thinking kind of person. He paid attention to minute details." For all his convictions for serious crimes, the amazing thing is how little time Jenkins served in prison.

Lester Pugh, Albert McDonald, and Bob Jenkins were among the roughest members of the Dixie Mafia in northeastern Oklahoma. The membership graded down to, say, a tavern owner who might handle a hot item from time to time, but the network was extensive, at one point reaching, as we saw earlier, as high as the Tulsa chief of police. Daddy was a central figure, if anything so amorphous as the Dixie Mafia could be said to have a center. He is said to have known everything that was going on. As one friend put it, "He knew a lot of things and a lot of people, who confided in him, because they knew he would keep his mouth shut. He was not a snitch. He hated snitches."

He was just the kind of guy the big boys were looking for. Daddy once told me about the most bone-chilling business meeting he had ever taken part in, in the 1960s or 1970s. He had received a call from a man of Italian descent who wanted to meet with him, in the man's private jet out at the airport. Apparently, the man couldn't be touched by the Tulsa police as long as he didn't set foot on the ground. In the meeting, the man "offered him the whole area." Before then, northeastern Oklahoma hadn't been a sufficient market for the Italian Mafia, but with the rise in drug use on both coasts and in big cities like Chicago and St. Louis, the Cosa Nostra figured it was time to stake their claim to a territory that in the coming years would prove more lucrative. Daddy was not only adamantly against drugs, he was chilled by the look in the man's eyes. "They were steel hard," he told me, "inhuman. I don't scare easy, but I have to admit that looking into his eyes scared me. Those people play for keeps, and they include your family." As diplomatically as possible, Daddy declined their offer.

A source told me that the man was Nick Savelli, of the Kansas City Mafia.

It wasn't Daddy's first or last contact with the Italian Mob. Over the years he made numerous trips to Chicago and Kansas City to get rid of stolen goods, especially jewelry.

According to Kam, "He would never have anything to do with any drugs, even though that's where the money was. His big thing was jewelry. He could 'turn' it real easy. Twenty cents on the dollar, maybe, sometimes less, and it was easy to get rid of. He had a helluva connection, right here in Tulsa. I went with him a half a dozen times, maybe more, to Kansas City. We went to the Italian district and I just sat in the car." She also accompanied him to Chicago.

Daddy got connected in Chicago by Bob Deck, an East Side Tulsa boy from way back. Deck had co-owned a bar in South Beloit, Illinois, with the son of a big shot in the Teamsters Union in Chicago.

The Kansas City connection was more byzantine. A bank robber named Glen Roy Wright was doing time in McAlester State Penitentiary, where he made the acquaintance of an oldtime mobster named "Jew" Eddie Snyder. While in prison, Jew Eddie connected Glen Roy's brother Harold to Kansas City. According to Bobby Bluejacket, Harold "Fats" Wright "was a hustler, never worked. A helluva guy. When I lived in Tulsa, I'd see Fats every day. We'd go out to dinner or he'd come by my tire shop. Later he bought Doc's Pool Hall downtown. Anyway, Fats helped Wayne make the connections in Kansas City. Friendship deals worked that way. Back then, if you was a decent person, people would connect you up." (A "decent person": Bluejacket is invoking the honor-among-thieves principle here.)

Daddy also was connected to mobsters in southern Illinois: the Shelton mob around Peoria and the Buster Workman gang in St. Louis. The connection to these two groups is rather ironic. In Chapter 8, I told about Daddy's being robbed at gunpoint. Two of the robbers were Indians, one named George and the other Joe "Crookedleg Joe" Crow. When police stopped the bandits' car, George was no longer in it, but another Indian named Charlie Squirrel was. To save Joe and to keep George out of it, Charlie Squirrel took the rap for both of them. He got ten years in McAlester, which in those days meant serving a flat five. When Charlie got out of prison, Daddy was ready to level the score with him, but when the whole situation was explained, he and Charlie became friends, and Charlie hooked Daddy up with the Shelton mob and Workman gang.

It has never been clear how Daddy became involved in the Mullendore case. By 1970, E. C. Mullendore III, the owner of a huge northeastern Oklahoma ranch, had fallen into serious debt. He turned to a series of "investors," including dubious and even criminal figures. When the financial details of repayment became more and more ambiguous, some of the investors started to snarl at each other and at Mullendore and to make threats. At a meeting in Ponca City, one of the investors, George Aycock, a gray-haired, well-dressed wheeler-dealer in his sixties, arrived with some men whose appearance scared Mullendore so much that he called the police, who came to the meeting place and searched the men but found no weapons. The men described themselves simply as bodyguards. One of them was later identified as Wayne Padgett. Some months later, Mullendore was shot and killed in his own home. The finger pointed to Mullendore's chauffeur, but he was not charged. The case has never been solved.

From time to time, Daddy did serve as a freelance bodyguard. If someone was going down to Texas to play in a high-stakes poker game, he hired Daddy to come along and just stand around. If someone was going to meet with people who might prove dangerous, he took Daddy along. Daddy used his reputation, fearlessness, and sheer physical presence as sources of legal income.

The FBI failed to notice Daddy's two trips to Costa Rica. His California friend Pete James had made good money developing real estate there. Pete had an apartment in the ritziest suburb of San José, the neighborhood where the president of the country lived, and where he and Daddy stayed while on vacation. Pete had also gotten into the loan business there. At

OKLAHOMA TOUGH

that time, the interest rates in Costa Rica were unregulated. Pete borrowed money in the U.S. at 10 percent and loaned it in Costa Rica at twice that. His Costa Rican partner, a lawyer, had been holding out on him, though, on a technicality. Finally, Pete figured out that the guy was just stiffing him. My father offered to go to Costa Rica to collect the money. Pete gave him a round-trip ticket and the keys to his San José apartment. Daddy took along a football player, a large black man, to help with the strong-arming. When the lawyer proved to be recalcitrant, Daddy realized that if he and his sidekick inflicted serious damage on the guy, they might not ever get out of the country. He was not comfortable operating outside the U.S.

Later Daddy asked me if I'd like to meet him in San José and spend a week or so there, just for fun, but it turned out that he never went back.

Since 1969 I had been earning a living mostly by teaching poetry writing to elementary schoolchildren. It was freelance work that I did once or twice a week, just enough to sustain my family at a level that could be described as bohemian, though we always had some money in the bank. I was not a regular, certified teacher, but Daddy ignored the distinction, proudly telling his friends that his son had become a teacher.

Throughout most of Daddy's Dixie Mafia years, he wasn't simply a crook. He also continued his legitimate business ventures in real estate and bail bonds; for example, with business partner Fred Stone he obtained a $450,000 bank loan to build an apartment complex. And he continued to hunt and fish and to help out his family and friends, at one point spending months doing manual labor on a friend's demolition project. In March of 1973 he even helped Daisy, his ex-mother-in-law and old nemesis, get a new car at a discount, and another one for Mother at just a little above cost. Of course, he continued to look after his own mother, who, after becoming in 1957 the first female school-crossing guard in Tulsa's history, was still at her post, age seventy-three.

Verna worried about her son's health. As early as 1971, she wrote me that he was having pain in his forehead, which he ascribed to sinusitis.

But she suspected it was something worse, and kept after him to go to the doctor.

There were other problems. In 1972 or 1973, Daddy, ever intensely jealous, accused Kam of infidelity. Kam said, "One of his worst nightmares in the world was that I'd sleep with somebody besides him. That's what bothered him more than anything that you could ever imagine. That was *the* thing." There are some who think that he had good reason to suspect her. Kam denies it. In any event, one night his jealousy peaked and he shot holes in the kitchen. Kam recounted: "One of the bullets lodged in the butcher block, others went into the Formica. He didn't intend to shoot me. He was shooting all around me. Shot the coffee pot off the stove, pow. And then the baby woke up and started crying, so he sat him on the bar and shot again to show him he was just playing. But he had just 'lost it' in a violent rage. That's when I started getting fed up."

According to her, he never hit her, but one time he grabbed her by the hair and dragged her toward the bathtub, telling her he was going to kill her there so he wouldn't get blood on the floor. Instead, he shot up the house again.

As Kam told me about these incidents, she picked up a photo of him and said, "He was a *handsome* devil, wasn't he? He was beautiful." Then, laughing, she added, "It was a shame he had to be abusive."

The times I visited the house on Eighty-first Street, I saw no hint of all this discord. Daddy and Kam seemed to be getting along fine. Little Wayne was big and healthy. In fact, by the age of four he was so big and healthy that Daddy bought him a three-wheeled Honda motorbike to ride around the property. (That he had driven it into a barbed-wire fence was no reason to take it away from him.) Friends and relatives dropped by to have coffee and to chat. Sometimes some of us would shoot a game of eight-ball, using the pool table that overlooked the sunken living room area. The atmosphere was free and easy, with a lot of good-natured joking. No one seemed remotely concerned when the policeman saw the garage filled with "hot" merchandise. As he had when I was a child, Daddy put a good front on everything.

But his jealousy never subsided, and as Kam grew older she began to resent his oppressive control. She was now in her thirties, beginning to realize that she had a mind of her own. He interpreted her desire for independence as a cover for infidelity. Actually, the night he had threatened to kill her, something in her had snapped. The overwhelming love she had felt for him was suddenly not so overwhelming. Being a gangster's moll had lost its charm.

In 1973, he kicked her out and filed for divorce, putting the house on the market at an attractive price. I recall Daddy's telling me the property was worth $100,000, a figure confirmed by an evaluation in an FBI file. The FBI heard that he had sold it for $91,000 cash. His 1973 tax return gave the selling price as $85,206.50. Although the buyer got a good deal, it was as if there were bad karma in the place. A few years after moving in, he got in bed and shot himself to death.

The final divorce decree was granted on July 27. Kam was given custody of Wayne Jr., but Daddy was granted reasonable visitation rights. Kam kept her 1972 Cadillac, her personal possessions, and whatever money she had on her when she was kicked out. According to Kam, she was to receive no alimony and no child support. Daddy retained all the real estate. As in his previous divorce, a single lawyer represented both parties, this time Daddy's associate Paul Garrison, and again Daddy got the lion's share. This was one way to punish the ex-wives.

Kam took their five-year-old boy and went to her sister Joan's house in Biloxi, Mississippi. By September Daddy was living in the Liberty Towers, a respectable apartment building just south of downtown. It was all over with Kam.

And so I was surprised to receive a letter from her, dated September 16 and with Mom's return address: "Well what can I say except I am home with the man I love and things have worked out just fine. We don't have our show home, but who needs it! We are staying with Wayne in his apartment, but we will have to move soon and get the boy back in school. . . . I only hope I didn't completely ruin your summer vacation. . . . Don't worry about your Daddy, I will take excellent care of him." The divorce was voided.

A few months later, in the fall of 1973, Daddy, Kam, and Wayne Jr. were living in their new home, a comfortable two-bedroom ranch-style house in a middle-class neighborhood, at 8856 East 39th. When my wife, son, and I visited the new home one summer, some of Kam's relatives were there, and someone pointed out that there were four Wayne Padgetts in the room: Daddy, me (my middle name is Wayne), my son, and Daddy's son. Not only were the last three of us named after him, but Kam's nephew, also present, was too! Such was his charisma.

Meanwhile, the FBI kept an eye on him. In 1974 they noted that he used pay phones, making it impossible to track his toll calls. Some of his favorite pay phones were at a Dairy Queen (he loved ice cream), Dick & Dovie's Restaurant, the Pit Bar-B-Q, the Avalon Night Club, and Virgil Edgar's Conoco service station. As we shall soon see, it was at the gas station that he would receive a phone call with serious consequences for him. In the meantime, he was supervising his construction projects, such as an industrial complex called Wolf Point, and looking after friends and family. When Daisy was hospitalized in November of 1974, he was solicitous, which Mother appreciated. She wrote to me: "I talked to your father a nite or two ago and he is fine. He is so funny sometimes. But he always was one to joke." In June he attended a Tucker family reunion, and in August sent me my new Oklahoma registration and license plate sticker for the Volkswagon he had helped me find that summer. I didn't know that his obtaining the renewals was not kosher. Later I learned that he had a "friend" in the Motor Vehicle Department. He was also doing a little fencing on the side.

But the FBI wasn't getting anywhere in its investigations. Is it possible they decided to stir things up a bit? Or did one agent just temporarily go haywire?

In April of 1974, agent W. B. Henderson had given testimony that violated agency guidelines on confidentiality. Henderson was testifying at the trial of Rex Brinlee, a Tulsa criminal who was serving a life term for blowing up the wife of an accomplice. During a prison riot, Brinlee had slipped away. He was later arrested in Mississippi. How had the FBI found him?

On the way back to prison, Brinlee reportedly told agent Henderson, "I made only one call to Oklahoma—to Wayne Padgett. You must have had his phone tapped."

"No. He's an FBI informant. He's the one who turned you around," Henderson told him.

At first Brinlee refused to believe it, but then he began to wonder. How else did they find him? It must have been Padgett. Later Brinlee openly vowed to kill Daddy, his wife, and children at the first opportunity. Daddy called the *Tulsa Daily World* and said, "I've never turned anybody in to the police in my life. I couldn't live with myself if I was a rat." He went on to state that agent Henderson's statement was a "cold-blooded lie" and blamed former state Crime Bureau Director Frank Hagedorn for being the instigator.

According to one source I spoke with, Brinlee *had* telephoned Daddy, asking that a handgun and fake driver's license be mailed to him: "When Rex broke out of McAlester, he called my place [of business] and talked to Wayne, and then he called me at home and wanted a driver's license and a pistol. Wayne didn't send him the pistol, but he did send him the driver's license. Wayne had access to driver's licenses, car tags, birth certificates, anything. He could get anything he wanted."

In fingering Daddy, was the FBI simply trying to put some heat on him? Bobby Bluejacket thought so. "Sure. Sometimes it does work. It depends on the individual and your known integrity. It's an old ploy." The agency couldn't pin anything on Daddy legally, so they were resorting to other means, sowing seeds of distrust to get the crooks fighting among themselves.

An April 5, 1974, agency file had noted an unnamed person's description of Daddy as "an intelligent, cunning individual and completely unpredictable in his routine." The person added, though, that "in his opinion Padgett could be trapped by a surveillance of his residence." An October 11 teletype from the Oklahoma City bureau to J. Edgar Hoover's office in Washington said that Daddy "is acutely surveillance conscious and has been observed by bureau agents on numerous occasions to go through extensive maneuvers to identify and lose surveillances. Numerous previous attempts by Oklahoma City division to conduct surveillances on the subject have been generally unsuccessful in view of *his extreme sensitivity to surveillance*" (emphasis mine).

The Oklahoma City Field Office asked that special surveillance equipment be flown to Tulsa, and on October 17, 1974, a Braniff International flight arrived with the equipment and a special agent to show local agents how to operate it. For five straight nights the agents conducted a concentrated surveillance of Daddy's residence. One night he and another person went to a bar and then a supper club. The other four nights he stayed at home. Local agents had gotten the special equipment by telling

Washington that Daddy conducted stealing and fencing operations on an almost nightly basis, but instead here he was at home watching TV. In one terse paragraph, the Oklahoma City field office report concluded, "No criminal activities were conducted by Padgett during the surveillance period."

The following month, however, an event was to take place that would enable a frustrated FBI to stop worrying about the elusive Wayne Padgett.

18 *The Sears Deal*

THE MAN HELD THE GUN AT Daddy's head and ordered him to spread his feet, lean forward, and place his hands on the cab of the truck. He was Tulsa city police officer Jim Aud and he was making an arrest in a parking area at the Sundowner Apartments, Ninth and Sheridan, between 3:30 and 4 P.M. on Wednesday, November 20, 1974, the climax of a three-month investigation. It sounds simple enough, but actually it is quite a tangled tale.

Also arrested that afternoon were Ferrell Kirtley and Pete Nicklau. Although Kirtley, thirty-two, worked as a salesman at a Sears, Roebuck warehouse, he acted as manager every Wednesday, his superiors' day off. At some point he had no longer been able to resist the temptation of appropriating certain goods for use in the six rental properties he owned. This practice led to his selling merchandise on the side to friends, right off the loading dock at the warehouse.

One of those friends was Jerry Todd, who introduced Kirtley to a fellow named Pete Nicklau. Beginning in early 1974, Kirtley supplied Nicklau with major appliances, all, of course, at very low prices. Nicklau picked up the goods on Wednesdays, and on Fridays, Kirtley's day off, the two of them met in Nicklau's pawnshop or at a restaurant called Dick and Dovie's.

Daddy was present at some of these meetings, and though he never gave Kirtley any money, Kirtley assumed that he was in on the deal. After all, Daddy was an old friend of Nicklau's. Kirtley had even played cards with them at the pawnshop, just a social game, Tonk at fifty cents a hand. The financial level of the transactions for appliances was considerably higher: Kirtley later estimated the retail value of the goods he embezzled that year at around $15,000 to $20,000, and that he netted around $4,000 from it.

On November 20, Ron Marsh arrived at the Sears warehouse at 6:15 A.M., before the other employees. He positioned his pickup truck, climbed into the camper in the back, noted the time, and took out his binoculars. Formerly a Tulsa police officer, Marsh was now the security manager for Sears. His suspicions about Kirtley had been aroused. The night before, Marsh had taken a detailed inventory of the major appliances in Kirtley's division, and now he was waiting and watching. Occasionally he used his walkie-talkie to speak with his assistant, Mr. Woodall, who was parked a block away, ready to tail any suspects.

At 10:39 A.M. he saw a man, later identified as Pete Nicklau, drive up in a blue pickup and go inside the warehouse salesroom. A few minutes later Nicklau emerged with Kirtley, who wheeled a white clothes dryer out onto the loading dock. Nicklau had trouble starting his truck, but when it finally did start, he backed up to the loading dock and Kirtley brought out the matching washer and loaded the set onto the pickup. Nicklau drove away.

At approximately 11:30 he returned, staying for about ten minutes. He came back again around 12:15. Kirtley loaded another washer-dryer set and Nicklau drove away.

The tenacious Marsh did not budge from the camper. He waited until 1:58 P.M., when a new Chevrolet pickup pulled into the parking area. Daddy got out of the truck, went into the warehouse salesroom, and emerged a minute or so later with a portable television set, which he put on the seat on the passenger side. He started to drive away, but Kirtley came out and waved for him to stop. Daddy backed the truck up and Kirtley went back in, soon reemerging with a large green refrigerator, which he loaded onto the truck. Daddy drove away.

Marsh immediately went to phone his colleague, Carrol Gatlin, a Tulsa police officer assigned to the anti-racketeering squad who moonlighted as a security agent for Sears. He knew that Marsh had planned the stakeout. Marsh returned to his lookout post in the camper.

At around 3:20, a Volkswagon pulled into the warehouse parking area and Daddy got out. Inside the showroom, Kirtley gave him a plastic box for holding the cubes in an automatic icemaker. The two of them had forgotten it on the previous run. Daddy got back in the VW and drove away.

Seven minutes later, officer Gatlin and his partner Jim Aud arrived and spoke with Marsh. Marsh then went into the showroom to begin a second inventory, and the officers sped away.

They drove directly to Daddy's apartment complex at Ninth and Sheridan, where they saw him unloading the green refrigerator with another man. By the time they turned their car around, he had begun to drive away, but they blocked his exit and ordered him from his truck. That's when officer Aud placed the pistol to his head and spread-eagled him. When Daddy asked him what the arrest was for, Aud said nothing. Police also arrested Pete Nicklau, near the apartment office, and then Ferrell Kirtley at the warehouse. The three were charged conjointly with embezzlement by employee, a felony.

A few days later Kirtley turned state's evidence and, a week before the trial, went into hiding, fearful for his safety. Although the three of them had been charged, Daddy was tried first and separately.

The prosecuting team was headed by District Attorney S. M. "Buddy" Fallis, who saw this as a rare opportunity to nail a kingpin of crime. Fallis was well aware of Daddy's reputation. Although twelve years younger than Daddy, he had grown up in the same neighborhood, worked just as Daddy had at Archer Park, and attended the same public schools. In his law school days, Buddy had even bought an occasional bottle from Daddy's brother Tommie. Buddy and Daddy's paths had crossed at the county courthouse, where Buddy had been a clerk and where Daddy posted bonds. Now Buddy lived just a few blocks from Daddy, and both their sons attended Fulton Elementary School. In Daddy's thirty or so years of crime, this was the first time the state had any felony case against him, and the pressure was on Fallis to get a conviction.

He was aided by Assistant District Attorney Pat Thompson and several others from the D.A.'s office. The prosecution's witnesses were Kirtley, Marsh, and officers Gatlin, Aud, and David Harrison.

Daddy's defense team of Paul Garrison and Tom Hanlon called four witnesses: Jerry Todd, the man who had introduced Kirtley to Nicklau; Patrick Murphy, who had been charged in a separate scheme with Kirtley; Clemens Laurrell, Daddy's friend since childhood; and Daddy himself.

For reasons that have never been explained satisfactorily, Pete Nicklau did not testify.

The trial began on September 17, 1975.

Daddy's story was that on November 20 of the previous year, Pete had called him at the Conoco station where Daddy hung out, to say that his pickup wouldn't start. Would Daddy do him the favor of picking up a TV set for him? Daddy told him he was busy at the moment, but that he would do it as soon as he was finished. An hour or so later he drove to Sears to pick up the TV, but at the last moment the salesman remembered that Pete had also wanted him to pick up a refrigerator. Well, okay. Daddy took the items to his nearby apartment complex, where Pete would pick them up. Suddenly he had a gun pointed at his head and he was under arrest. For what? For helping a friend?

This is not only the story he told the court, it is the story he told me, the story he told Kam, and the story he insisted was true, years later, to his old friend Bobby Bluejacket as they walked along a beach in Vancouver on vacation. By then, there was no reason for him to lie about it.

But it wasn't quite that simple. What about the washer-dryer set that police had seen being removed from his garage the week before? It was, he said, something he got from Pete for a friend. He didn't make anything on it. He didn't know it was stolen. How about the washer-dryer set that police found being removed from his garage on the evening of his arrest? Daddy said he had no idea how that set got there: how could he? He was in police custody.

Then there was the matter of Kirtley's testimony, which strongly suggested that Daddy was in on the deal. But perhaps most damaging was the exchange between Daddy and Buddy Fallis near the end of Daddy's testimony, recorded in the trial transcript:

Q: Do you, Mr. Padgett, have a washer and dyer in your garage?
A: Yes, sir.
Q: Did you back in November of 1974?
A: Yes, sir.
Q: What was the brand name?
A: Sears.
Q: Do you have a refrigerator in your house?
A: Yes, sir.

THE SEARS DEAL

Q: What's the brand name?

A: Sears.

Q: Did you have a television in your house back in November of 1974?

A: Yes, sir.

Q: What's the brand name?

A: Sears.

It then came out that Daddy also had a Sears trash compactor. Daddy's explanation was simple: "We trade at Sears." When Fallis asked him if he had any cancelled checks to prove the appliances were obtained legally, Daddy answered that, except for his utility bills, he always dealt in cash. This was true, but in light of the entire testimony, it sounded bad. When asked if he had any receipts, Daddy said that his wife did all the shopping. His answers appeared more and more convenient, less and less likely.

Daddy's feckless lawyers raised no objection to this line of questioning. Added to this, they allowed the prosecution to bring up Daddy's bootlegging record, his reckless driving arrests, his jail time for refusing to cooperate with a grand jury, his arrest for assault and battery in 1971, and his arrest for harboring a fugitive. Fallis concluded by waving what purportedly was a long list of Daddy's crimes and declaiming, "I could go on for two hours." This tactic had worked for Senator Joseph McCarthy, why not try it again?

The trial lasted four days. After an hour and a half of deliberation, the jury returned with a verdict of guilty, with a recommended sentence of five years in the penitentiary, the maximum. Daddy was remanded into custody.

The trial actually raised more questions than it answered. If Daddy was as innocent as he claimed, why hadn't Pete Nicklau testified on his behalf? Was the D.A.'s office, before going ahead and deciding what to do with Ferrell Kirtley, waiting to see how good he was at helping them nail Padgett? Why was Daddy tried first, when Kirtley was the instigator and Nicklau was the principal buyer? What had Nicklau meant when Daddy asked him, in the corridor outside the courtroom, if he had cut a deal with Fallis, and Nicklau had answered, "I don't know"? Why did the Sears security manager wait until Daddy came to Sears to call the police? If he

OKLAHOMA TOUGH

was looking for accomplices of Nicklau's, why didn't he wait longer? And, ultimately, why was Daddy, of the three men charged in this case, *the only one to receive jail time*? Kirtley pleaded guilty and was given a suspended sentence and ordered to make financial restitution to Sears. Nicklau pleaded guilty, but his sentencing mysteriously never happened. A year later his case was, as the appearance docket for criminal court succinctly put it, "dismissed."

Daddy came to the logical conclusion: he had been set up. Kirtley had been confronted weeks before November 20 and converted into a stooge. Maybe even Pete had gone over. Daddy's suspicions were strengthened when he got wind that law enforcement officers had plotted against him. One source told me, "It was a vendetta thing. Not just Fallis, it was [Sheriff] Frank Thurmond and all of 'em. The room where they were discussing all this had all kinds of officers and policemen and old veterans, and one of them—I don't know his name—liked Wayne and went to him after this discussion about how they were going to do something to trap him. They'd been after him for years and years and never caught him. They were going to trap him, and they were going to use his boyhood friend Pete Nicklau to do it. Pete Nicklau was good friends with an FBI agent. And Pete was going to set Wayne up." Later, when Sheriff Thurmond, who had been Daddy's friend, happened to walk past his cell in the county jail, Thurmond appeared to be ashamed, unable to look him in the eye.

The final entry in Daddy's FBI file was in February of 1975. There is no legible mention anywhere of Nicklau's friendship with an FBI agent. Had a few frustrated members of the agency decided unofficially to help nail Daddy by leaning on Pete? Or was it simply a plot among local law enforcement officials?

And exactly how guilty was Daddy, anyway? It is safe to assume that he was aware of the general arrangement between Kirtley and Nicklau. But it is quite possible that Daddy, on the day in question, felt that he was simply doing Pete the favor of picking up a TV for him, the kind of helpful favor he was well known for. Even Kirtley, the prosecution's star witness, could not say for certain that Daddy had knowledge of the embezzlement scheme. And there was nothing in the trial testimony to rule out reasonable doubt. If I'm correct, Daddy had been convicted of a crime he didn't commit, technically speaking.

THE SEARS DEAL

Two days after the verdict and before formal sentencing, the Honorable Ronald N. Ricketts, acting on the defense's motion for a new trial, declared a mistrial, on the grounds that because he had improperly instructed the jury, the state Court of Criminal Appeals would certainly vacate the first trial. "It was just one of the unusual cases where we needed a little more adequate instruction," he explained rather cavalierly. But, according to Kam, this was merely a cover-up for his real reason for granting a new trial: he was scared. Daddy had phoned Ricketts and threatened him enough to scare the daylights out of him. Or maybe this was just a story that Daddy put out, to help reestablish his fearsome reputation, which had been diminished by the trial.

The new trial date was rescheduled for January 26, 1976. Because he needed a lawyer with more muscle, he hired Gene Stipe, a state senator and a power in Oklahoma politics who had an outstanding reputation as a defense attorney. Daddy knew that Stipe was going to be expensive. In a letter postmarked December 12, 1975, he wrote me: "On my case I got the new trial—hired a better lawyer—I can get it put off until next summer—looks better but I hired Sen. Gene Stipes [*sic*]—costly but I decided I had better. What I done in 5 minutes took the police over 4 days to tell. They really are beautiful liars. . . . This trouble has cost me about 40 or 50 thousand. Might sound big but I am saddled with my cases, Pete's, Don & Jerry—6 charges in all. I think it will work out now." Daddy was paying *all* the legal fees, including, oddly, Nicklau's.

But who were Don and Jerry? They were the ones who had attempted to remove a washer-dryer and TV set from Daddy's garage the night of his arrest. On January 30, 1976, Jerry "Joker" Estep, thirty-six, and Don Goodson, forty-seven, each received a two-year sentence for knowingly concealing stolen property. No charge was brought against Daddy for his part, if any, in the disposition of that merchandise, though the prosecution had brandished that episode during his trial.

In June, just as Daddy's new trial was about to get underway, Robert Green, the new judge, ordered a continuance to September 28 "for various circumstances beyond control." The circumstances consisted of the fact that Rex Brinlee, the killer who had put both Daddy and the D.A. at the top of his hit list, had once again escaped from McAlester Penitentiary. I remember visiting Tulsa that summer, and Daddy's telling me that a guy had threatened to kill him and his family. I was to keep my eyes open, but

OKLAHOMA TOUGH

not to worry, because it was an empty threat. Right. I recall thinking that maybe I should have stayed in New York, where it was nice and safe.

In October, Grandma ("Mom") wrote to tell me that Daddy "was really glad to get your nice letter. It's amazing what a letter can do for our morale sometimes." As usual, she had dismissed the charges against him as nonsense. All her life, she was unaware of the depth of his criminal life. All she knew was that he and Tommie had sold whiskey, which she, although a nondrinker, did not think of as being any different from selling Dr. Pepper. Like the mothers of a number of the Ozarks' and Southwest's criminal brothers—the Jameses, the Youngers, the Daltons, the Barkers, the Barrows—Mom was unable or unwilling to condemn her sons' behavior. She felt that her sons were unjustly persecuted by the police. Besides, she was more concerned about Daddy's health: "He is getting along OK. I notice he still has cotton in his ear."

Partly to gain time for his defense, Daddy had elected to have surgery on his inner ear. In November, Kam wrote to say that the ear was healing very well. With characteristic bounciness, she added, "Maybe when he's completely well he can hear me fuss at him better." She had started playing basketball in a local women's league. Little Wayne, taking after his father, was riding a Honda 70, a street and trail motorbike—at age eight.

That fall, there was a certain amount of legal maneuvering between Stipe and the D.A.'s office, and on November 22, after two days of intense plea-bargaining, Daddy pleaded guilty. As part of the deal, the state dropped the companion charge, the one that Estep and Goodson had gone to jail for. District Judge Richard Armstrong was to study the possibility of probation and then conduct formal sentencing.

When court reconvened on February 4, 1977, the judge pronounced sentence: three years in prison. Daddy's jaw dropped and his eyes widened. He was supposed to get no jail time, just probation. Stipe had told him so. Stipe had a deal with Buddy Fallis. Daddy looked over at Fallis, but "Little Caesar," as Fallis was referred to by his detractors around the courthouse, remained mute. Three years it was. As Kam put it, "They took him right from the courtroom, boots, suit, and all."

Later that day, Daddy tried to withdraw his plea. He claimed that he had pleaded guilty only to spare his family the embarrassment of further bad publicity. There is some truth to this: Wayne Jr. *was* finding it hard to face the kids at school, among whom was Buddy Fallis's son. Daddy also claimed that the judge had been prejudiced by a lengthy and erroneous pre-sentencing rap sheet that the D.A.'s office had compiled. The sheet listed not only Daddy's entire police record, but also linked him to any number of other criminals and crimes, even unsolved ones. It also linked him to crimes he didn't commit. And even though this was his first felony conviction, and a nonviolent one at that, he was getting noticeable jail time. His reputation as a kingpin of crime had caught up with him.

And worst of all, according to Daddy, Buddy Fallis had sold him out. Their agreement had called for probation. "Do you have that in writing?" Judge Armstrong asked. Stipe did not. And, of course, it wouldn't have occurred to Daddy. He believed that a deal is a deal.

Stipe had gathered letters supporting Daddy from Tulsa businessmen and friends, including the manager of an evangelistic association. And to demonstrate the unreliability of the rap sheet, Bobby Bluejacket had flown down from Minneapolis to testify as to Daddy's innocence in one of the Minnesota crimes mentioned on the sheet: the robbery of an armored car.

Daddy *had* been in Minnesota at the time of the robbery, but for a different purpose. Kam explained, "My mom asked Wayne to go up to Minnesota because Julie, the girl she had adopted, had gotten married to a kid from Minnesota and had a baby. Julie was separated from him, he was a druggie, and she probably was too. My mom asked Wayne to go up there and get Julie and the baby. Wayne flew up there by himself—she even gave him the plane ticket money. He got hold of Bobby Bluejacket, who had a live-in girl named Velvet, a stripper, I'm sure. Bobby and Velvet drove him and Julie out to where this baby was—the husband's mother had taken Julie's baby out to her house and wouldn't let Julie come and get her. So Velvet pretended to be a caseworker and asked the women if she could come in and check on the baby. Once this lady let Velvet in, Wayne had Julie walk in and pick up her own child out of this playpen and take her out. So that's what he was doing in Minnesota. And the report said Armored Car Robbery. Probably an armored car did get robbed. And they found out that Wayne was in Minnesota, so: 'He did it!'"

Despite such protestations, the judge followed the recommendation of the probation officer who had studied the matter and who concluded: "Considering the preponderance of information gathered from various law enforcement agencies concerning the defendant's lengthy involvement in organized crime and with criminal figures, this officer does not feel that the defendant would be amenable to the rehabilitative designation of a probationary program nor can he meet society's expectations of a law-abiding citizen." Daddy was remanded to the county jail, pending a request for appeal and bond. Both were denied, and on March 2 he was transferred from the Tulsa County Jail to the McAlester State Penitentiary. Two days later he turned fifty-five. The prison barber gave him a buzz cut.

"Damn! I should never have stopped them," Daddy later told Kam. He was referring to a plot cooked up a year or so before the Sears arrest. Some members of the Dixie Mafia, fed up with what they felt to be Buddy Fallis's cocky and duplicious behavior, had decided to take action. As Fallis came out the door of his home some morning, or drove into his driveway some evening, they would walk up and blow his brains out. Or maybe they would wire his car and watch it go boom. "No, leave him alone," Daddy had told them. "He lives in my neighborhood, and I don't want anything like that happening there. Besides, it would put too much heat on all of us." The Dixie Mafia abandoned the idea.

Daddy had taken a financial beating from legal fees—he later claimed a cost of $70,000. I was told that originally he could have bought his way out for $25,000. And when he stopped to think about how he had hired a high-powered lawyer (Stipe) and the guy hadn't even thought to get the plea-bargain agreement in writing, he began to feel that Stipe had been brought in on the whole conspiracy against him. While Daddy was in prison, Stipe's wife was robbed of her big diamond ring at gunpoint, and some of Stipe's prize racehorses were found shot to death in their pasture. Some observers are still convinced that Daddy had retaliated.

Lee Eller confirmed that Daddy was quite capable of retaliation: "You didn't cross him. Just like the Evans boys, Gomer and Jerome. We were gambling one time and they beat both of us out of some money, using a crooked top. They got us, but it cost them, and cost them, and cost them, and kept costing them. Like acid all over their automobiles, different things like that. Old Buster Cullison crossed him for a thousand dollars and wouldn't pay him. His barns went up in flames. Wayne had a way of knowing what was going to happen. I'm not saying he did it personally, but it seemed to happen and he was aware of it. Kind of a coincidence, heh heh."

After a two-week stay in McAlester State Penitentiary for administrative purposes, Daddy was sent to the Lexington Regional Treatment Center in Lexington, Oklahoma, about twenty miles south of Oklahoma City and, ironically, only a few miles from the little town of Wayne. Located in a flat, dry part of the state, the Lexington facility is a minimum security prison that looks like a small army base, with a front gate and rows of barracks. I wrote to him often, more often than usual, to help keep his spirits up.

He wrote back from Lexington, as prisoner #94420:

[March 28, 1977]

Dear Son,

I don't know how I got this smart but here I am. I know you probably think I'm in trouble but this isn't that bad of a deal. If I was in The Walls [McAlester] in a cage it would be the shits. This place has a 12' or 14' fence but no one hardly leaves—they're all short termers here. It's more like an army camp, but you don't get paid.

I was supposed to get 3 yrs probation on a guilty plea but got doublecrossed at the last—oh well, you can't have everything.

I'll be out of here in 4 or 5 months, don't worry I have all I need. Kam drives down every week, we visit for 4 hours once a week, it takes 6 hrs driving for her—sorry about that. Sometimes she drives half way and stays with her brother.

I hope Patty and the grandson is OK. I always know they are taken care of. Hope you have a good place for the summer.

I haven't heard about Patty's mother lately. Hope she is better.

Don't bother to answer—write to Kam if you can. She is lonesome. Maybe you can cheer her up.

This place here is so ugly it would make a freight train take a dirt road.

I'll be home at the end of summer, so that won't be bad at all.

I'm starting to welding school tomorrow and taking time this next few days and will take my G.E.D. course. I need a diploma?

Take care of all and I'll see you sometime later this year.

Love you all. W.P.

P.S. Don't worry a minute. I'm fine, meeting lots of crooks to improve my image.

On April 6, he wrote:

Dear Son,

Received your letter today, it's nice to get them once in a while when you are "captured." I'm as lost as Pres. Carter would be without his teeth. Not really, that was supposed to be funny. I'm kinda like you are, I like to be free and do as I like. It hasn't worked out this time. The papers lied and the whole thing was a bunch of B.S. Whether people believe what they read or not I couldn't care less. I'm going to worry about me for a while instead of other people.

This is not a bad place, I work all day and don't have time to worry. I stay busy until bedtime, you know me. I don't mind working.

I really don't have time to read. People have sent books, so I don't need any more. They have a library here, also a law library.

If you plan to visit here you will have to write a letter and tell them about what time you can be here. Saturday is the day Kam comes, so you and Pat and Wayne could ride down with her. If you don't get permission you can't come. I really think you should enjoy your visit in Tulsa and not worry about me. I can see you later. Kam comes every week and I work the rest of the time. I'll be out by Sept. so it's no big deal. You just live this life and don't think about outside or time and it's easier.

When visitors leave, it bothers you but it does that to everyone in here.

You can't take pictures in here. They have cameras inside.

I don't want people being upset because I am not, myself. I can stand this real nice. I'm adjusted and know about when I will get out. It is hard on Kam, and kids say bad things to Wayne but that should make him tough. He always wanted to be a policeman so if this changes his mind it will be worth it for that alone. I would never want him to be one of those things at all.

Senator Young of Sapulpa spoke here at a welding graduation class (not mine) and looked at me and said hello. Also told me he had a phone call from Lee Eller asking him to help me.

Ron, don't worry about writing. I get 5 or 6 letters per week and can't answer them all. You should know how I hate to write by now.

I'm laying on my back writing on a book. I guess you can tell that, can't you?

Hope you are all O.K. Tell Pat and Wayne hello and I'll see you later.

Kam can tell you how things are.

Take care.

Wayne

He included a drawing of himself behind bars, with the caption "Your dad."

On May 13, he received his high school diploma.

A month later I went back to Tulsa and drove down with Mom, Kam, and my wife to see him. Security at Lexington was light, and we soon found ourselves inside the grounds, where inmates and their visitors, mostly family members, were already mingling, both outside at a picnic area and inside in a lounge. In many cases I couldn't tell the visitors from the inmates, all of whom were nonviolent offenders. In fact, communiqués from the superintendent of the facility referred to inmates as "residents."

Daddy looked great. He was wearing white cotton pants, a white shirt with the sleeves rolled up, and a red and white baseball cap. He had dropped some extra weight and his general tone was excellent.

He kissed Kam and Pat, shook my hand and gave me that beautiful little smile of his and said, "Howdy, pardner." It was as if we had just walked into his living room.

We strolled over to a picnic table and sat down. Kids were running and playing around us. The day was sunny but not hot, with a few rags of white cloud in the distance. The general atmosphere was festive.

"You look great," I said.

"I feel pretty good," he said. "You know I've had high blood pressure for all these years, but after a while they tested me here and found that it had dropped down to normal. I don't even take the medicine now." He also talked about how relaxing it was not to have to carry money, and how most of the guys there were pretty good fellows.

"Oh, there was one guy who thought he could whip me. We went around back and I straightened him out."

He then talked about the welding classes he was taking, describing different kinds of welds. It was part of his rehabilitation program. He mentioned getting his high school diploma.

"Now I'll be able to get a better job," he said, shooting us a look.

I began to wonder. Maybe this stay in jail *was* good for him. It seemed to be having the effect of a vacation spa. I hadn't seen him this relaxed and happy in years. Or was he putting a good face on it for our benefit? No, he really looked good.

Even without his teeth he looked good, in a photograph that appeared in the July 14, 1977, *Tulsa Tribune*. It accompanied the one and only interview he ever gave a reporter.

The article begins: "Wayne M. Padgett. The name means muscle. To policemen, it conjures up an image of underworld influence, power, and organized crime. To Padgett's friends, his name means an always ready helping hand, a needed loan, or a stern word to a man who is not spending enough time with his family. Who is Wayne Padgett, the man with the 'Godfather' image?"

After reciting the names of his underworld friends and quoting the police's description of him as the "Kingpin" of crime in Tulsa County, the article admiringly points out that "Padgett, at age 55, is strong enough to whip two men half his age."

In the article, Daddy denied that he had ever cooperated with the FBI: "I've never told the FBI, the state crime bureau, city police, or anybody else any information about anybody in my whole life. I just don't believe in that and I never have. I'm dead set against people being like that. I know we have to have them, but I'm not going to be one of them. To me, they're worse than the people violating the law." He added that "at Rex Brinlee's trial, a crime bureau agent got up and volunteered that I informed on Brinlee—they didn't even ask him, he just volunteered it. They did that to make me look bad."

As for the presence of organized crime in Tulsa, Daddy said that it would never happen as long as Jack Purdie was police chief. "Purdie is a tough cop—but he is honest and fair. He's what's keeping those guys out." Notice Daddy's discrimination between the two types of criminals, the Mafia and the local boys.

When the reporter asked Daddy "why some persons in and around Tulsa drop the Padgett name as a show of muscle, Padgett pulled back his sleeve, pointed to his ripping bicep and said, 'I guess it's sitting right here.'"

In talking about his bootlegging days, he said, "This room wouldn't hold all the whiskey I sold to police officers."

Not surprisingly, Daddy had uncomplimentary things to say about the Tulsa D.A.: "Buddy Fallis told my attorney that he should plead me out for probation. That sounded good, so we decided to do it. But when I came to court that day and saw all those policemen, I knew I was trapped. I knew I had been turned around. The court later ruled the deal wasn't any good because it wasn't in writing. Where I come from, a deal is a deal. I'm here because Buddy Fallis tricked me into this. He outsmarted me, but I'll tell you what, he'll never get another shot at me."

The camaraderie of prison life appealed to him: "The people in here are great, they help each other. They share—it's not like on the outside."

Daddy also talked about his personal life: "The worst part is being away from your family. A man needs to be with his son when he is this age," referring to Wayne Jr., then age eight. Perhaps without realizing it, Daddy was talking about his own childhood and adolescence without a father.

The lengthy *Tribune* article gave a surprisingly balanced portrait of Daddy, allowing him ample space to respond to charges and to show the world that he was, deep down, a right guy. It even provided matching photographs of him, smiling affably, and Kam, "an attractive former dancer."

Daddy had granted the interview solely at the urging of his new lawyer, Al Benningfield, who felt that if Daddy wanted parole, he had better get some good publicity for a change. The article was a start.

Meanwhile, letters urging Daddy's release had been pouring in at the parole board, more than forty so far. The letters were from friends, family members, business associates, and even a minister, portraying him as the Robin Hood they knew him to be.

His old friend Lee Eller described him as "a real gentleman and true friend. Wayne has always been anxious to do his best for his friends and to help them in any way he possibly could." Tony Hampton, vice president of Riverside Industries, had known Daddy since ironworking days. He told the parole board that he had a job available for Daddy anytime he wanted it. Fred Stone described Daddy as "the best business partner and personal friend I have ever had. I would do anything I could for Wayne. Personal or financial. He can have anything I have. I think that much of him." Turner Burnette wrote that "Wayne has done things for my family which very few longtime friends would have done," adding how he had provided emergency cars to family members and helped them recover from a fire.

OKLAHOMA TOUGH

Lee Baehler wrote, "He is one of the most wonderful men I have ever had the pleasure of meeting," and "he is very unique in that he has very high morals." She echoed others in saying "he does good things sometimes without anyone knowing, like a policeman was injured in a car wreck and Wayne loaded his pick-up with groceries and took them to the family, without giving his name or anything." Oliver Marler of Tulsa Manufacturing Jewelers called him "one of the most honest and fair men possible" who had "helped a larger number of friends." Howard Brown at Ramsey Chevrolet wrote, "I think Wayne would give a man the shirt off his back if he thought it was for a good cause." Kam's sister Gen reaffirmed that "Wayne puts everyone's welfare above his own."

Pete James said that Daddy is "a very dedicated family man, a gentleman in the true sense of the word, and a sincere, sober, salt of the earth type person. He has helped so many people in time of need." Mike San Miguel, a neighbor on East 39th Street, called him "a good neighbor and friend who is always willing to lend a hand." San Miguel also mentioned how kind Daddy was with his children, taking them fishing or to the park. Minister Jerry O'Dell said, "I have found him willing to put himself out on numerous occasions in assisting people with needs or problems." Paul Denton offered Daddy a job at his Ford dealership, pointing out how he was "the greatest help and consolation to family and friends alike, completely fair and honorable." Gail Schulte wrote movingly about how Daddy had helped her pull through when her father died, adding, "I can say without hesitation that I would trust Wayne with the lives and raising of my two little girls."

Dan Thompson pointed out how, when his father died, Daddy bought a house and let Dan's mother live in it rent-free until she remarried. Clemens Laurrell described coming home on leave from the army during World War II: "I didn't have any money or car and Wayne loaned me money and a car. He also helped many other people. At Christmas he would take food to the poor. I know, because I went with him." Robert Cottingim wrote: "Wayne has really kept me on the straight and narrow path throughout all the years I've known him. When I first got married I was having a hard time making ends meet. I had a chance to do some contract lumber hauling, but I couldn't afford a truck. Wayne loaned me a truck and bought my gasoline and then he wouldn't accept anything in return. He has kept after me all my life and several times when I began to stray he has reminded me of what he has always said should be every man's policy in life: 'Always be honest and never try to put the screws to your friends and you'll never have to cover up for something you've said or done.'"

Daddy's attorney, Al Benningfield, wrote that "he has always truly epitomized the very essence of the Judeo-Christian ethic," and "Wayne's reputation for truthfulness and ethics within the business community is unsurpassed. Any businessman or banker who has dealt with Wayne will tell you that truly his word is his bond. I personally know that Wayne Padgett's handshake is worth more than any set of multi-exhibited written contracts that could be produced by a whole covey of Philadelphia lawyers." Ed Elias, the owner of Eddy's Steak House, said, "I think he is a wonderful human being and I would do anything I could for Wayne. He has helped me as well as other members of my family in the past." David Sisson, Daddy's partner at Midamerica Powerguard, pointed out that "we have operated our business with no written agreements as I have always found Wayne to be an honorable man and his word is as strong as any contract. My wife and I have always considered him to be hard-working, fair, and of good character." In my own letter, I wrote, "My father taught me to be honest, to work hard, to be obedient, to stay out of trouble, not to lie, to be fair, courteous, respectful, sober, and decent. He was firm with me when firmness was called for, but he was also generous and sweet. His word was as solid as steel, and he acquired a reputation as a man whom you could count on, a reputation he maintains." Kam and several others pointed out how good he was with children. And many people emphasized what good care he took of his mother, now seventy-seven. Billie Sue Brewer, a family friend, summed it all up with "I don't think I have ever met a finer man than Wayne Padgett."

Perhaps the letter that carried the greatest weight among parole board members came from Gene Stipe, who had continued to represent Daddy a short while after the guilty plea. Stipe's letter got a respectful and optimistic reply from at least one board member. Pardon and Parole Board Chairman Charles Chesnut promptly placed Daddy on the docket for a hearing. He had been in prison for only four months.

Letters or no letters, Tulsa law officials were outraged. The D.A.'s office described Buddy Fallis as "quite upset," and an officer in the organized crime unit said, "It took us nearly forty years to nail him on a felony and now they are thinking about letting him go. We'll come down personally and tell them about Padgett if they would like." Criminals speculated that Daddy might have cut a deal with the FBI. One thug said that Lester Pugh, Jerry James, and Don Sparks planned to kill Daddy, believing that he was an FBI informant—exactly the reaction the FBI agent had hoped for. Regardless, Tulsa police sent the parole board a petition signed by hundreds of police officers, and on July 24 his bid was denied by a vote of five to zero.

Daddy's attorney, Al Benningfield—who incidentally had been my classmate in elementary school—had told the board that of course Daddy had been a bootlegger years ago, but added that "the street talk that has followed this man around has come from the lowest and most incredible sources," that is, from riffraft and stool pigeons. Benningfield pointed out that the pre-sentencing police rap sheet on Daddy was filled with such garbage: "Judge Armstrong [who had pronounced sentence] did personally authorize me to say to the parole board that never in his history on the bench had such hearsay [the tainted rap sheet] been introduced at a sentencing hearing, and that it did influence his decision, and that in retrospect he didn't think it should have." Benningfield also pointed out that "Wayne Padgett's word is his bond," describing him as a "strong, close-knit family man who has helped several persons overcome difficulties." One parole board member replied that there is "no doubt that he has been an asset to any number of people," but told Daddy, "you can't erase reputation. Some people think you are connected with the Mafia . . . the criminal . . . everything that's big in Oklahoma. I'm not saying it's true." At least this board member was showing signs of waffling. The public relations campaign was paying off. In fact, the board assured Daddy that they would grant parole at his next hearing.

The next day the public relations war intensified. A July 25, 1977, *Tribune* article quoted Floyd Cumbey, a convicted killer serving two life sentences, as saying that Daddy had engineered an armed robbery in Joplin, then sold them out. Cumbey also believed that Daddy had betrayed Rex Brinlee: "The FBI said he did."

Around this time, Daddy sold his one-half interest in Midamerica Powerguard, a Tulsa firm that marketed, distributed, and installed electrical energy conservation devices. He had bought into the company in April 1976 for $14,000 and by the end of the year had earned $11,500. The total value of the company had grown to around $100,000. Not surprisingly,

Daddy and his partner David Sisson had conducted their business with no written agreements. When Sisson later decided that he wanted to buy out Daddy's interest, Kam wrote to me that Sisson "gave me an offer and I gave it to Wayne and then when Wayne set a price, I jacked it a thousand and sold. Wayne just laughed, I told him I needed some mad money for the rest of the summer."

On September 23, Daddy was transferred to an even lower security facility, the Oklahoma City Community Corrections Center, and six days later he was moved to a comparable facility in Muskogee, where he was assigned to drive work-release prisoners to and from their jobs on weekdays. The Muskogee officials described him as a "model prisoner." Because of good behavior, he was allowed to spend nearly every weekend in Tulsa, working at a car lot.

He and Fred Stone had dissolved their real estate partnership in 1975 because of Fred's health, and Daddy was trying to work out the financial mess he had gotten himself into when he invested in a Kentucky coal mining operation with a friend named Jake Loggins. Apparently, Daddy had been able to convince farmers to sell their mineral rights, the same farmers who, according to one source, "would run bigshot college graduate geologists right off their land." But it turned out to be a losing proposition. According to Lee Eller, both Daddy and Johnny Eller lost money, but "there wasn't any hellfire and brimstone about it, it was just a poor investment— the knots just weren't tied at the end of the rope. They got screwed." Daddy was also extricating himself from a Tulsa real-estate venture with Loggins.

Meanwhile, Kam had been earning a little money by making costumes for barmaids and club waitresses.

On November 13, the state parole board voted four to one in favor of Daddy's parole, much to the distress of Tulsa law authorities. They took the matter straight to Governor David Boren, who promptly denied parole, on the grounds that the "law enforcement community" was strongly against it.

But life became a little easier when Daddy was transferred to the Tulsa Community Corrections Center, on January 5, 1978. The Center consisted of the top two floors of the old John 3:16 Mission building on a rundown street on the north edge of downtown. The John 3:16 Mission was directed by a guy named Homer "Tree Top" Still, so called because in his prime he stood six foot seven and weighed nearly three hundred pounds. A former policeman and now a Baptist minister, Still wasn't crazy about having

Daddy in the facility: "I arrested Wayne when he was a bootlegger. In fact I was about the only officer that would arrest him, because I didn't take his payoff." Daddy was allowed to leave the building on work release during the day, returning only to sleep there on weekday nights.

Things were looking up. On April 22, the Pardon and Parole Board voted once again 4–1 in favor of parole, and this time Governor Boren signed the papers. On June 27, 1978, the "model prisoner" was released on parole, and six months later was discharged. He had paid his debt—twenty-three months—to society.

He felt, though, that he owed a moral debt to Lee Eller for what had happened in the meantime to his son Johnny. Daddy, Johnny's godfather, had saved him from any number of scrapes. Some of Johnny's deals were borderline legal, others actually crossed the line. Al Benningfield recalled that "Johnny hired me to do legal work for him, for the land promotion deals he was doing up at Grand Lake. Every once in a while I'd go on trips with him, and he'd have Wayne along as 'protection.' Trips to Springfield and Las Vegas. Then there were other times when Wayne and Johnny'd go on trips together, and Johnny'd tell me, 'I've got Wayne with me because I'm doing business with people who might want to hurt me. They ain't gonna hurt me if Wayne's there.'"

But not long after Daddy went to prison, Johnny was found dead with a bullet in his head. According to Benningfield: "A lot of people said that had Wayne not been in prison, this probably wouldn't have happened."

Soon after his release, Daddy went to Lee and offered to pursue the matter, but Lee, now a born-again Christian, wasn't interested in revenge.

This moral debt aside, there was another "debt" that had been silently accruing, one that Daddy would never be able to settle.

19   *Slowing Down*

ON THE WAY TO TULSA FROM Tucson with a load of hot merchandise back in 1967, Daddy had blown his nose and felt a terrible pain in his head, and when he looked down at the Kleenex, he saw blood on it, a lot of blood. When the pain and bleeding persisted, he and Kam went to the nearest hospital emergency room, where the bleeding finally was staunched. After the two got to Tulsa, he went to a doctor, who removed some cartilege or bone in the sinuses, to widen a passage.

But when the condition didn't improve, a surgeon performed a biopsy. One sample was a harmless growth, but two others revealed adenoidal cystic carcinoma: sinus cancer, of a rare type. Shortly thereafter, most of the tumor was removed. When Daddy told me about it on the phone, he dismissed it as "nothing." And when I saw him the following summer, indeed over the next ten years, he looked strong and healthy. His hair turned from silver to a radiant snowy white, but otherwise he seemed to age very little.

But eventually Daddy acknowledged that his sinuses had grown tighter and tighter. Tests dated July 26, 1978, suggested that the tumor had reappeared. Four months later, an X-ray showed its dimensions and location. When he went into the hospital for a biopsy, Kam called me with the news, and I flew to Tulsa. It was a shock to see him flat on his back in a hospital bed, unshaven, his hair mussed, his eyes black, breathing through his mouth because of the wadding stuffed into his nostrils.

"Hey," I said.

He smiled wanly and waved a finger in the direction of a man standing at the foot of his bed. It was his old friend Clemens Laurrell. Some years back Clemens had given up drinking and become a born-again Christian.

"You remember me don't you, Ronnie?" Clemens said.

"Of course I do, Clemens. How are you?" We shook hands.

"It's been a while, ain't it?" he answered.

"Sure has. But you look good." I went over to the bedside. "But *you*, you look like you had a rough night on the town."

Daddy started to smile and said in a muffled voice, "Worst thing I ever felt."

Then he described the biopsy procedure, which involved going deep up into his sinuses, almost as far as the brain. Slowly he pulled out a long strand of wadding. It was darkened with blood.

After a while Clemens said, "Ronnie, I gotta go. It sure was good seeing you again. Wayne, take care of yourself. Let me know if you need anything. I mean *anything at all*." They shook hands.

"I'll walk you to the elevator, Clemens," I said.

We walked down to a waiting area near the nurses' station.

"What can you tell me, Clemens?"

OKLAHOMA TOUGH

"Well, Ronnie, it don't look good. I ain't never seen Wayne like this, and I just about can't stand it." He put his hand to his eyes and started to cry quietly. "I'd do anything for Wayne. I'd take his place right now in that bed if I could. You know, I've had a couple of heart attacks. I just can't stand seeing him like this." Clemens was the same gentle soul he had been when he had delivered whiskey for Daddy thirty years ago.

We said goodbye and I went back to the room.

"Son, this is rough." Daddy was referring not only to the physical pain of the biopsy, but also to the anguished hallucinations induced by the sedatives. "At one point I opened my eyes and all I could see was black, but the black was full of black worms, millions of them, twisting and crawling around one another, millions of them all glistening, and I knew that was Death." As he spoke, his face had taken on a wild look. "It was horrible. The most horrible thing I ever saw. . . . But how about you? What's new in New York? How's your wife and the boy?" He wasn't a hallucinatory type of guy.

I made some conversation and then said, "I can stay in town as long as you need me. How long are you going to be in here?"

"I think they'll let me go home tomorrow. Then I'll have to come back for treatments."

"What kind?"

"Cobalt. It's like an X-ray, it doesn't hurt, but it has some side effects. It causes your hair to fall out, but I don't need any hair. You know, I could die now without any regrets. I've had a good life, a full life, and I have nothing to complain about." His voice was getting weaker. I suggested he get some rest.

The next day he was home, looking remarkably better, and a day or so after that I drove him back to the hospital for his first radiation treatment. It was a lengthy preliminary session in which the radiologists positioned him carefully and marked, with a dye, big red lines across his face to serve as guides for the bombardment. Dr. Brownson, his oncologist, had offered surgery as an alternative, but my father had refused: it would have required the virtual demolition of his face and many rounds of reconstructive surgery. Because of the tumor's proximity to the brain—another quarter of an inch and treatment would have been useless—the rays had to be aimed very carefully.

When he emerged from the radiology department, people gaped. The bold red lines on his face made him look like an Indian in a sort of New

Age war paint, and on the ride home he began to enjoy the startled expressions of drivers next to us at stoplights.

"Scares the shit out of 'em," he laughed.

The next day he received his first in a series of cobalt treatments, something called Clinac-18, "utilizing 10meV photons" in medical parlance. What it came down to was a ray that could go into his head and stop the growth of the tumor, we hoped. Without treatment, the cancer would reach his brain and kill him. Dr. Brownson told him that the radiation offered approximately a one-in-ten chance of his living more than a year.

"What have I got to lose?" was Daddy's response.

By the end of the year he had received eight bombardments. His friend Pete James suggested that he also try a special cancer clinic in Tijuana. The place was said to have had some successes, due to a combination of Laetrile, vitamin C, and a strict low-fat diet. Daddy decided to give it a try.

In April he flew out to stay with Pete in Los Angeles, then drove down to the clinic for a one-week stay of intensive treatment. After commuting from Pete's to the clinic for five or six weeks, he returned to Tulsa with a suitcase full of Laetrile and instructions for his diet. He looked much better.

Subsequent tests showed that the tumor had gone into remission. It had not metastasized. Five years later Daddy told me, "It was like I died back then. Now this is like being in heaven. It's all gravy."

Of course, it wasn't entirely paradisal. The radiation had permanently destroyed his salivation glands, causing an unremitting dryness in the mouth and throat. Occasionally he took a sip of olive oil, to keep his throat lubricated. He continued to suffer from sinus headaches, which medication could only partly assuage. At some point he also got some relief through acupuncture, apparently from an Asian specialist in California. I was very surprised that he had even tried acupuncture, which at that time was relegated to the quack or weirdo category by most Americans.

The temporary loss of his hair didn't bother him at all. Nor did he seem to be bothered by the impotence that such treatments cause. For one year he had no sexual function. "It's as if you're dead down there," he told me matter-of-factly. But all in all, it looked as though he might "lick the Big C," as John Wayne, to whom he was often compared, had put it.

One benefit of his condition was that he was listed as a terminal cancer patient and thus eligible for disability support from the government. He used the monthly checks to cover his basic living expenses.

Sometime in mid-1979, Kam stunned everyone. She left Daddy. She had stood by him throughout his imprisonment, but the accumulated weight of his jealousy and control had become too heavy, and it's also possible that she could not face the prospect of watching him slowly die. She was nearing thirty-seven. There was still time for her to start a new life. She was even desperate enough to leave her ten-year-old son behind. Daddy tore up her clothes and threw out the shoebox full of letters he had written to her from prison. When I heard Kam had left—especially at such a critical time—I was shocked. I knew she would never return, or rather, that Daddy would never forgive her.

But I was wrong again, for by December she was back and, as Mom put it in a letter, "everyone seems to be happy." When I came to Tulsa to buy a pickup truck, which he had found for me, I noticed nothing unusual about their relationship. As usual, Kam was lively and he was amiably laconic. In any case, neither of them would have talked to me about their personal problems, Kam because of my bloodlines, Daddy because he was of the old school: you don't discuss or analyze your feelings.

Despite appearances, by March of the next year he was back in the hospital for exploratory tests. He had always had "stomach trouble," and the doctors wanted to take a look. An endoscopy showed some scar tissue in the stomach, but no cancer.

In mid-April Mom wrote me, "Everyone here is very well. Wayne is looking better and gaining strength." With typical spunk, she described how she herself had recently gotten three strikes in one game of bowling, at the age of eighty.

According to Kam, throughout most of the 1980s, periodic checkups showed that the cancer was still in remission. In the early 1980s, Daddy seemed to mellow a little. He even did something unthinkable: he let his hair grow long. A two-haircuts-a-month guy all his adult life, he now adopted what I, recalling the locks of President Johnson in the early 1970s, called the late-LBJ look. He also came around to the idea that marijuana wasn't any worse than alcohol, though he never smoked marijuana and he continued to have no tolerance for other illicit drugs. In general, he seemed to take the view that some things that had gotten him hot under the collar in the past weren't really very important. He even mellowed about my mother. Her remarriages didn't seem to bother him.

But with Kam it was a different story. Although he took her back after each of their splits, he was never free of jealousy. His jealousy may have been exacerbated by his continuing impairment of sexual function. In August of 1983 he threw her out once again and filed for divorce. This time it was for real: the divorce became legal and final.

Kam quickly married a guy named Wes Littlefield, but soon discovered he was not to her liking. It's lucky for him that she did, because Daddy had arranged for a close friend to "have a talk" with Littlefield. That is, a *final* talk.

At the same time, Daddy required his friends to have no contact with Kam, an order Pete James ignored by having Kam continue as his barber. Daddy went into a rage and vowed to have nothing further to do with him. But gradually Daddy did start speaking to Pete again.

A few years after their rift, Pete was blown up against his bedroom ceiling. A bomb placed under his house blew out an entire wall and the back porch. Pete suffered only a broken leg and multiple cuts: his box spring and thick mattress had absorbed the shrapnel. Pete told the Bureau of Alcohol, Firearms, and Tobacco that he had received no threats, but that a silent caller had phoned around midnight. Privately Pete felt that he knew the identity of one of the two men whom neighbors had seen driving away in an old pickup truck an hour before the explosion. Wayne Padgett.

"Oh no," Bobby Bluejacket told me. "Your dad told me it was a deal out of California. It was a man and his son or maybe two brothers that Pete got crossways with in a business deal. I'll tell you what: if your dad had wanted him killed, the guyda got killed."

I believe the Bluejacket version, mainly because Daddy was not the kind of person to have someone killed because of a haircut.

A week after the bombing, Daddy called Pete to say that he knew who was behind it, but that he couldn't disclose their identities. Pete replied, "A fine fucking friend you are!" and their rift became permanent.

The loss of Pete's friendship was nothing compared to the news Daddy got in July of 1986: his brother Bob was diagnosed as having a glioblastoma, a rapidly growing brain lesion. In Bob's case, it was inoperable. Three and a half weeks later he died from it, at his home in San Mateo, California. Mom, now eighty-six and retired, was devastated. When Daddy gave me the news of Bob's death, he did so with manly calm, but I knew that he was concealing his real feelings, perhaps even from himself.

Daddy and Kam had not seen or spoken with each other for two and a half years when, in August of 1987, she knocked on his door.

"I didn't say anything, I just stood there looking at him."

He said, 'What are you doing here?'"

"I'm here to see my son."

"What about your old husband?"

"I'm just here to see Wayne Jr."

"He's not here, but come on in and let's have a cup of coffee. I've got to run up to the lease. You got time to run up there?"

Still divorced, they were soon back together. Kam: "I never remembered the bad, I'd just block it out," said Kam. "All I remembered was how warm and sweet and wonderful he was, and loving."

In November of 1988, Daddy had another biopsy. The old tumor was still there, but it had spread into the sinus cavity and into the bone. In fact, it had become inoperable. The doctor told him that surgery would result in his bleeding to death on the operating table.

There were no visible signs of his illness, but at this point he just didn't have the energy it takes to be a major criminal. He did some minor fencing, but mostly he was living on his disability checks and the trickle of income from his oil lease, which he himself worked. He still had an appetite for physical work. Bobby Bluejacket remembered seeing him "work so hard and get so tired he couldn't even get in the pickup. He'd have to sit down in the shade and rest before he could drive home. And he was in his late sixties."

Preparing for the inevitable, he had put everything he owned—his house, oil lease, truck, and car—in Wayne Jr.'s name. In his spare time, he continued to hunt with his old friend Al Haddock and to drop by to see friends such as Lee Eller, always bringing a pie or bag of doughnuts.

At one point, Lee's assets had been frozen. Eller recalled: "For about three months he made sure I had anything I needed. He'd come to our home and stay all day, he and I would ride around, we'd go to Sapulpa, just talk old times and laugh, we'd have our shotguns and dogs in the back. He didn't have anything particular to do."

Private detective B. T. Cook remembered that Daddy dropped by his wife's pawnshop once a week, just to shoot the breeze. "Wayne loved to talk. I told him, 'The older you get, the more you like to talk.'"

Daddy also liked to drive around town with Bobby Bluejacket, who recalled that "he and I'd run around all day long, daylight to dark, seven o'clock in the morning until eleven o'clock at night. Just driving everywhere all over town, in this business and over to this business. He had a big thing about going by Bama Pie and buying great big boxes of cookies and pies, and we'd pull up here and go in and he'd give people two or three bags of cookies, and we'd go over there and he'd give 'em a couple of pies. Every day we'd go around doing that!"

The two of them also liked to drive around and talk about old times. Kam recalled that as early as 1987, "all Bobby and Wayne would do is drive down through Archer Park and reminisce until you was up to here with their childhood things." They would slowly cruise up and down every street, pointing out, house by house, who had lived where, and what had happened to them. They could have compiled a gigantic oral history of the neighborhood.

Sometime around 1988 I was visiting Tulsa. Daddy invited me out to dinner with him and Bobby. The three of us drove to a steakhouse. When we stepped inside, the owner greeted us with, "Hi, Wayne, how's everything?" and told a waiter to show us to a table. I noticed that as soon as we had entered, Daddy and Bobby's demeanors had altered. They walked slower, their eyes scanning the diners with a cool, measured confidence, as if they were claiming this as *their* territory.

We ordered steaks with baked potatoes, maybe a beer or iced tea. Bobby and I fell into conversation. He told me that at Daddy's house he had seen a book I had coedited called *The Whole Word Catalogue 2*, a collection of essays about teaching writing. "I read the part about haiku," he said. "My daughter up in Minnesota was assigned to write haiku for school, and I helped her write a bunch of 'em. They're really interesting." He then went on to discuss the haiku form with an acuity that surpassed that of many of the teachers I had worked with. Then somehow we started talking about hair transplants.

Meanwhile, Daddy had polished off a slice of pie with whipped cream, and was signing the credit card receipt. I had never known him to have a credit card, and upon closer inspection I saw that he still didn't have one. It was in someone else's name. Of course, the management accepted it, since the owner was one of Daddy's cronies. (Years later Bobby explained that probably somebody had owed Daddy some money, and, being unable to repay him, had let him run up a certain amount on the card.) Regardless, I had thoroughly enjoyed the night out, with its weird blend of gangsterism and literature.

During another Tulsa visit, though, I caught Daddy in a far less mellow mood. It was sometime in the 1980s, and I don't know why it stands out in my memory. As always, he met my flight. We walked straight out to his car and drove toward the parking lot exit. Only one of two toll-booth windows was open, and there was a long line of cars ahead of us. It took us five or ten minutes to inch up to the window, by which time the cost for his parking had risen into the next thirty-minute increment. He was furious that *he* had to pay an extra fifty cents because the lot had only one window open. The young attendant recoiled in the face of Daddy's tirade. As we squealed away, I pointed out that it wasn't the kid's fault. "I don't give a shit," was his reply.

We pulled up to a stop sign, around which were other signs, symbols, and numbers pointing in various directions.

"You see those goddamned signs?" he began. "I got a ticket because of those fucking signs. They put them in a while back, and hell, I didn't know what those things mean. The policeman told me they were international symbols, and we needed them because of all the foreigners who can't read English. So why the hell don't they learn English or go back to where they fucking came from?"

"Hey, Daddy," I butted in, "you know I have no use for this line of talk. What is this anyway? *Welcome to Tulsa?*"

At that he cooled down. I knew that he was just scapegoating foreigners because he had gotten a traffic citation. Maybe I had just caught him on a bad day. Maybe his illness was wearing him down. Maybe things weren't going well at home.

At some point he and Kam had a huge argument because Kam's sister Joan left his friend Don Goodson and married someone else. Daddy went into a rage and inflicted some damage on the house.

Kam described another of his outbursts: "I'd been out Christmas shopping. He thought I'd been out sleeping with somebody. He *destroyed* the house on Thirty-ninth. That marbletop table? He took off the top, stuck it up against the door and tried to break it, went through the kitchen cabinets throwing beans and rice and flour, just knocking everything off. Took the double mirror from the dresser and bent it double over the TV. He never beat me up, but he was so strong! That night I had on a suede jacket. He picked me up by the lapels and just thumped me. Then I got mad and told him to go to hell, got in the car and drove off. That's when he tore up my pictures and slashed my clothes. He told some people later, 'I was going to cut *all* her clothes up, but I got tired, because she had so damned many.'" In retelling this ugly incident, even Kam laughed at his joke.

Yet another domestic dispute ended in laughter. Kam related: "One time he grabbed me and I was so mad that I was going to try to whip him with my bare hands, and he was gonna leave because he didn't want to hurt me, and I flung myself up against the door, and I know I looked like a *wild* person—he had me crazy! I would have killed him with anything I could have got my hands on before he got out that door. He wasn't gonna do this to me and run out the door again. And he started laughing! There I was trying to block this 200-something pound man and fire was coming out of my nose, and he started laughing. And I got to thinking as to how I must have looked, and I got to laughing. I said, 'You're driving me to be a stark raving maniac!'"

In November of 1988, Kam bought half-interest in a bar called Bottoms Up, not far from their home. Her idea was to give them an additional source of income from a business they could gradually turn over to Little Wayne, who, at twenty-one, had earned a brown belt in karate and was bench pressing huge weights, and could handle himself in a bar. But owning a bar also meant Kam's spending long hours there among guys on the make. Daddy's jealousy resurfaced, and the two argued repeatedly. Three months after buying the bar, Kam came home and found a pillow outside the closed bedroom door. On the pillow was a note that read: "If your new partner can't buy you out, go to Romine [Tulsa vending machine mogul] and he will get it financed for you. Get me my money. Move out today. W.P." She took her clothes and left.

The next month, he and Mom flew down to Houston to visit Tommie, who for some years with his new wife had organized Junior Miss pageants across the Southwest. But now he too was being treated for cancer. Mom wrote to me, "Wayne and I had a nice trip to Houston. It helped Tom so much. We ate all meals out and drove around a lot, two hours, before we left. He had to check in the hospital for more chemo treatments, which make him very ill for three or four days. He is out now for a while, but a long way to go according to the doctor."

Kam moved into an apartment and continued running the bar. But another type of cancer was eating at Daddy, a vendetta against her. Kam is certain that it was he who slashed all the tires in the bar's parking lot one night. She feels certain that it was he who smashed the club's front-door glass and sign. "I'm going to bust you," she recalled his telling her. According to her, he kept coming by the club, telling her he was going to shoot her, that because he had terminal cancer he had nothing to lose. When she locked up the bar at 2 A.M., she'd see him just sitting in his car across the street, looking at her. He was watching one night when she and a guy named Dale Wygant, who dropped into the bar from time to time, were leaving the club. Dale was about Kam's age. A good-natured, slow-talking good old boy, he was running his own service station. Kam recalled: "Dale and I were having our first date. We were in two separate cars, delivering one to a friend of his. Wayne saw me get in my little Honda and Dale in a brown Chevrolet. We took off out the back way of the club and he cut Dale off." A tremendous fistfight ensued. Sixty-seven years old and weakened by his worsening cancer—in fact only a year away from death—Daddy was still powerful enough to get the better of his strongly built opponent. Daddy told me about it on the phone.

"I got pretty well banged up," he said, "but you should see the other guy."

According to Kam, "Dale was beat up really bad. His face was just, oh shit—I mean horrible, horrible." Apparently, Daddy also hit Dale in the head with a pipe, leaving a permanent indentation in his skull. The three of them ended up in jail.

Daddy got a $500 fine and a warning from the judge that if he came near Kam again he would go to prison for a year.

In November of 1989, Kam and Dale got married.

Kam believes that Daddy fully intended to kill her, but that the suddenness of his final illness prevented it. The fact is that if he had really wanted her dead, she would be dead today.

When Tommie's condition worsened, Daddy and Wayne Jr. took Mom back to Houston. In 1990, Tommie finally died. Wayne was the only child Mom had left.

At some point not too long after Kam's departure in 1989, Daddy invited Nancy Bluejacket (née Mann) out to dinner. In her early thirties, Nancy was a lively Tulsa girl who had grown up in a middle-class family of Holy Rollers. Her father had worked his way up from bagging groceries at a local supermarket chain to serving as its president. He extended his work ethic to his children: after high school they were entirely on their own, financially speaking. Daddy had first met her when she was fifteen and doing odd jobs for his friend Charley Corley, who owned a car lot and a swimming pool company.

"Wayne helped me out of a lot of messes," Nancy recalled, "especially with nasty boyfriends and bad husbands. He was my protector, my best friend. There wasn't anything I couldn't tell him."

After high school Nancy audited nursing courses at the University of Tulsa and at the Oklahoma State University Medical School, enabling her to pass a state certification test and become a home-health-care aide.

It was through Daddy and Charley Corley that she met and married Bobby Bluejacket. By 1989 she was divorced from Bobby, who was at that time a guest of the federal government in one of its penal institutions. In the late 1980s, Daddy, Kam, Bobby, and Nancy had spent a lot of time together. Now, with Kam gone, Daddy was lonely, so he invited Nancy out for dinner. According to her, she saw it simply as spending time with an old friend who was going through a bad time.

They had dinner at a nice supper club called The Palace, and they even danced a little, which was unusual for him. Afterward she drove him home. Before getting out of the car he leaned over and kissed her, and she thought, "Oh, my." When she got home she found his message on her phone machine, asking if she'd like to go up to his oil lease the next morning. From then on, they were constant companions.

There was a genuine affection between them, based on years of trust and friendship. And he was more than happy to be around her three daughters, who were crazy about him. It is uncertain how Wayne Jr. felt about the new situation, but it is unlikely that he approved.

Nancy and Daddy seemed made for each other. She was ready to jump in the truck and go up to the lease with him, or rummage through abandoned houses for things that he could give to others, or just stay home with the girls.

It was not as if his wild streak had died out. In fact, she recalled several pyrotechnical adventures. "Wayne loved fires. He was a fire freak. I remember one night when the oil lease had sprung a big leak. We wadded up newspapers and lit and threw them out onto the oil slick. Suddenly I realized, 'We're at an oil well, and there's oil all over the ground, and it is pumping, and we have these oil tanks. . . .' I walked out into the field and looked around: the fire was the most beautiful red and orange, and black billows of smoke were going everywhere. It was gorgeous. He said, 'Now you can see why I like fires.'" Fortunately he had started a backfire, which controlled the flames.

In another incident, the flames almost got the better of him. A young woman was having financial difficulties, including car payments, so to help her he drove her car out to a remote field and doused it with gasoline. He then lit a match and threw it onto the front seat, and took off running. The impact of the explosion threw him forward, and when he got back to his truck he noticed that all the hair had been singed off his arms.

But after one particular trip to Kansas City, even he had to admit that his "running" days were numbered. He had gone there expecting to be included in some big action, but the new Mob there—younger men with college educations and three-piece suits—told him he was too old. Dealing with such rejection was very hard for him, but finally he began to think of just taking it easy. He and Nancy started talking about traveling, maybe taking some cruises. He was especially keen on taking her to Alaska, the most beautiful place he had ever seen. She would love it.

20 *Last Days*

WHO WOULD HAVE THOUGHT THAT Daddy would die in a hail of bullets in a final shootout with twenty-two FBI agents atop the Empire State Building? No one, because it didn't happen. For the purposes of bestsellers and action films, that would have been a better ending, but in my father's case, we have only that blazing series of moments known as real life.

Daddy's oil lease was near Collinsville, about twenty miles north of Tulsa. In February of 1991, working alone at the lease, he had slipped and fallen against the side of his pickup truck, banging his ribs. The resulting pain did not go away, and as the weeks went by he grew shorter and shorter of breath. Finally, after much urging on the part of Nancy, he went to see a doctor, who hospitalized him at Saint John Medical Center for tests. An X-ray showed a partially collapsed left lung, with fluid buildup. It also showed a tumor the size of a fist. The sinus cancer, tired of waiting, had finally sent its emissary to another region.

The doctor drained off the excess fluid and did what he could to reinflate the lung. It wasn't until April that Nancy called to tell me that Daddy was seriously ill. I flew down to Tulsa and went straight to her house. He was lying in bed, groggy from medication, but when he saw me he scooted upright in bed and said hello. We talked about his stay in the hospital. The doctor had made an incision in his side, inserted what looked like a chromium crowbar, and pried and pried. It was the most painful thing he had ever felt. Daddy showed me the incision: it looked like the slit in Christ's side. Chemotherapy had burned his lips, lending them a darker cast. It also caused intense nausea. There was a small plastic basin next to the bed.

Nancy's daughters—around fifteen, thirteen, and nine—were undaunted by his illness. They hugged and kissed him with genuine affection every time they came in the room, as if he were their beloved father.

The going had been rough. He had even started asking Nancy, a Christian, a lot of questions about God. One night they were in bed, when Nancy heard a loud crash. She got up and found him in the closet. He had fled there and torn the clothes down onto himself, on the floor. When she asked him what was wrong, he said that men in black hoods were chasing him. He was terrified. She explained that it was a hallucination caused by Dilaudid, and they began to talk about death, the hereafter, and God. She told him that it was important for him to believe in God, that if he was going to leave this earth, he needed to go with God. According to her, he accepted that, and for the first time in his adult life did not deny the existence of God.

Nancy told me that the cancer had spread down to one lung, but that the doctors thought there was a slim chance that chemotherapy would help. After all, he had beaten the odds before. In any event, he had some time left. I told Daddy that I was at his disposal for as long as he wanted, but when he found out that my wife and I had plane tickets to visit our son in Italy, he insisted that we go. Nancy's boundless energy seemed almost depleted, but she too insisted. Daddy also told me to keep the bad news from Mom. He was calling her every day and telling her he had the flu or giving some other excuse for not dropping by. After a few days I went back to New York and on to Varenna, a village on Lake Como.

A week later, coming back to my son's apartment house there, I saw the landlady waiting outside, and I knew something was wrong. Looking very subdued, she told me that I had received a phone call: *Su papa è molto, molto grave.* The signora allowed me to use her phone to call America. Nancy gave me the details. He had been hospitalized, due to his inability to eat enough or to keep hydrated. A week into his stay, his blood pressure shot up, his breathing became labored, and he began to sweat profusely. A massive blood clot was lodged in his right lung. The doctors feared that at any moment the clot might break loose, travel to his brain and kill him.

Two days later, in his hospital room, I wrote the following:

Though his legs are skinnier, he is not shrivelled and wasted. His big-boned presence takes up the entire bed—big shoulders, broad chest, solid forearms, and best of all, a large, fine head, perfectly shaped, with a white stubble. I never knew what a beautifully rounded head he has. And his face has good color, a ruddy, tanned, open-air color, and I realize that there is something of the older Walt Whitman in his look—even the blue-gray eyes—just as there is something of Whitman in this description of him. Without his teeth he resembles a lot of nineteenth-century men. Whitman's death mask has that same look around the mouth, as did my father's grandfather.

But then there are the frequent changes of bedding by firm, sweet, cheerful nurses, the tubes, the machines clicking and blinking the night away. Hooked up to a constant flow of morphine, he wanders in and out of consciousness. I was surprised by how easy it was to sit with him all night the first night, watching him breathe, watching the strobe lights of the hospital heliport outside, watching the dark, and feeling myself fall in love with him. The nurses come in and say, "What a handsome man he is!" and I look down at him and see that even now, even here, he does have that big bold cowboy aura, that largeness of gesture, the weird beauty of being what used to be called "a real man."

This afternoon, he suddenly opened his eyes, looked up at me, stuck out his hand, and said, with perfect lucidity, "Howdy, pardner." I had to grip back hard, just to keep his hand from crunching mine. Then his grip grew slack and he drifted off again.

That week, I would arrive at the hospital each afternoon around five, stay all night, and leave at nine or ten the next morning, when Nancy took over the watch. After breakfast, I crashed at my mother's or at Mom's (she still didn't know he was in the hospital). Friends came to visit him, some spending hours and hours. When Roger Eller (Lee's son and Johnny's brother) came by, Daddy told me that Roger had just sold the oil lease for him, and to be sure that Roger got his commission.

Daddy had his lucid moments, but much of the time he was either asleep or experiencing delusions from morphine. At one point he even said to me, "I'm hallucinating." Periodically he would sit up and, ignoring his intravenous and oxygen hookups, start to climb out of bed. When I stopped him and asked him where he was going, he would say in a conspiratorial tone, "I'm busting out."

"Out of where?"

"*Jail*," he would say, without the slightest trace of irony.

At one point he furtively waved me to his bedside and whispered, "See that man over there?"

"Where?" I asked, looking around the empty room.

"The one sitting in that chair." The chair was empty. "He's a U.S. marshall."

At first I tried to explain that this is a hospital, and that he was being well cared for, and that he was going to be all right. These explanations caused him to look confused for a moment, then sink back into sleep. Eventually, when the hallucinations became more frequent, I began to go along with them, while giving them a positive spin.

"Daddy, I'll get rid of the marshall. You just relax a minute and I'll go kick him out."

Or: "There's no need to bust out of jail, because your parole has come through. They're just doing the paperwork. All you have to do now is lie back and relax, take a nap."

I remember one odd moment in particular. It was around ten at night, the floor was quiet, and Daddy was asleep. In the dark, I switched on the television, keeping the sound muted. The screen lit up: a basketball game. Oh yes, the Celtics-Pistons playoffs. I recognized the parquet floors of the Boston Garden and the green uniforms of the Celtics. One of the players stole the ball, raced downcourt, took off at the free-throw line, and dunked the ball.

"Look at that!" I heard Daddy say.

He was watching the game.

Then he added, "Those guys are really something, aren't they?"

The only other television program that elicited his lucidity was a feature on water skiing, which he had done many times up at Grand Lake.

He had also been relatively lucid when, finally, someone brought Mom to see him, against his wishes. He didn't want her to be upset by seeing him like this, and he assured her that he was going to be okay. But soon he tired.

Every time I arrived he would become lucid, at least for a while. Some of his old friends also brought him into focus, but then he would fade out. A while later I would notice that once again he was slowly and gently rubbing the tips of his thumb, index finger, and middle finger together, examining them, and bringing them to his lips, rounded as if sipping water. He also tended to bunch the sheets with his fingertips. From time to time, the morphine caused him to give a sudden twitch or jerk.

Then, after a while, he'd open his eyes and wink at me, or just smile.

He was taking very little real food, mostly chocolate milk and a few spoons of ice cream. From time to time he could handle a water glass or a spoon or apply Carmex balm to his lips or squirt artificial saliva into his mouth, but mostly people did these things for him. For breakfast he might take a few spoonsful of cream of wheat or oatmeal, but when he didn't want any more, he would refuse it with his customary stubbornness. Most of his nutrition was coming through an IV tube.

As the days went by, he gradually rejected his hospital gown. There were long periods of his lying there naked, but whenever he was aware that someone had entered the room, he would quickly pull the gown over his groin. At first he had been distressed by his incontinence, but eventually he seemed to accept it, or perhaps he simply grew tired of being distressed.

It was hard to predict what his mood would be. He would show unexpected flashes of wit and humor, followed by conversations such as the following:

"Got a pocket knife?" he asked me.

"No. Why do you want a pocket knife?"

"To cut my fucking throat."

At another point, looking like a child who has just had a great idea, he said to me, "Lemme die."

"No," I answered firmly.

"Okay," he said, somewhat cheerfully.

I almost laughed. But one night, alone with him as he slept and muttered, I heard inside my head a pleading voice—my own—that said, "*Please* go ahead and die." The next morning, when Nancy arrived and we stood at the door together, we both admitted for the first time that the chemotherapy was not going to work and that he was going to die. We threw our arms around each other and sobbed heavily.

The doctors gave him "weeks or months." At my job in New York, my absence was starting to pose problems. I decided to go back to New York for a few days, meet some pressing deadlines, and return to Tulsa.

Two days later Nancy had, as usual, spent the night on a cot next to Daddy's bed. They were both awakened when a nurse came in the room. He gave Nancy a wink. She told him she loved him, and he told her he loved her. Then they said a few other things, at which point Nancy looked up to say something to the nurse. When she looked back at him, he let out a big sigh. The nurse checked and found no vital signs. A resident doctor confirmed the death.

Nancy was left alone with him in the silent room. Suddenly he let out another sigh, and Nancy, thinking he had revived, dashed out in the hall, calling for a doctor. It was around five A.M., May 21, 1991.

Later that day, it was quiet and cool inside Moore's Funeral Home. The top half of the coffin lid was open, down to his waist. He was wearing a light blue short-sleeved shirt with the words *Bill Blass* embroidered on the pocket. The thought crossed my mind that someday someone would mistake Daddy for the famous fashion designer. As usual, he was not wearing a tie. I let the fingertips of my right hand rest lightly on his bare arm. He felt like a statue. He looked like a statue. I suddenly realized that he wasn't "there." Wherever he was, he certainly wasn't there. This made me feel better.

The next morning, the parking lot was jammed with the cars of the more than 250 people who filled the chapel. Kam was not among them. Daddy had told Little Wayne not to allow her in. But he had also told him, "She's your mother, so be good to her."

The coffin was flanked by huge banks of flowers. The eulogy was delivered by Virgil Adams, the East Side boy who had attended Mom's Sunday school and, after many adventures, become a minister, now retired. Virgil gave exactly the kind of eulogy Daddy would have appreciated: honest, down-home, and compassionate.

So here was my father, the subject of a Christian funeral, the religion he had denied until just before the end of his life. I wasn't sure that he qualified.

Some years back, the wife of his friend Lee Eller had been in the hospital with a terminal illness, given one year to live (she lived seven). A Christian, she had long tried to convert Daddy, who was visiting her every day, sometimes twice a day. He told her, "If your faith is true, and you get cured, I'll convert." When later she walked out of the hospital and asked him to uphold his promise, he became evasive, telling Lee, "The kind of business I'm in, I can't handle religion right now. You and I are very good friends, so don't worry about me."

Two of Daddy's other friends were also interested in his spiritual well-being, Dale Baehler and his wife, Lee, who, after years of playing high-stakes poker, saw the light and became born-again Christians.

One time Daddy told Lee, "You know I had that medicine the doctor gave me and I was hallucinating? I dozed off and this old guy with a long white beard and white robe who came by and looked at me and said, 'You're nothing but a flick in time.'"

Lee said, "The Lord visited you."

Daddy replied, "Lee, I told you I had a *dream*."

Until near the end, he did not give in to the Christianity that had surrounded him since childhood, when he had volunteered for baptism.

On an ethical level, he was a mass of contradictions. He hated hypocrites and liars, but bent the truth when it served his purposes. He showed great pride in my school accomplishments, but he had scoffed at the one credit he needed for a high school diploma. As a husband he could be an angel, tender and sweet, or a devil. He was gentle and respectful with old people and children, but ready to wreak havoc on any guy who crossed him. He was extraordinarily generous and altruistic, but also capable of narrow-minded egocentricity. He taught me to be good and obedient, but freely broke the law himself.

Of course, the seam between criminal and lawful behavior can be very thin. On opposite ends of the spectrum are the violent sociopath and the saint, and for the rest of us the difference is, at any given moment, a question of degree. There are many law-abiding citizens who are lousy people and many criminals who are generous, loyal, and even kind. I put my father in the latter category.

Author Susan Berman, in doing research on the life of her Mafia father —a man who treated her with the utmost love and care—eventually had to face the terrible possibility that he might have murdered someone: "The thing that I feared most was that I would find out something that would make me love my father less, that would tamper with the idealized, romanticized view I had of him as a child. I was afraid I would find out he had a barbarous nature." I had not suffered from that fear, for I felt, from childhood onward, that although my dad was a crook, he drew the line this side of barbarous.

And so when I first heard that he said he had killed a man by blowing up Wilder's Restaurant, I was shocked, then relieved when the facts showed that his claim was fictitious. The scare came back when a colleague of his said that Daddy had told him he had killed E. C. Mullendore. Then a more reliable source told me that Daddy most certainly hadn't, that, in fact, the killer was still at large. But Daddy told the same reliable source that he had performed "hits" in California for a mobster. By this point I began to discern a pattern in Daddy's claiming to have killed somebody when he thought there would be no proof to the contrary. It was a way of developing his fearsome reputation. Actually, throughout his life, there are many instances of his telling people *not* to commit murders. Once when a friend suggested "doing" somebody, Daddy cautioned him, "You gotta be careful. A few times is O.K., but then you'll reach a point where it's a way of life: you'll just want to do everybody." As the friend told me, "You can become hardened in your thinking, with a total lack of respect for life." I don't think Daddy ever quite reached that point, though some of his associates did.

Throughout my childhood, both my parents had spoken about men who would "just soon kill you as look at you," cold-blooded, inhuman men. Daddy was not one of them. But much later I realized that I had left Tulsa at the age of eighteen, at the point when my father was edging into a more violent milieu, and that it is possible that later he did arrange some hits on people he thought "deserved" it. As hard as this is for me to accept, it does fit Daddy's tendency to hire other people to do the dirty work. He preferred to be a gray eminence, which is one of the reasons that law enforcement took nearly forty years to convict him of a felony.

Another reason was that he was well liked, trusted, and feared. Even one of his main adversaries, former Tulsa District Attorney Buddy Fallis, described him as "a man who appeared very handsome, very neat, very well kempt, meticulous in his personal habits, and always appeared to be physically strong. . . . He was always a type A person, very gregarious, people liked him. Liked him a lot. Always friendly. . . . And I heard that he was very generous. He was also a very clever person . . . [and] well liked—that created some problems for law enforcement, from the standpoint of people saying things about him. He was a dashing-looking guy. The nickname I always heard was The Silver Fox. If you're liked, you're less likely to hear a disparaging word."

Fallis was right. Although there were a few informants, there were a great many others who flatly refused to say anything incriminating about him, or anything at all. He had a huge network of friends, including law-abiding Christians, who felt fiercely loyal to him because of his many kindnesses over the years and the sense of integrity he radiated. It may sound odd to use a word such as *integrity* in describing him, but how else do you describe someone who had such a strong code of ethics?

As his friend Bobby Bluejacket, who spent many years in prison, put it: "They always say, 'The kid went bad because he had no love in his childhood. He had no values.' Who could you possibly know that had a more loving mother than Wayne's? Who could you possibly know that had a mother more industrious than my mother, who walked three or four miles across town when bus tokens were three for a dime, to scrub floors for thirty-five or forty cents a day? She'd save the bus money to buy bread for her kids. Who could you possibly know that would set their grandchildren on their lap and hug 'em and love 'em more than my grandma and grandpa, old dear Quaker people who fed hundreds of people out here in East Tulsa back during the depression. These people had a hand in raising me. My integrity is boundless when it comes to not abusing old people, children, or women. Other than that, the world's a great big apple. All you have to do is take a bite of it."

People such as Bobby Bluejacket and Daddy came to believe that the odds had been stacked against them by the "haves" of society, and that the only way they themselves could make real headway in the world was to operate by a different set of rules—their own. Asked how he could morally justify robbing people at gunpoint, my father answered that they were rich and that their insurance covered the losses anyway. When told that insurance rates and taxes were higher because of such robberies, he replied that insurance companies and politicians were out to screw you anyway, crime or no crime. In other words, he had an answer for every-thing, an answer that always had some truth to it, but was too convenient to be fully credible. For he rarely, if ever, examined his rationalizations from any point of view other than his own. When Nancy asked him how he justified some of the things he did, he answered, "I just don't think about it, but I don't do anything to anybody who doesn't deserve it." Larger issues, such as the relationship between law and social and polit-ical structure, probably never crossed his mind.

Whether or not his thinking was right—and to what degree—is not the point here. It was the moral basis of his behavior, a basis necessary for a per-son of his upbringing. Despite his blatantly criminal behavior, his sense of morality allowed him to feel that deep down he was one of the good guys.

But over the decades, times changed, and "honor among thieves" grad-ually disappeared. As Bluejacket put it, "In the old days you knew what a guy was made of. You don't know what they're made of anymore."

In his autobiography, Joseph Bonanno, the former Mafia Father, noted a similar degeneration among his associates: "Friendships, connections, family ties, trust, loyalty, obedience—this was the 'glue' that held us [Sicil-ian mafiosi] together. In America, however, and increasingly throughout the industrialized world, the glue that holds people together is their eco-nomic relationship."[1]

Friendships, connections, family ties, trust, loyalty, and obedience—relationships with other people—these were my father's forte. On the other hand, neither introspection nor self-awareness was his strong suit. He knew that his criminal life began when his father died; he told police investigators as much when they were compiling his pre-sentencing report. He relegated it to the level of "I had no father to keep me on the straight and narrow," which was true, as far as it went. But he never gave any indication of understanding how Grover's suicide, like a bloody hand, had plunged into his emotional system, squeezed hard, and given it a violent yank.

This sudden attack from the outside world had given the child the usual two options: flight or fight. Daddy chose to fight, never looking back to analyze the source of what was, deep down, his fear and rage. From his father's suicide came his anti-social, criminal, and sometimes violent behavior; from his mother's love and decency came his generosity, hard work, and personal integrity. These two sides of his personality blended to form a self that had nuance, color, and power, a man who for some seemed larger than life.

But it's more complicated than that. There was also the sheer momentum of his life. He hadn't made a transition from bootlegging to a fully legitimate profession partly because he had lived his entire adult life outside the law, and it was too late for him even to try to take on a shopkeeper mentality. He was too much the outsider to accept the humdrum of legitimate business. A legal high-stakes profession, such as currency speculation or day trading, might have satisfied his taste for risk, but he had no access to such professions. And, aside from everything else, crime was adrenalizing, and it was only very late in life that he began to wean himself away from living on that edge. What Mother had said about his being too wild for marriage at a young age—"wild and . . . too young to be tied down"—applied to most of his later years as well: deep down he stayed wild, as if some part of his personality had stopped growing at the moment of his father's death, making it impossible for him to assume a mature, lawful role in society. This refusal or inability to "settle down" was at the root of his restlessness and lawlessness, but also his impish sense of humor. In some ways he remained eleven years old.

And so, unable to build a life *in* society, he had improvised one that allowed him to get *through* society. He was always looking for an opening through which he could slip into the next day of his life. Thus he grew to be alert, enterprising, and, when it served his purposes, elusive, evading the law, refusing to confront his personal flaws, masking the breakup of his marriage to Mother, and for years denying the painful truth about his father's death. Being an outsider who was in some ways running even from himself made it impossible for him to construct a stable, bourgeois life, with a steady job, church affiliation, or country club membership to give him the feeling of belonging to a society. His anti-social behavior was confirmed, however, by the many people who admired him precisely because he was a living example of a person who created his own life instead of accepting the life of subjugation that society tends to impose the have-nots.

Because Daddy passed much of his attitude toward society on to me, it is hard for me to say, even after discovering the depth of his criminality, that he should have done otherwise, though it is obvious that he should have done so. But who was to guide him to the otherwise? His father was long dead, and I, even had I known of the nefarious doings of his later years, would have been unable to deter him. This fact only partially relieves the guilt I sometimes feel for not having "saved" him.

Besides, a life can take on an aura of predestination. I suspect that deep down Daddy regretted not having conventional respectability but felt that it was just not in the cards for him. Something he once told Kam is revealing. She had asked him what he would do with his life if he had it to live all over again. What would he be?

"I'd be an agent that guards the President, a secret service agent. I think I'd have been a good one."

Given his extraordinary instincts, his taste for danger, and his fierce loyalty, he could have been an outstanding one. But on a deeper level, his answer could be understood as, "I would protect my father from harm." That was his great unsatisfied irrational and no doubt unconscious desire: to restore his father to life.

The mourners filed past the casket for a last good-bye. Some glanced, others stopped and touched him. There were quiet tears. When my mother approached the casket, she let out a loud sob as she gasped, "Good-bye, Wayne." Mom, sitting beside me and crying quietly like a kitten, looked all of her years, now ninety-one.

It had rained that morning, and the sky was still overcast. The cortege drove to Rose Hill Cemetery, where Virgil Adams said a few more words at the graveside. Then close friends and family gave their condolences to Mom, me, and Little Wayne, and we drove back to Mom's.

My cousin Dean and I went out and brought back fried chicken for the relatives who had accompanied Mom home. The lunch conversation included quite a few funny stories and memories, as such conversations often do.

After everyone left, Mom asked me to drive her back to the cemetery. By now the clouds had been blown away by a pleasant breeze. The clear sunlight on the flowers, now heaped high on the grave, gave them a lovely radiance. Mom cried again, but this time she seemed to feel a little better, and that night she and I, accompanied by Robert's daughter Penny, went out for barbeque at the down-home Knotty Pine, Robert's favorite restaurant in Tulsa.

The next day the three of us drove up to Claremore to see the house where Mom's parents had lived, the house Robert was born in, and the gravesites of Verna's and Grover's parents. Mom had outlived all her children, but memories of her youth momentarily brought the place back to life, and seemed to comfort her.

Appendix A

A Brief History of Law and Order, Crime and Punishment in Oklahoma and Tulsa (up to 1945)

Because this appendix deals only with the lawless and sometimes violent side of Oklahoma's and Tulsa's histories, the reader should keep in mind that at least by the end of World War II, Tulsa was a relatively safe city, with what one commentator described as many "Dick-and-Jane neighborhoods." But this was not always so. In fact, the area has quite a history both of crime and of legalized plunder.

In the Louisiana Purchase (1804), the United States bought from France the huge area that included present-day Oklahoma. At that time, the eastern half of Oklahoma was the hunting ground of the Quapaw and Osage Indians, but by 1818 both tribes had been "induced" to cede the land to the U.S. government. In 1824, two forts in eastern Oklahoma were established to counter Indian raids against whites and other Indians.

Under the Indian Removal Act of 1830, all Indians east of the Mississippi were required to cede their land in return for land in the West. The main period of the removal of these Indians to Oklahoma was 1830–40. Their migration west, known later as the Trail of Tears, was devastating for them. For example, in 1835, thirty-five hundred of fifteen thousand migrating Creeks died of exposure and illness; in 1838, the Cherokees lost four thousand of thirteen thousand in a similar manner. The survivors created farms and little communities in the eastern part of what would become the state.

The western part was inhabited by prairie tribes, the so-called wild tribes, such as the Comanche, Wichita, and Kiowa. An 1835 treaty brought a certain measure of peace to that area.

During the Civil War, many Indian farms were pillaged and houses burned, and because at least a part of every tribe had sided with the Confederacy, at the end of the war *all* the tribes were required to pay a penalty: namely, to cede control of the western half of the future state. This area, renamed Oklahoma Lands, was then set aside for Indian settlers, but some of them resisted control, and a lot of blood was shed before order was restored. Though prohibited by law, white settlers began filtering into the Oklahoma Lands, and finally, through political pressure, the area was thrown open to white settlers, resulting in the famous "run" of March 23, 1889. But the sixty thousand settlers who poured in had to live without a government for over a year. Congress had forgotten to establish one! The Organic Act of 1890 remedied that, and changed the area's name to the Territory of Oklahoma.

Eastern Oklahoma (Indian Territory) had remained under the control of the Five Civilized Tribes (Cherokee, Choctaw, Creek, Chickasaw, and Seminole), who lived under their own constitutional governments. But there were no local laws governing the whites who drifted in. Technically, the area was under the judicial control of the U.S. Court in Fort Smith, Arkansas, from which federal marshals were given the impossible task of maintaining law and order. Thus the area became a haven for criminals, who could raid the bordering states (Kansas, Missouri, Texas, and Arkansas) and abscond to Indian Territory with virtual impunity. Michael Wallis wrote, "Folks who lived in Oklahoma recognized that it was a land conceived in violence, the last frontier of the outlaw. This was particularly true in eastern Oklahoma . . . [which] acted as a true refuge for the lawless and untamed."[1]

During a period of more than nine years, beginning with the Dawes Commission in 1893, Congress pressured the Indians out of control of their land. Against the strenuous objections of the Five Civilized Tribes, the Territory of Oklahoma and Indian Territory were united in statehood, on November 16, 1907. It's hard not to see this entire history as one of strong-arm tactics and legislated larceny by the federal government. Oklahoma had become as desirable for white ranchers, farmers, and businessmen as it had been for outlaws.

Tulsa was originally a Lockapoka Creek Indian settlement called Tulsy, a name probably derived from the Creek words for *town* ("tulwa") and *old*

APPENDIX A

("ahassee"). The Indian Removal Act of 1830 had provided for the forcible removal of these Creeks from Tallassee, Alabama, their original town. The Tulsa Creek village was destroyed during the Civil War, and the area was raided by guerilla gangs after the war. The Creeks, however, continued to farm their land.

The first white settlers didn't come until 1882, when construction of the Frisco Railroad line began through what was to become the town of Tulsa. One year later, illegal liquor was being smuggled down the Arkansas River and into the little town. The first known killing in Tulsa occurred in 1883, when a man was stabbed during a fight in a gambling tent. "Outlaw gangs seemed to be rather fashionable during the last twenty years of the nineteenth century. This was partially due to the lack of law enforcement officers in Indian Territory. . . . Outlaws were familiar with the horses that the marshals rode, so when the outlaws came near Tulsa, they rode to Standpipe Hill (approximately today's 400 North Cincinnati) and used their field glasses to see if the marshalls' horses were tied up in town. . . . The outlaws always pulled their crimes outside of Tulsa but lived near Tulsa and often walked the streets of Tulsa."[2]

When a railroad bridge was built across the Arkansas River in 1883, Tulsa became a cow town, attracting cowboys looking for work. Some of those who remained unemployed found other ways of getting a dollar. Tulsa's first gang was the Glass gang, dealing in booze and stolen horses. There were even Indian gangs that indulged in robbery and illegal liquor. The Dalton gang (led by Bob, Grat, and Emmett Dalton) lived in the Tulsa area. Bob and Grat were killed attempting to rob two banks simultaneously just across the state line in Coffeyville, Kansas, in 1892. Emmett was later captured and sent to prison.

Another wild character was U.S. Marshal Bill Cook, who lost his commission in 1884 because he was selling whiskey on the side. Cook then organized a violent gang of robbers and killers. Other notable outlaws were the Bill Doolin gang (which included characters with names such as Tulsa Jack, Dynamite Dick, Red Buck, and Bitter Creek) and the short-lived Rufus Buck gang, whose ten-day rape, robbery, and murder spree resulted in their execution by hanging.

In the 1880s and 1890s, Tulsa was a wild cow town, with plenty of liquor, gambling, and prostitution. As one historian noted, "When the cowboys came to town in the evening, they got drunk and rode through the town firing their revolvers, breaking out windows and lights of businesses as well as residences. Many of the residents had to turn out their kerosene lamps and lie on the floor to avoid being struck by a wild bullet. Even churches and their members were fired upon."[3]

Such shenanigans prompted the federal court to appoint Lon Lewis and Bryl Cox as Tulsa's first deputy U.S. marshals, in 1895. Several years later, Cox, no longer a marshal, seized a shack belonging to a Chinese cook, who resisted. Cox shot him dead.

The City of Tulsa was incorporated in January of 1898, and the position of city marshal was created. This elected official was assisted by a night watchman and perhaps one other man.

In 1889, the first U.S. Court in Indian Territory was finally established. Along with other courts, it helped calm the area down.

Tulsa, with around 1,400 inhabitants, became a boom town when oil was discovered just north of nearby Red Fork in 1901. Tulsa businessmen erected the first vehicular and pedestrian bridge across the Arkansas River, which opened in 1904, funneling Red Fork oil and refinery money into Tulsa, instead of Sapulpa, which was across the river and twelve miles to the west.

By then, Tulsa had three police officers and one city marshal. The oil boom continued. By 1905, the population had jumped to 7,200. Liquor, gambling, and prostitution remained popular. The city marshal, Charles Robertson, was embarrassed when U.S. Marshal Bud Ledbetter raided Tulsa gambling dens. Robertson claimed not to have known of the presence of gambling in Tulsa; later he said that he had been aware of it, but hadn't quite gotten around to doing anything about it. He got the boot. The force added two new officers. The city built a new City Hall and police and fire station, all in a single two-story brick structure. In 1905, the Glenn Pool of oil was discovered fifteen miles south of town, and Tulsa boomed even more.

The town began to take on a progressive look, with paved streets, a trolley line, and street lights along Main. But things were still a bit ragged. In 1907 Tulsa saw an influx of gamblers, and City Marshal William J. Baber was fined and dismissed for pistol-whipping a man he didn't like.

With statehood (1907), Oklahoma formally adopted prohibition, and in the following year the City Council added tough gambling laws. In 1908, Oklahoma went so far as to abolish all uses of alcoholic drinks, even medicinal. The Tulsa police force numbered sixteen. Tulsa's Commercial Club —a forerunner of the Chamber of Commerce—made a booster trip back east, featuring former outlaw Emmett Dalton as one of its attractions!

It wasn't until 1909 that Geronimo—for many whites the last living symbol of Indian resistance—died at Fort Sill, in Lawton, Oklahoma.

By 1910 Tulsa was booming along (pop. 18,182), with an abundance of booze, gambling, and floozies along First Street. Now even "narcotics" were available. Respectable people and churchgoers mounted various clean-up drives against lawlessness.

Every two years the citizens elected a new mayor, who appointed a new police and fire commissioner, who appointed new officers. It was a prototype of the spoils system that later became virtually institutionalized in Tulsa.

In 1912 the force, now with thirty-five officers, confiscated 290 cases of whiskey and 40 barrels of beer from railroad stations and the Oklahoma State Bank building in the heart of downtown. By 1914, "Crime and vice were running rampant in the city."[4]

In the 1914 Democratic primary for governor, Al Jennings, former Oklahoma outlaw, ran for office. He "boasted that the people of Oklahoma could trust a train robber far more than the dishonest politicians. That made perfect sense to some Oklahomans."[5] He got 24 percent of the vote, not bad for a confessed outlaw. The next year Police Chief Foster Burns was removed from office on indictments that he was lax in enforcement, especially with the manufacturing and sale of liquor in Tulsa and with prostitution payoffs.

In 1915 the notorious Barker gang—originally Ma Barker and her five sons—moved to Tulsa, to 401 North Cincinnati, coincidentally the old outlaws' vantage point. Back in 1892, Ma, whose maiden name was Arizona Donnie Clark, had married George Barker in the small town of Aurora, Arkansas, and lived there until 1903. (Verna's family would move to Aurora only a few years later.) The Barker brothers and seventeen other kids made up Tulsa's Central Park gang that hung out at Sixth Street and Peoria Avenue. As they got older, the gang graduated to bank robbery, kidnapping, and murder. Ma, the matriarch of this crime family, took in other crooks, such as Alvin Karpis. Tulsa police raided Karpis's residence and the Barker's home, but after a gun battle the crooks escaped. In 1928, Oklahoma bootlegger George Kelly Barnes, Jr., a.k.a. "Machine Gun" Kelly, came to Tulsa and joined the Barker gang. Actually, he never killed anyone, but he did brandish a machine gun in committing his crimes, and was said to have used it to shoot his name into a wall. Ma left Tulsa in the early 1930s.

Other early area gangsters included Frank Holloway (bank and train robberies in the early 1920s), Frank Nash (bank robbery and murder), and Wilber Underhill (bank robbery and murder).

By 1917, a new kind of crime had surfaced. In November, police arrested members of the International Workers of the World, who were then seized by the Knights of Liberty, a Klan-like group that beat, tarred, and feathered these "radicals," and ran them out of town, with the tacit approval of the police and the encouragement of the *Tulsa Daily World*, which had strongly recommended the lynching of "unpatriotic radicals."

By 1918, there were fifty officers, with salaries starting at $106 per month. The underpaid and demoralized officers formed a Police Union and went on strike. The population had mushroomed to 42,000, a fair number of whom were crooks and idlers of various sorts.

All over America, on January 16, 1920, the Eighteenth Amendment (Prohibition) went into effect, but it meant little to Oklahoma, which had been dry since statehood thirteen years before. In fact, by 1916 almost half the U.S. was already dry.

In 1921, Henry Starr, notorious Oklahoma outlaw, was wounded in a shootout. Born in Indian Territory in 1873, Starr grew up a cowboy, but at seventeen began a life of rustling and robbery. He hid out in Osage County (to the immediate northwest of Tulsa), aided by friends and acquaintances, and always got out of his predicaments by escapes and pardons (even one from President Theodore Roosevelt).

In 1921, Tulsa's most horrific act of lawlessness—the Tulsa Race Riot—broke out (see Chapter 3). This took place during the tenure of new Chief of Police John ("I'll clean up the city or quit!") Gustafson, who, afterward convicted of failing to organize the police or citizenry, was ousted. He was also convicted of participating in a stolen car conspiracy.

The Ku Klux Klan had become active in Tulsa in 1917. A year after the riots, the Klan held a march right down Main Street—1,741 strong. The group claimed to have 4,000 city members, a thousand more in the county, and a total of 70,000 in the state. A few months after the march, 1,020 new local members were inducted. Apparently, the race riot had boosted the Klan's popularity. In Tulsa's elections that fall, both the Republican and Democratic candidates for sheriff and county attorney were Klan members.

In 1923—the year after Wayne's birth—Klan violence and terrorism finally prompted the governor to place Tulsa under martial law. The mayor defied the governor's order, so the governor closed all the stores and restaurants in Tulsa and placed the entire state under martial law. When the state legislature tried to convene, the governor gave orders to shoot to kill anyone trying to hold a legislative session. Finally, the city police began to disarm the state troops. Three months later, the state health commissioner testified that not only was he a KKK member but that the governor was too, an assertion confirmed by a former Klan official. The governor denied it, but was removed from office by impeachment.

In the 1920s, many Tulsa police officers had been rough: "The police department had been criticized for excessive physical force used on prisoners during arrest, detention, and interrogation. It was not uncommon that the accused appeared before the court with bruises and bloodied clothing, but remained silent."[6]

In 1924, a new police station opened. Made of Bedford stone, it had three levels: the municipal court and the jail cells on the second (top) floor; administrative offices and the booking area on the street level, and in the basement a pistol range, drill room, and boiler room. The entire building had marble floors, marble steps, and marble walls. Years later, for Wayne and his friends, this was *the* police station. They would refer to it simply as "Fourth and Elgin," its location. "You don't want to go down to Fourth and Elgin."

In 1926, County Commissioner J. S. Shaver, his son Harold, and Phil B. Stone, captain of the Tulsa County Highway Patrol, were found guilty of conspiracy to violate prohibition laws. Shaver and Stone became part of the tradition of corrupt politicians and law enforcement officers in cahoots with local criminals.

The 1928 elections saw the virtual institutionalization of the spoils system, which was to operate for thirty years. Under it, officers of the victorious political party were retained, the others dismissed. The new chief dismissed 66 of 137 officers and hired 65 new ones (of his political persuasion, of course). Even a new slate of the same party would result in mass dismissals. This system had a devastating effect on the officers' loyalty to the job and their ability to coordinate long-term efforts.

After the stock market crash of 1929, Tulsa stopped growing. Over the next decade, its population (141,258) increased by only 1,000. The Great Depression and the Dust Bowl had arrived.

In the first week of 1932, Oklahoma country boy Charles Arthur "Pretty Boy" Floyd had moved with his wife and young son to Tulsa. Floyd was primarily a bank robber, which, if things got out of hand, involved shooting and killing. Floyd had two running gun battles with Tulsa police. On February 7, Floyd and his accomplice George Birdwell shot their way out of a confrontation with police on the north side of town. Three days later, police fired their sawed-off shotguns at Floyd and Birdwell as the two drove along. In the early morning hours of February 11, a large number of officers closed in on the Floyd house, but the two bandits eluded them by slipping out the back door and along rows of laundry hanging from clotheslines.

That same month, Fire and Police Commissioner Thomas Munroe was indicted by a federal grand jury for being part of a protection scheme for bootleggers. The alleged payoff man and state's star witness, former officer R. G. Kennedy, died of a suspicious "flu" in jail three weeks before the trial, in which the commissioner was found not guilty. Two months later, budget cuts reduced the force from 190 to 140 officers.

To many citizens, the prohibition of *all* alcoholic beverages was too extreme. In light of Wayne's future profession, the large front-page headline of the *Tulsa Daily World* for May 30, 1933—two days after his father's death—takes on an ironic glow: "Beer Forces Gain Victory in House." The article described another step in Oklahoma's march toward the legalization of 3.2 beer, that is, beer with 3.2 percent alcohol content. The repeal of national Prohibition in December of 1933 had no visible effect on Oklahoma's liquor business: the state remained dry and bootleggers continued to do a good business.

During the mid-1930s, cars were hard to come by, and the Tulsa police force lost some of its mobility. In 1935, officers worked twelve-hour shifts, seven days a week.

During World War II, with many officers gone to war, there was a lack of serious law enforcement. It was an opportune time to pursue an illegal business such as bootlegging.

APPENDIX A

After the war, soldiers who had been policemen were discharged immediately. Thirty-two returned to Tulsa. The police force then beefed itself up even more. Police morale began to pick up a bit. So did Wayne's whiskey business.

He felt no pangs of conscience about selling hooch. A large number of Tulsans—people of all walks of life, including policemen—had winked at the state's liquor laws for decades. The only ones adamantly against liquor were the Bible thumpers. And if preachers drank whiskey—as Wayne knew that some did—then why should he have any moral compunctions about selling it? Besides, in repealing Prohibition, hadn't the very Congress of the United States said that whiskey was okay?

Appendix B

Names of Key People

Adams, Virgil. Longtime acquaintance of W. P. and eulogist at his funeral.

Amos, Bob. Co-owner, with W. P., of the Sheridan Club.

Armstrong, Richard. Judge in W. P.'s second trial for Sears embezzlement.

Benningfield, Al. Friend and lawyer of W. P.

Berrigan, Ted. Poet and friend of Ron Padgett.

Bluejacket, Bobby. Friend of W. P.

Bluejacket, Nancy. Née Mann. Wife of Bobby Bluejacket, later girlfriend of W. P.

Brainard, Joe. Artist and friend of Ron Padgett.

Brinlee, Rex. Tulsa criminal and prison escapee.

Bulloch, Nolen. Tulsa journalist.

Cates, Raymond. Tulsa car dealer and reputed small-time crook. Enemy of W. P.

Cochrane, John. One of W. P.'s lawyers.

Cook, B. T. Private investigator and friend of W. P.

Dillon, John. A member of the Dixie Mafia, auto mechanic, farmer, etc. Found murdered.

Dillon, Lorine. Née Bryson. Wife of John Dillon.

Donahue, Howard. Old friend of W. P., welder, race car driver.

Downing, Gene. Co-owner, with W. P., of the Sheridan Club, and auto dealer.

Easley, Claude. Tulsa bootlegger and father of Priscilla Griffing.

Edgar, Virgil. Service station owner and friend of W. P.

Edwards, Bill. Criminal and brother of Martin Edwards.

Edwards, Martin. Tulsa criminal. Found murdered.

Eller, Johnny Lee. Godson of W. P. and son of Lee Eller. Found murdered.

Eller, Lee. Friend of W. P. and businessman.

Eller, Pat. Tulsa businessman and friend of W. P.

Eller, Roger. Oilman and friend of W. P.

Epps, Cleo. Esteemed friend of W. P. Known as "Queen of the Bootleggers." Found murdered.

Estep, Jerry ("Joker"). Associate of W. P. who, along with Don Goodson, was convicted of concealing stolen property.

Fallis, S. M. "Buddy." Tulsa district attorney. Adversary of W. P.

Gafford, Homer. Friend of W. P. and husband first of Bobbie Hood and then of Jackie Hood.

Garrison, Paul. One of W. P.'s attorneys.

Goodson, Don. Criminal and husband of Joan Thompson (sister of Kam Padgett) and friend of W. P.

Gott, Jack. Tulsa police officer, brother of Jim.

Gott, Jim. Tulsa police officer, brother of Jack.

Griffing, Fred Austin ("Griff"). Tulsa bootlegger and associate of W. P.

Griffing, Priscilla. Née Easley. Wife of Fred Griffing and girlfriend of W. P.

Haddock, Al. Hunting buddy of W. P. and Tulsa police officer.

Hanlon, Tom. One of W. P.'s attorneys in the first Sears embezzlement case.

Henderson, W. B. FBI agent who offered (probably untrue) information to the press.

Hood, Bessie. Mother of Jackie and Bobbie Hood.

Hood, Bob. Father of Jackie and Bobbie Hood.

Hood, Bobbie. Friend of Wayne and Lucille Padgett. Tulsa bootlegger.

Hood, Jackie. Friend of Wayne and Lucille Padgett. Tulsa bootlegger.

Huey, Daisy. Mother of Lucille Huey.

Huey, Noah. Father of Lucille Huey.

James, Jerry. Robber and one of FBI's Ten Most Wanted. Accomplice of Don Sparks. W. P. served as his fence. No relation to Pete James.

James, Pete. Businessman and friend of W. P.

Jenkins, Ruby Charles ("Bob"). Murderer, thief, bootlegger, etc., and associate of W. P.

King, Pete. Tulsa bondsman and hotel owner. Friend of W. P.

Kirtley, Ferrell. Sears employee in embezzlement scheme.

Littlefield, Wes. Kam Padgett's second husband.

Loggins, Jake. Business associate of W. P.

Laurrell, Clemens. Old friend and employee of W. P.

Marsh, Ron. Sears security manager and former Tulsa police officer.

McBride, Jack. Criminal and friend of W. P.

McCall, John. Northeast Oklahoma whiskey hauler and friend of W. P.

McDonald, Albert. Member of the Dixie Mafia and partner in crime with Lester Pugh. Killed in prison.

Martin, Bill. Old friend and employee of W. P.

Martin, Edith. Tulsa bootlegger. No relation to Bill Martin.

Miller, Nick. Second husband of Verna Padgett and stepfather of W. P.

Mitchell, Pat. The author's wife.

Mitchell, Ricky. Friend of W. P. and second husband of Bobbie Hood.

Montgomery, Alma. Née Padgett, daughter of Roy Padgett and cousin of W. P.

Montgomery, Tom. Husband of Alma Montgomery. Bootlegger and later security guard.

Mullendore, E. C. III. Wealthy Oklahoma rancher. Found murdered.

Newton, Willis. Old-time criminal and Tulsa club owner. Friend of W. P.

Nicklau, Pete. Friend of W. P. since high school, owner of pawnshop, involved in Sears embezzlement scheme.

Noble, Henry. Tulsa club owner and friend of W. P.

Padgett, Elda. Née Powers. Third wife of Tommie Padgett.

Padgett, George. Father of Grover Padgett.

Padgett, Grover. Father of W. P.

Padgett, Kam. Née Louise Thompson. Second wife of W. P.

Padgett, Lucille. Née Huey. First wife of W. P. and mother of Ron Padgett.

Padgett, Mary Margaret. Née Fletcher. Wife of Robert Padgett.

Padgett, Patricia. Née Mitchell. Wife of Ron Padgett.

Padgett, Robert. Older brother of W. P.

Padgett, Ron. First son of W. P. and author of this book.

Padgett, Roy. Brother of Grover Padgett.

Padgett, Tommie. Younger brother of W. P.

Padgett, Verna ("Mom"). Née Tucker. Mother of W. P.

Padgett, Wayne Merriott. The subject of this book.

Padgett, Wayne Merriott, Jr. Second son of Wayne Merriott Padgett.

Padgett, Wayne Mitchell. Son of Ron Padgett.

Pilkington, Gladys ("Happy"). Sister of Noah Huey and great-aunt of Lucille Padgett.

Pilkington, Jimmy. Son of Wesley and Gladys Pilkington.

Pilkington, Wesley. Husband of Gladys Pilkington.

Popovich, Billie. Owner of the Avalon restaurant and friend of W. P.

Pugh, Lester. Member of the Dixie Mafia and partner in crime with Albert McDonald, among others.

Purdy, Jack. Tulsa's straight-arrow chief of police.

Rains, Roy. Tulsa County police officer, head of Raiding Squad.

Ricketts, Ronald. Judge in W. P.'s first trial for Sears embezzlement.

Sparks, Don. Robber and one of FBI's Ten Most Wanted. Accomplice of Jerry James. W. P. served as his fence.

Stipe, Gene. Lawyer of W. P. in second Sears embezzlement case and Oklahoma State Senator.

APPENDIX B

Stone, Fred. Business associate of W. P.

Thompson, Pat. Assistant district attorney who, with D.A. Buddy Fallis, prosecuted W. P. in Sears embezzlement case.

Thompson, Titanic. Legendary old-time con artist and gambler.

Thurmond, Frank. Tulsa sheriff, one-time friend of W. P.

Tucker, Eva. Née Lester. Mother of Verna Padgett.

Tucker, Jesse. Father of Verna Padgett.

VanDeventer, J. N. (Ned). Tulsa sportsman, businessman, and gambler.

Vardeman, Tommy. Friend and employee of W. P., race car driver.

Wood, Charley. Acquaintance of W. P. since childhood. Glazier and union official.

Wygant, Dale. Kam Padgett's third husband. Owner of service station and towing service.

Notes

Grover and Verna: Married Life

1. Trekell, 43.

2. For an excellent account of the Tulsa Race Riot, see Scott Ellsworth's book *Death in a Promised Land*. See also Tim Madigan's account, *The Burning*, as well as *Tulsa Race Riot: A Report by the Oklahoma Commission to Study the Tulsa Race Riot of 1921*.

3. *Goin' Back to T' Town*, a PBS documentary.

4. *Tulsa: A Guide to the Oil Capital*, 69.

Fourth Street

1. Kellner, 136–37.

2. Ibid., 136.

Out and About

1. David Snell, "The Newton Gang Rides Again," *Life*, April 19, 1968, 54.

Family

1. Wallis, *Pretty Boy*, 227–28.

2. Quoted in Wallis, op. cit., 228.

3. Wallis, ibid., 228.

Things Fall Apart . . .

1. Roger Devlin, "The Rambler," *Tulsa Tribune*, undated clipping, after 1959.

New Life, New Wife

1. "Cleo Epps: Warm, Gentle Woman and Friend of Criminals," *Tulsa Tribune*, June 26, 1974.

The Dixie Mafia

1. "Cleo Epps: Warm, Gentle Woman . . . ," *Tulsa Tribune*, June 26, 1974.
2. "No Probe Link Seen in Edwards Slaying," *Tulsa World,* September 29, 1971.

Last Days

1. Bonanno, *A Man of Honor*, 404.

Appendix A

1. Wallis, op. cit., 36.
2. Ibid., 15.
3. Trekell, 20.
4. Ibid., 40.
5. Wallis, op. cit., 115.
6. Trekell, 94.

Annotated Bibliography

Books

I have listed the following books for various reasons. Some books I quoted from. Others provided context for the story of my father's life. Others, notably the memoirs by children of criminal fathers, I refrained from reading until I had finished the first draft of this book.

Abbott, Shirley. *The Bookmaker's Daughter*. New York: Ticknor & Fields, 1991. A well-written, bittersweet memoir about growing up in Hot Springs, Arkansas.

Berman, Susan. *Easy Street: The True Story of a Mob Family*. New York: Dial Press, 1981. Growing up as the daughter of an operator of a big Las Vegas casino hotel with Mob ties.

Blaise, Clark. *I Had a Father*. Reading, Mass.: Addison-Wesley, 1993. A somewhat post-modernist slant.

Bonanno, Joseph. *A Man of Honor*. New York: Simon and Schuster, 1983. A self-serving but interesting autobiography by the Father of one of New York's top crime "families." Written with Sergio Lalli.

Bradshaw, Jon. *Fast Company*. New York: Vintage, 1987. Devotes one chapter to the legendary gambler and con artist Titanic Thompson.

Brainard, Joe. *Selected Writings*. New York: Kulchur Foundation, 1971. A brilliant collection by the writer and artist originally from Tulsa.

Butler, William. *Tulsa 75*. Tulsa, Okla.: Metropolitan Tulsa Chamber of Commerce, 1974.

Chaix, Marie. *The Laurels of Lake Constance*. Translated by Harry Mathews. New York: Viking, 1977. A beautifully written memoir of growing up in France during and after World War II with a father who had collaborated with the Germans.

Corbett, William. *Furthering My Education*. Cambridge, Mass.: Zoland Books, 1997. An emotional account of growing up as the son of a successful doctor who abruptly abandoned his family and career and went to Baghdad.

Debo, Angie. *Tulsa: From Creek Town to Oil Capital*. Norman: University of Oklahoma Press, 1943.

Dunn, Nina Lane. *Tulsa's Magic Roots*. Tulsa, Okla.: Oklahoma Book Publishing Co., 1979. Valuable photographs and some useful information.

Ellsworth, Scott. *Death in a Promised Land: The Tulsa Race Riot of 1921*. Baton Rouge: Louisiana State University Press, 1982. An outstanding account.

Everly-Douze, Susan. *Tulsa Times: A Pictorial History*. Tulsa: World Publishing Co., 1988, 1997. An extraordinary three-volume set of photographs from the Beryl D. Ford Collection and the *Tulsa World* archives.

Federal Writers' Project [Thompson, Jim?]. *Tulsa: A Guide to the Oil Capital*. Tulsa: Mid-West Printing Co., 1938.

Gifford, Barry. *A Good Man to Know*. Livingston, Mont.: Clark City Press, 1992. A good book about growing up with a semi-criminal father.

Goble, Danny. *Tulsa! The Biography of a City*. Tulsa: Council Oak Books, 1997. Excellent survey with great photographs.

Joyce, Davis D. *"An Oklahoma I Had Never Seen Before."* Norman: University of Oklahoma Press, 1994. Subtitled *Alternative Views of Oklahoma History*, this volume has a particularly interesting chapter by Nigel Sellars on the fate of the Wobblies in Oklahoma.

Kellner, Esther. *Moonshine, Its History and Folklore*. Indianapolis and New York: Bobbs-Merrill, 1971.

Kent, Ruth, et al. *Oklahoma: A Guide to the Sooner State*. Norman: University of Oklahoma Press, 1957.

Kwitney, Jonathan. *The Mullendore Murder Case*. New York: Warner Books, 1974. A detailed account, in which my father is mentioned once, as a bodyguard.

Madigan, Tim. *The Burning*. New York: Thomas Dunne Books, 2001. Continues the work of Scott Ellsworth's pioneering *Death in a Promised Land*, with more eyewitness accounts that paint an even more tragic picture of the Tulsa Race Riot of 1921.

McReynolds, Edwin C. *Oklahoma: A History of the Sooner State*. Norman: University of Oklahoma Press, 1954.

Offit, Sidney. *Memoir of a Bookie's Son*. New York: St. Martin's Press, 1995. A pleasant and agreeable memoir.

Padgett, Ron. *The Big Something*. Great Barrington, Mass.: The Figures, 1990. Contains the seed work, "Coors," quoted in the preface of the current volume.

———. *Bloodwork: Selected Prose*. Flint, Mich.: Bamberger Books, 1993. Contains the full text of my diaristic account of my father's final hospitalization.

Randel, William Pierce. *The Ku Klux Klan: A Century of Infamy*. Philadelphia: Chilton, 1965.

Roth, Philip. *Patrimony*. New York: Vintage Books, 1996. An absorbing account of the author's father's final illness and last days.

Seybold, David, ed. *Fathers and Sons*. New York: Grove Weidenfeld, 1992. An interesting anthology, with outstanding pieces by Stratis Haviaras and Kent Nelson.

Switzer, Barry. *Bootlegger's Boy*. New York: William Morrow, 1990. Mostly about the author's football and coaching career.

Trekell, Ronald. *History of the Tulsa Police Department*. Self-published, [Tulsa], no date. An invaluable resource for local researchers and historians.

Tulsa Fire Department History Book Committee [Pete Faulkenberry, George Coble, and Woody McKenzie]. *Tulsa Fire Department Yearbook 1905–1973*. No publisher, no date. Good photographs.

Tulsa Race Riot: A Report by the Oklahoma Commission to Study the Tulsa Race Riot of 1921. [Oklahoma City: Oklahoma Historical Society, 2001.] Printed in an edition limited to fifty copies, this valuable collection of essays and photographs is scheduled for publication by the University of Oklahoma Press.

Wallis, Michael. *Pretty Boy*. New York: St. Martin's, 1992. An entertaining and well-researched life of bank robber and folk hero Charles Arthur "Pretty Boy" Floyd.

———. *Route 66: The Mother Road*. New York: St. Martin's, 1990.

Wolff, Geoffrey. *The Duke of Deception: Memories of My Father*. New York: Random House, 1979. A skillful and amazingly detailed (and fictionalized?) memoir.

Videotapes

Goin' Back to T' Town. Produced by Sam Pollard and Joyce Vaughn. 1992. A solid PBS documentary on Tulsa's Greenwood District and the Race Riot of 1921.

Tulsa History Series. Eight documentaries made in the early 1990s by Jack Frank: *Tulsa Memories, Things Not in Tulsa Anymore, Let's Go Downtown, Stuff That's Gone, More Tulsa Memories, Holy Tulsa!, Tulsa's Uncommon Houses*, and *Tulsa Art Deco*. Some fluff and boosterism along with invaluable footage. Available from Vintage Films, PO Box 14155, Tulsa, OK 74159-1155.

Internet Source

Useful and interesting is the Oklahombres Online Research Forum, the Web site of the journal *Oklahombres*, devoted to Oklahoma lawmen and outlaws. The Web address is <http://www.oklahombres.org>. The postal address is Oklahombres, Ron Trekell, 8286 East 34th St., Tulsa, OK 74145-1427.

Printed in the USA
CPSIA information can be obtained
at www.ICGtesting.com
LVHW040628220524
780858LV00001B/108

9 780806 137322